SHADOW OVER PARIS

by

Michael Parker

Charlotte de la Cour returns to France in the late Spring of 1940 after two years studying languages at Oxford in England. She has been recruited as an SOE agent to be embedded in Paris before the expected occupation by Nazi Germany, which followed in June of that year. Her work as a waitress at the Hotel Metropole brings her face to face with many senior German Officers where her lip-reading and language skills are used to learn as much as she can from their unguarded loose talk. But her life outside of the hotel draws her closer to the unsung heroes of the budding resistance movement in France, where she learns what living on the edge is really like and the price she would pay if she failed.

Dedicated to the memory of my late wife, Patricia.
1942-2020

Copyright Michael Parker 2024

Book jacket — thebooktypesetters.com

Chapter 1

April 1940

London

The storm clouds had long since gathered over Europe as the Nazis swept towards the glittering prize of Paris. Nothing and no-one had been able to stand in their way. Poland had been brushed aside, swiftly followed by Denmark and Norway and then the Benelux countries of Holland, Belgium and Luxemburg. All that stood in their way was a huge, French army and a token British force gathered along the Maginot Line to stop Hitler's devastating fighting machine.

Very little of this was on the mind of Charlotte de la Cour as she walked out of the London Underground at Baker Street station and into the chilly April wind. She tugged her coat around her in an attempt to retain some of the Underground warmth and stood there for a while gathering her thoughts before asking someone for directions to the Inter Service Bureau. She had an appointment at the Bureau for a job interview as a translator. The woman she asked pointed along the street and told her the Bureau was a short walk. Charlotte thanked her and, head down, walked briskly against the wind.

There was precious little to inspire Charlotte as she stared up at the old building. It's Victorian façade echoed a past that intimated a kind of heroic stoicism for which the British Empire was renowned. But now it was simply a dreary looking structure that held secrets few people knew of and would hardly be interested in anyway.

She looked at the slip of paper in her hand and stepped up to the front door. It wasn't until she rattled the heavy knocker against the dull, brass plate that she saw a poster in an adjacent window with an arrow and a message to use the door in the passageway alongside the building.

She frowned and took herself along the pavement, stepping into the narrow alleyway still clutching her slip of paper and walked ten yards or so to a plain looking door. A small plate carried the words *Inter Service Bureau*. She wrapped her knuckles on the dull brown wood and waited. Presently the door opened and an elderly looking man peered at her.

"Yes?"

Charlotte immediately opened her handbag and pulled out the letter she'd received from the Bureau and showed it to him. "I have an appointment," she said. "It's for a job interview."

"And what is your name?"

"Charlotte de la Cour."

He stood back and pulled the door open wider. "This way," he said.

The daylight, what there was of it from the dingy alleyway, disappeared as he closed the door. The grim looking corridor was only lit by a single bulb, which made the place look gloomier than ever. He pointed to a row of chairs and asked her to wait there. Then he wandered off.

Charlotte sat down. She heard muffled voices coming from a closed door facing her. Suddenly the door opened, and a young woman came out, called out her thanks and smiled briefly at her. Charlotte smiled back. She could see a small scar at the corner of the woman's mouth. As she smiled, it distorted her lips a little but did nothing to change her vivacious looks. The woman walked off down the corridor as an unseen hand closed the door behind her. Charlotte began to wonder what kind of place it was she'd come to; all she wanted was a job as a translator, but everything seemed so quiet and gloomy she wasn't sure she would like to work in such a dull environment.

She let her mind drift back to her younger days in France, long before the war started, thinking about her life there before her father died. She thought of the fun filled days as a youngster living in the suburbs of Paris, her friends, her life and her mother — her very English mother who always encouraged Charlotte to use the English language when the two of them were on their own. Once father was home, she always reverted to her native French tongue.

Before he died, Charlotte's father had worked for the *Fonction publique de l'État*, the French Civil Service, and was based in the heart of the city. Charlotte loved travelling up from the suburbs on occasions to meet him when he had finished work for the day. In the summer it was such a joy to spend time walking with him along the banks of the River Seine, and she loved walking alongside the stalls selling stamps. She would stop at each one and gaze in sheer joy at the scenes from countries all over the world. She loved the Notre Dame cathedral with its towering columns and a roof so high that she felt you could step from there into heaven. Sometimes, especially when her mother was with them, they would spend an evening in the vibrant streets of the Latin Quarter, popular among students from the Sorbonne University, listening to the laughing voices, the street singers, and the sounds from the cafes and restaurants.

She could almost feel herself breaking into song when suddenly the door opened.

"Mademoiselle De La Cour?"

Charlotte snapped out of her daydream and looked up at the man who was standing there holding the door open. He was quite tall, a little cadaverous looking but well dressed in a suit, collar and tie. He was holding a pipe in his hand.

"Good morning, he said. "I'm Mister Jefson. This way please."

He let Charlotte through into a small office that was filled with the aroma of his pipe tobacco. Like the corridor, there was only a single light battling against the dull brown walls and sparse furnishing. He indicated the one chair facing the desk as he sat down in the chair opposite.

"Please," he said.

Charlotte sat down and held her handbag on her lap,

unable to relax enough to feel comfortable. She waited for him to speak and watched as he opened a slim folder in front of him.

"Thank you for coming, Mademoiselle De La Cour." He said that in French, and surprisingly good French as far as Charlotte was concerned. "Good journey up?"

"It was only from Crawley," she answered. "Not far."

"So, let me see…" He ran the tip of his pipe down the top page in the file. "Charlotte de la Cour. French national. Lived in France until you came to England to study languages at Oxford." He looked up. "You remained in England. Why didn't you go back to France when you finished your degree?"

Charlotte shifted a little on the hard, wooden chair. "When my father died, my mother decided she would come to England with me while I studied at Oxford. The plan was to return to France once I'd graduated." She shrugged. "But the outbreak of war…" She left it unsaid.

"Made it difficult for you to return?"

She shook her head briefly. "I wanted to go back, but my mother was unsure. The newspapers were telling us it would all be over by Christmas, so we decided to wait until then."

"Why did you want to go back?" he asked.

"I wanted to see my Aunt Matilde."

Jefson's shaggy eyebrows lifted. "Oh. And this Aunt Matilde?"

"My father's sister," Charlotte explained. "She lives

in Paris in the fourteenth *arrondissement*. That's on the outer suburbs —."

"Yes, I know where it is," Jefson interrupted. "Please go on."

"I wanted to persuade Aunt Matilde to come and live with us. I thought it would be wise," she added.

He nodded. "I can understand that. Have you thought how safe a journey to France might be?"

Charlotte looked down at her hands. "I thought while I'm here in London I could speak to someone we know in the French Embassy. He was a friend of my father; they worked together in the Civil Service in Paris."

Jefson picked up a pen and wrote something on the top page of the folder. He put the pen down and smiled at Charlotte. "Just updating your file," he explained.

"Does your mother know you will be seeing this friend of your late father?"

Charlotte frowned, wondering why he'd asked the question, but she answered anyway. "No; I told her I was meeting one of my university friends in London. A girl's day out if you like."

"Do you find it easy to…" He glanced up towards the ceiling, looking thoughtful for a brief moment. "To be economical with the truth?"

"Do you mean do I find it easy to lie?"

"That would be another way of putting it," he admitted. "It leads me to believe that you were very keen to go back to France, even to the point of lying to your mother."

Charlotte chuckled softly. "You make me sound

quite mean, but yes, I was very keen. Still am in fact if I could find a way of doing it without my mother knowing."

"That's interesting," he said, and looked back at the folder. "Now, you came to England to study languages at Oxford. English and German, I understand?"

She nodded. "Yes."

"Would you tell me why you chose those particular languages?"

Charlotte shuffled her bottom again in the chair. "Well, my mother is English, which made that choice easy. And we always spoke in that language when there was just the two of us at home. And because English is allied to the Germanic tongue, Teutonic of course, it made sense to study that as a second language. And Queen Victoria was married to Prince Albert, a German, which did rather cement the languages together, and I could see the advantage of being able to speak the three most important languages in Europe. Why do you ask?"

"How fluent are you in English and German?" he asked, ignoring Charlotte's question.

She shrugged. "Well, by studying in England rather than the Sorbonne in Paris it exposed me to the colloquial English tongue. Consequently, I speak fairly good English."

He held his pipe up. "Then we'll continue in English. Please go on."

"Okay," she answered in English. "You'll be able to judge for yourself how well I speak it. As for my German, I've yet to test myself alongside a native

German, but my tutor at Oxford was well pleased with me whenever we conversed in that language. So, I'm quite confident about working as a translator, which is why I've applied for this job."

Jefson did not respond to that, but looked back at the folder, then closed it. He leaned back in his chair, put the pipe in his mouth and studied Charlotte for a while. There was little that made her stand out; she was quite small, not big boned at all. Her brunette hair was cut in the fashion of the day, the top was brushed to give it volume, while the bottom looked as though it had been curled with a heated roller or iron. Her hair framed her face beautifully, which he had missed on his first appraisal when she walked into the office. One thing Jefson prided himself on was the ability to assess someone quite accurately on their first encounter. And in his position, it was vital he made the right assessment. He breathed in sharply through his nose and sat forward.

"You have listed on your application that you can lip read. Why did you put that?"

She shrugged. "You asked for any other interesting or useful skills, so I put that down."

"How did you come to learn that. Or why?"

"My mother has been partially deaf all her life. When I was a toddler, I had a speech impediment. My mother assumed I had inherited her deafness, so she taught me to lip read."

"And the impediment?"

She shook her head. "I grew out of it."

"And was your lip-reading skill of any use."

She laughed. "Only when the boys were making lurid remarks about me at school. I could use it as a weapon against them. Same at university"

He smiled broadly. "I can imagine." He tapped the folder. "Leaving aside your lip-reading skill and the young boys, do you have any idea how things are going in Europe? The war, I mean?"

Charlotte sighed heavily. "Not very well by all accounts. We can only believe what we read in the newspapers, but they do say that the first casualty of war is the truth. So, no, I don't really know."

"Then let me tell you. At the moment, the war in Europe is going very badly for the Allies. Our intelligence leads us to believe the Germans will be in Paris within the next three or four weeks considering how fast they are moving. Unfortunately, the French Army seems unable to stop them despite the help from the British Expeditionary Force. And we believe France will be seeking a surrender before they are completely overwhelmed."

He stopped there and leaned forward to pick up a box of matches. He took one out and relit his pipe. "One thing we are desperately short of is good intelligence." He shook the burning match and dropped the dead ember into an ash tray. "And also, a way of communicating it," he added.

Charlotte wondered if this was the reason her language skills were needed — to translate any information received from France. Or Germany for that matter. She began to feel a trifle uncomfortable about being there. Jefson had quite skilfully meandered around the details he had in front of him; mostly supplied by Charlotte in her application letter. She hoped it wouldn't be too long before he came to the point of the interview.

Suddenly, he switched to French, and a dark, serious look came over his face. "Mademoiselle De La Cour, do you feel that France is ready for an all-out war against Germany?"

Charlotte wondered what her opinion mattered when all she wanted to do was work as a translator. But he had asked the question, so she felt it warranted an answer.

"Well, France has almost three million men at arms, so yes."

He nodded his head thoughtfully. "If you was back in France now, would you be concerned, bearing in mind what I've just told you?"

She smiled. "I think I might be blissfully unaware until I knew more."

"The information you get from the newspapers; is that what you mean?"

She shook her head. "They rarely tell the truth and only go for dramatic news to sell newspapers."

Jefson put the pipe in his mouth and sucked in the smoke. Charlotte could see the tobacco flare in the bole of the pipe. He tipped his head back and blew the smoke up into the air.

"So, if you knew the truth, the stuff they don't print, how concerned would you be?"

Charlotte wondered where Jefson was going with this. "I don't know what truth we are talking about, unless it's the kind that governments never tell the people who voted them into power."

"Secret stuff?" he suggested.

Charlotte shrugged. "For those who are privy to that kind of information I would imagine, but I can't see how that could affect a low-grade clerk working as a translator."

He leaned forward, his arms on the desk.

Charlotte caught the aroma of the pipe tobacco quite strongly because it was much closer to her now.

"If you worked for the Ministry of Information," he told her, "you would have some important, as well as highly classified information in front of you that would get you closer to the truth and a greater understanding of how strong France is. Or at least, could be. And that, Charlotte, would bring you to a deeper awareness of how well the war is going."

"So let me understand this, Charlotte said. "As a translator I would be privy to a lot of information the Bureau receives from France, or Germany."

He smiled thinly. "Not working here in the Bureau," he said. "But somewhere else."

Charlotte frowned. "Then where?"

He waited a few seconds before answering.

"In France."

Chapter 2

The last time Charlotte had travelled to France was a year earlier. There was no hint of war then; people were going about their business in much the same way as they had always done. The rise of Nazi Germany worried a few intellectuals, but the common man had no such fear. But now it was different. Her interview with Jefson had lasted two hours; two hours in which he had painted a picture that both inspired and frightened her. Charlotte knew she belonged back in France, but she knew the risks now. She was thankful that Jefson had been fair and given her plenty of time to consider what lay ahead. The damning thing was that she wanted to talk to her mother about it, but he had warned Charlotte that to do so would be tantamount to treason.

She had walked away from the Bureau with mixed feelings, although she knew she had made the right choice. Her immediate problem was to go home and lie to her mother: something she'd never done before — not seriously anyway.

With so much going through her head, Charlotte took some time before boarding her train back to Crawley to stop at a café and reflect on the choice she'd made: to work for the defence of France. By looking at it that way, she felt much happier despite the trickle of apprehension that had taken root in her heart.

She rang her mother from Crawley station who arrived in less than thirty minutes and bombarded her with questions on the drive home in her Austin Seven motor car. Sometimes Charlotte thought she was in more danger as a passenger in the car while her mother spent more time talking and not concentrating on the narrow country roads along which they were travelling. But they made it safely back to the farm cottage they rented from a family member. Once they were both settled in the house, her mother started with the questions again.

"I will be working for a chap called Jefson in one of the government ministries, Mother," Charlotte explained for the umpteenth time. "And no, I will not be a secret agent. I will simply act as an interpreter, or translator if you prefer, on anything they feel is of particular interest to them." It was a banal explanation, but necessary.

"But why can't you stay here?" her mother asked. "You can travel up to London each day, surely."

"I have to sign the Official Secrets Act, which means I am basically their property. That is why I have to be billeted in London. Oh, and I will not be allowed to communicate with you by telephone."

Her mother frowned. "Why on earth not?"

"In case anyone is listening in. We may be on a party line, so you can imagine the difficulty."

"Well how will I know you are okay?"

Charlotte was finding this difficult. She could see her mother was genuinely worried, but Jefson's words kept ringing in her ears; she had to say nothing about going back to France. She put her hand up. "I will write to you each week, but the letters might be opened and read. For security reasons," she added glibly. It was a pack of lies, but Jefson had insisted Charlotte used these excuses because she would never be allowed to communicate with her mother once she was in France. Any personal letters would be written by the Bureau.

And so the questions continued until Charlotte cried off and went to bed. Sleep did not come easily to her either despite feeling exhausted mentally. Instead, her dreams were filled with images of Paris and of her mother's scary driving along the country lanes around their home. And when the morning light filtered in slowly from behind her bedroom curtains, Charlotte stretched her limbs and thought of the journey back to London that morning, of saying goodbye to her mother and wondering when, if ever, she would see her again.

***

Charlotte stayed in London for one week for intensive briefing and instruction. Jefson had told her much about the Special Operations Executive, the SOE, that had been sanctioned by the Prime Minister, Neville Chamberlain, and that it was still in its infancy. The role of SOE agents would be to support the fledgling resistance groups that were secretly forming in France, ready to disrupt German operations should the Nazis occupy the country. But for Charlotte, Jefson envisaged a different role: one in which she could make use of her right to live and work in France, rather than become a covert agent in the field.

It wasn't until Charlotte was on the ferry to Calais when she realised something significant about the amount of empty seats and the rather small number of passengers travelling. Her mind went back to the train journey from London. There were barely any French people on the train. When she had travelled to France a year earlier, the train had been bustling and the French language was being spoken by almost everyone. She recalled how much it comforted her; hearing French being spoken so volubly. And as much as she enjoyed living in England, French was her native tongue and just hearing it gave her a warm feeling inside.

The sense of emptiness was reinforced when Charlotte walked on to the platform to catch the Paris train. There were just a few people there; nothing like the year before. And that was when it struck her about the news of people fleeing France. She cast her mind back to the moment she had stepped off the ferry and the long queue of passengers waiting to board for the crossing to England, and how she'd been surprised when she'd shown her passport at the point of entry and the look the officer gave her.

These thoughts trickled through her mind as she took her seat in an almost empty carriage. There were just a few passengers, mostly people on their own; certainly no children and families. Two women wearing a uniform that Charlotte didn't recognise sat in the seat on the opposite side to her. She looked around as she made herself comfortable hoping to see more people board the train until suddenly, with the blast of a whistle and a sharp tug, the train began to pull away and begin its journey to Paris. Charlotte frowned and shook her head as Jefson's words came back to her about what she would be facing. She'd been in France barely thirty minutes and the reality of his words was now beginning to make an impact.

While Charlotte was looking out across the open fields, the train slowed a little. She wrinkled her brow, thinking their might be a problem on the line, but it soon became obvious as the train crossed a road. A barrier had been lowered, but there was only one vehicle waiting at the crossing. It was a dull coloured box van with a red cross on the side. There were two women sitting in the front of the van, both wearing a uniform. Charlotte looked across at the two passengers she had acknowledged earlier. They were wearing the same uniform. She leaned over in her seat.

"Excuse me, what are those uniforms you're wearing?"

"I'm sorry, I don't speak French," the woman nearest answered.

Charlotte asked again in English.

"We're FANY nurses: First Aid Nursing Yeomanry," the woman replied.

Charlotte had never heard of the organisation. "Oh. So, what are you doing in France?"

"We pick up wounded soldiers from the battlefield..." She paused there for a moment. "Well, any nationality of course," she added. "We nurse them and get them back to England away from the fighting so they can be treated."

Charlotte wondered where these battlefields were

considering there was no fighting in France. She thanked the woman and returned her gaze to looking out over the green fields and hills, seeing sheep and cattle grazing and the occasional tractor. It added to the sense of tranquillity — nothing like the scaremongering stories she'd heard about the noise of war. She did miss not having families around her though. She remembered how she would often mischievously lip read some of the conversations going on, which added to the fun of being surrounded by people. But soon she was breathing a deep sigh and pulling a book out of her bag; something to offset the boredom of the lifeless carriage.

The book proved to be difficult to read and she soon fell asleep, woken only as the train was pulling into the Gare du Nord. Charlotte closed the book and pushed it back into her bag. Then she got up and retrieved her suitcase from the overhead luggage rack. She slung her bag over her shoulder, checked she'd left nothing on the seat and stepped out on to, once again, a very empty platform. Then she noticed the smell. She sniffed several times trying to figure out what it was, but it was difficult to define. She ignored it and made her way towards the exit.

Charlotte was relieved to finally be in Paris, the city she loved. She looked up at the station clock and figured she would be at her aunt's smallholding in about thirty minutes. But that was until she got out of the station and found herself standing at an empty taxi rank.

The sense of emptiness was slowly sinking in as she

looked around at the virtually lifeless roads. In the distance she could see a small group of people pushing what looked like a cart. It was piled high with what appeared to be clothing and furniture. A mattress was draped over the top, which a woman was battling gamely to stop from slipping off.

Then she began to feel the effects of the cloying smoke in her eyes and acrid taste in her mouth. She pulled a handkerchief from her pocket and held it to her face. She had to keep blinking to gain some comfort as her eyes started watering. She walked away from the station confines and the deserted taxi rank, finding a small measure of relief further along the street.

Charlotte's thoughts about the discomfort were interrupted when she saw a woman walking towards her. She had her head down and was holding a scarf to her face. Charlotte put a hand up.

"Excuse me, mademoiselle."

The woman stopped and lowered the scarf. "Yes?"

Charlotte wasn't sure how to begin. "Can you tell me, are there any taxis running?"

"You waiting for one?"

Charlotte nodded. "Yes."

The woman shook her head. "There aren't any. Everyone has left Paris."

Charlotte's mouth opened in surprise. "Left Paris?"

The woman took a step closer. "You must be new here."

"Well," Charlotte said, pointing back over her shoulder. "I've just arrived from England. I didn't..."

The woman shook her head. "Not a good idea, my

love. If you had any sense, you would go back."

Charlotte shrugged. "I can't; I've just arrived." She laughed lightly. "So, how can I get to Montrouge?"

The woman flicked her hand and pointed along the street. "You might be lucky and see someone willing to sell you a bicycle; otherwise, you'll have to walk." She looked at Charlotte's suitcase. "People will think you're heading south like everyone else running away from the Germans."

"What about buses?"

The woman shook her head. "They stopped a long time ago. Good luck my dear," the woman added and walked off.

As Charlotte watched the woman walk away, she looked again at the plumes of black smoke hovering above the city skyline. The soft wind was flattening the smoke and pushing it over the city like a blanket. The smell was noxious. And there were no birds: none whatsoever.

Charlotte's shoulders drooped; it was all so unexpected and unwelcome. She picked up her suitcase and started walking. At first she wasn't sure whether it was the right thing to do or not, but knowing she had little choice, she put up with it and started heading south for her aunt's home in Montrouge.

It wasn't long before Charlotte heard the sound of hoofs behind her. She turned and was surprised to see a horse and carriage drawing up alongside her. She stopped as the driver brought the carriage to a halt with a pull back on the reins and called the horse to a stop. He looked down at Charlotte.

"Do you want a lift, mademoiselle?" he asked.

Charlotte put her suitcase on the ground and straightened. "Are you for hire?"

"If mademoiselle wants. Where are you going?"

"Montrouge," she told him.

He gave it a moment's thought, pursed his lips and nodded. "Ten kilometres," he said. "I think we can manage that."

He climbed down from the carriage and helped Charlotte up on to the leather covered seat. Then he lifted her suitcase up and secured it to a panier at the rear of the carriage. He clambered up beside Charlotte, released the brake and flicked the reins. The horse pulled, causing the carriage to jerk suddenly. Charlotte almost toppled backwards. She laughed and sat up straight. She had inadvertently put her hand on the man's leg to steady herself. She took it away and apologised.

"Sorry about that," she said.

He smiled. "I'm not." He steered the horse away from the pavement and let it move at a gentle trot. He glanced sideways at Charlotte. "My name is Jacques," he told her, offering her his hand.

"Thank you for stopping, Jacques. My name is Charlotte." She shook his hand and then looked around at the emptiness. "Where is everybody? And what's that smoke?" she asked.

He glanced at her. "Most of the young men are in the Army or the Air Force. Those who could, have fled Paris. There are only key workers left: hospital staff, police, some Ministry people. The government, what's left of it, has ordered all files or anything that might be useful to be destroyed to prevent them falling into German hands." He pointed towards the smoke. "So, they are burning everything, even cooking oil, waste oil, anything and everything. The big companies are doing it as well, which is why there is so much pollution in the air." He shook his head disconsolately. "As for the people — there aren't many of us left. Those who could go have gone."

"Why are you still here then, Jacques? And what about your family?"

"I'm seventy years old, my family have left for Spain with my good wishes; it wasn't sensible for them to stay here. Now there's only me and Charles."

"Charles?"

He nodded ahead. "My horse. He's named after De Gaulle. I thought there was a similarity in their looks."

Charlotte laughed at the thought. "So what now, Jacques?"

He didn't answer straight away but looked ahead, his thoughts somewhere else. "Oh, I'll do my best to serve France in any way I can." He turned towards her. "But what about you, young lady? Why are you heading the wrong way?"

She couldn't tell him the truth, but her answer was a lie founded on an element of truth. "Me? Well, I live in England with my mother, and I've come over here to try and persuade my aunt to come back to England with me."

He shook his head. "There is a strong rumour that the Channel ferry to England will stop operating within the next few days. Your aunt must have a good reason for staying, otherwise she would have fled like everyone else."

"I guess I'll find out when I see her."

"Then I'll wait for you to persuade her and take you both back to the Gare Du Nord so you can catch the train to Calais before they cancel the crossings."

Charlotte chuckled at Jacques' attempt at humour, but it did reinforce the ugliness of the situation now building in France.

They talked on for the thirty minutes it took to reach Montrouge. Charlotte directed Jacques to her aunt's small holding situated in an uncluttered area just on the edge of the countryside. He pulled up and jumped down from the carriage, then turned and helped Charlotte down. He then went round to the panier and took her suitcase off. He handed it to her as she was rummaging through her shoulder bag for her purse so she could pay him.

"If I happen to come this way in the future, would you mind if I called? Just to see if you were able to persuade your aunt to go back to England," he explained.

"Of course, Jacques. And thank you for a such a lovely ride and lively conversation." She reached up and kissed him on the cheek.

He touched his cap and clambered back up on the coach seat. "Au revoir," he called and set Charles off in a gentle trot back towards an empty Paris.

***

Charlotte's Aunt Matilde came hurrying out of the old

farmhouse when she saw Charlotte being helped down from the carriage. She ran across the yard sending a couple of hens scurrying out of her way and threw her arms around Charlotte in a big hug. She wasn't a big woman but was able to wrap her arms around Charlotte's small frame with ease. She almost lifted Charlotte off her feet.

"Oh, my lovely Charlotte; it's such a pleasure to see you." She released her from the bear hug and stepped back opening her arms out wide. "I didn't know you was coming over." She half turned and hooked her arm round Charlotte's. "What are you doing here?"

Charlotte wanted to get into explanations slowly, so she suggested they wait until they were indoors with a cup of coffee, or tea, or even cognac; whatever her aunt preferred.

The hens were interested in the new arrival as the two women walked across the yard. Matilde shooshed them away and made Charlotte laugh with her antics. Once inside, Charlotte was relieved of her suitcase and offered a cognac.

"I'll take this up to your room," Matilde said, lifting the suitcase. "Then we can talk." She started walking away.

"My room? But you didn't know I was coming."

Matilde stopped. "Ah, you're right, but I always have a room ready should I ever need it."

Charlotte watched her aunt disappear upstairs and sat down at the large kitchen table thinking about the last twenty-four hours and what a shock it had been. She'd seen various newspaper reports and heard broadcasts from the BBC in London, but those reports failed to reveal the shocking state of Paris that Charlotte had now seen with her own eyes. It all made her wonder why her aunt had remained and not fled like most people.

Matilde came into the kitchen and served up two glasses of cognac. She sat opposite Charlotte at the large, wooden kitchen table and raised her glass.

"Santé!"

Charlotte acknowledged the toast and responded.

"Tchin-tchin."

Matilde smiled. "At least you still remember how to toast. Your French hasn't been distilled by your time in England."

"That could never happen," Charlotte assured her.

"So," Matilde said, leaning forward. "How is Constance and why are you here?"

"My mother is fine. She's happy being back in England since we lost Papa. And she would love to see you, Matilde, but she couldn't summon up the courage to come over with me, which is why I'm here; I would like you to come back to England with me. My mother believes it will be safer for you. And so do I."

Matilde reached her hand across the table and took hold of Charlotte's wrist.

"My dear Charlotte, my husband, your uncle, is serving with the French Army somewhere — there is no way I would leave France not knowing where he is or how he is. And if he was wounded, he would have to come back home to me so I could look after him. Do you understand that?"

Charlotte nodded and smiled. She put her hand on Matilde's. "Of course I do." Then she remembered the two FANY nurses on the train. She explained briefly what they did. "If Uncle Pierre was wounded, they might have to take him to England," she said. "then you would have to come over as well."

Matilde's expression changed and became a little grim. "Charlotte, the Germans will be in France within the week now. No-one, not even your wonderful FANY nurses will be taking wounded soldiers back to England."

"How will you know if anything happens to him?"

Matilde shook her head irritably. "God knows. Our government is falling apart. They are burning everything before they run. *Merde!*" She looked at Charlotte with a guilty glance. "What do the English say when they swear accidentally?"

"Pardon my French," Charlotte told her with a grin. "What about the man who worked with Papa? He's in London now. Couldn't he help?"

Matilde's frown deepened. "Pierre Baudet?"

"That's him. Mother spoke to him a few weeks ago. He's at the French Embassy."

Matilde got up from the table and brought the cognac over. She poured herself a small glass and offered the bottle to Charlotte who shook her head.

"Why do I get the feeling you don't like him, Matilde?" she asked.

"I've never liked him since he made a pass at me one evening. Your uncle was actually in the house too." She shook her head slowly as she recalled the moment. "I cannot repeat what he suggested, but he made me feel dirty. I told your uncle, but he said Baudet would have been drunk."

"And was he?"

"No, of course not. The man also has a gambling habit. An addiction. I don't know how his poor wife puts up with it. He's an altogether thoroughly nasty piece of work. And if he has anything to do with helping us against the Germans, God help us all."

"Well," Charlotte said with a deep sigh, "mother seems to like him."

"Then I hope she will soon find out that Pierre Baudet is not a man to be trusted."

Chapter 3

Pierre Baudet leaned up against the counter, his elbows on the polished walnut veneer and his hands clasped together on his head. Between his elbows was an empty glass. He had been sitting slumped like that for several minutes, lamenting the loss he had suffered at the Baccarat table and the consequence of gambling with borrowed money.

He could feel the stubble on his bald scalp, which only served to remind him that money was not the only thing he had lost. He'd also lost his dignity; something no self-respecting Frenchman could justify. He now had nowhere to go and no-one to turn to. His debts were beyond anything that he could manage, and he had no way and no answer as to how he was going to overcome what was an insurmountable problem.

Baudet was fifty-five years of age. He was married although that was a status in name only; his wife had moved back to France not long after he had been appointed as secretary to the French Ambassador in London. It was an appointment that offered him status, a good salary and opened doors for him that would otherwise have been difficult to pass through. But his wife knew the truth — the advantages had gained him access to places where wealth was an accepted and unspoken accoutrement; something that Baudet did not possess.

"Another drink?"

Baudet looked up at the barman, then down at his

empty glass. "Yes. A double please."

The barman took his glass away and returned with a fresh drink. Baudet thanked him and downed the brandy in one gulp. He slammed the empty glass on the counter and leaned back on the bar stool as someone spoke to him.

"Oh, that doesn't sound too good. You look like you lost a pound and found a penny."

Baudet looked up at the man standing beside him. He was holding two drinks, one in each hand. He was wearing a smartly tailored, double-breasted dark blue suit. His tie was the same colour, standing out against his pristine, white shirt.

"More like a hundred," Baudet answered with a snarl.

"That bad?"

Baudet gave him a withering look. "You wouldn't understand." He went to get off the bar stool when the man stopped him. "Try me," he said.

Baudet glared at him. "I beg your pardon?"

"Talk to me," the man answered and offered one of the drinks to Baudet. "Would you like a drink? I can always get another one."

"What is it?"

"Whiskey."

Baudet managed a chuckle and thought it kind of matched his luck and what were the odds of being offered the wrong drink?

"I'm a cognac man," he said.

The man looked over at the barman, lifted his chin and tipped his head towards Baudet. "My name is

Rudolf, by the way: Rudolf Havertz," he said to Baudet.

"German?"

Havertz smiled and shook his head. "Hardly; I'd be locked up by now if I was. No; I'm Swiss."

Baudet nodded slowly and smiled. He held his hand out. "Pierre Baudet. French."

Havertz put one of the drinks he was holding on the bar while he shook Baudet's hand. "It's unusual to see a Frenchman so dispirited; you always seem a happy bunch."

The barman came over and put Baudet's brandy in front of him. Baudet lifted it up and thanked Havertz, but this time he only took a sip of the cognac.

"I guess it must be the way the war is going for you?" Havertz suggested.

Baudet shook his head. "No; more like the way my luck is going."

"Can't you change it?" Havertz asked and glanced back towards the gaming tables. "Try a different table?"

Baudet frowned. "Really?" He laughed. "The way my luck is?"

Havertz put his hand in his pocket and pulled out a gaming chip. He looked at it, turned it over and then handed it to Baudet. "Try that," he said. "Call it a lucky chip."

Baudet took it from him and grinned. It had a value of twenty pounds. "Different table, you think?" he said looking up at Havertz.

Havertz shrugged and picked up his drinks. "Why not? Try the one by the exit. It brought me luck. Might work for you. Good luck." He turned and walked away.

Baudet watched him disappear into the busy club until he was lost to sight. Then he flicked the chip into the air, watched it spin and caught it in the palm of his hand. One more shot, he thought. One more shot.

As Havertz passed the table he'd recommended to Baudet, he nodded briefly at the courier who caught the movement and nodded back. He then walked over to a table where a woman was waiting for him.

Havertz sat beside her. "Worked like a charm," he said. "I'll be his friend for life if he wins."

"Will you be able to recruit him do you think?"

He nodded and leaned in a little closer, whispering into her ear. "He has nowhere to go, my love, and I know more about him than he knows himself. He's ready."

He kissed her on the cheek and lifted his glass in a silent toast.

Baudet finished his brandy and walked over to the table Havertz had suggested. He slid into an empty chair and put the chip on the table. He didn't expect to be there long. The croupier studied him briefly and dealt the cards. Baudet couldn't believe his luck with his first cards. After that the cards opened up for him and showered him with gains like wedding confetti. He made losses as well, but the prize was growing and his addiction was being fed, and that was all that mattered.

Until a woman slid into the seat beside him.

At first he didn't take too much notice of her other than the fragrance of her perfume. She smiled at him and placed a pile of chips on the table. As she played she made small, encouraging comments about her game and Baudet's. As time went by they became quite friendly, and Baudet found her company was giving him quite a lift, and it wasn't long before he began having thoughts about her that went way beyond the gaming tables. It soon became apparent to him by the kind of glances she was making towards him and also by some remarks she made that there was more than just a card game to come.

Eventually the woman stacked her cards, pulled her chips towards her and allowed an attendant member of staff to pull her chair back. As she got up, she leaned closer to Baudet.

"Why not join me for a drink?"

Baudet watched her walk away and immediately stacked his cards and pocketed his winning chips, dropping one in front of the croupier before following the woman across the club room to a quiet area. She smiled up at him as he sat down beside her.

"I think there can be more to fun than just a game of cards," she said to him. "Don't you agree?"

He said he did but didn't believe it as the words came out of his mouth. He beckoned a waiter over and ordered drinks. Once they had been delivered, he relaxed against the soft velvet padding of the curved bench on which they were sitting and allowed the evening to develop as he believed they both knew it would.

***

Charlotte woke up with the early morning sun just bringing enough light to brighten an already cloudy sky, and rolled over on to her back, her thoughts going over the last seven days she'd been in France. Jefson told her that someone would be in touch. It would be unexpected and not as soon as she might have thought. What Charlotte couldn't figure out was how anyone could find her here at her aunt's place. She'd seen a couple of Matilde's neighbours, which she had expected, but nothing and no-one else. All she could do was wait until it happened.

Charlotte had made herself useful though; helping feed the chickens and run errands for Matilde. She'd managed to buy a bicycle, which was helpful. Each day her and her aunt had listened to the radio broadcasts from the BBC in London, and each day Charlotte caught her aunt in a reflective mood as she worried about her husband putting his life on the line in defence of their beloved country.

She threw back the covers and swung her legs out of bed, pushed her feet into a pair of slippers and went through to the bathroom. She came out, slipped a dressing gown over her pyjamas and went down to the kitchen where she found her aunt listening to the radio.

Matilde looked up as Charlotte walked in.

"Winston Churchill has been made Prime Minister," she said.

Charlotte wrinkled her brow. "Has Neville Chamberlain resigned then?"

"He had to, Charlotte. Like our useless politicians, he was too weak to fight Hitler. Churchill will be much stronger."

She got up and went over to the black stove, which was throwing out a welcoming warmth into the kitchen.

She lifted a pot and brought it over to the table and poured a cup of coffee for Charlotte.

"And the Channel ferries have stopped operating."

Charlotte looked stunned for a moment. *"Mon Dieu!"* She immediately thought of her mother back in England. "My mother will be worried about me."

Matilde looked at Charlotte rather sharply. "You should have gone back while you had the chance. Now you're stuck here."

Charlotte had not told her aunt the real reason she was in France, and, very naively, had somehow expected the channel link to always be available. Step by step, she was beginning to see the real danger.

"I will have to write to her," she said. "Let her know I'm safe."

Matilde gave her a blank look. "And how do you expect your letter be sent? There will be no foreign mail, and there is certainly no airmail. Unless you can send your letter through the British Embassy before they shut down."

Jefson had warned her how often she would be tripped up by the small things in the detail, and Charlotte could see how difficult it would be to let her mother know she was fine without revealing the fact that she was in France.

"You look lost, Charlotte," Matilde said as she took the coffee pot away and put it back on the stove. "Something bothering you?"

Charlotte shook her head briskly. "No, Matilde, just a little stunned at how quickly things are moving I guess."

"Well, try not to let it worry you. Now," she said suddenly, all business-like. "What do you want for breakfast? We have plenty of eggs."

Charlotte laughed and got up from the table. "I'll do them, then I think I'll get washed up and changed."

"Do you have anything planned?" Matilde asked.

Charlotte stopped and looked thoughtful, one hand on the table. "I'm going to write to mother and cycle into Paris."

"And where, pray, will you post your letter?"

"I thought I would try the British Embassy; after all, they must still be operating."

"Not for long I would imagine," Matilde said brutally. "Best you cycle quickly in case they shut down today."

Charlotte laughed and spun round. "Eggs then, Matilde," she said and got on with making a couple of omelettes.

It was almost an hour later when Charlotte sat down and wrote the letter, but this time with a difference. She folded the finished letter and put it into an envelope addressed to *Mr. S. Jefson, Imperial Service Bureau, Baker Street, London, WC1*. She then added a note explaining the circumstances and asking Jefson to post the letter to her mother. This was the only way Charlotte could make sure there would be an English stamp and postmark on the letter her mother received. She knew that Jefson would put the letter into an envelope. The reason Charlotte didn't do this herself was because she knew that her letter would have to be read and approved before Jefson could send it.

The May weather was being kind with a few clouds and a gentle breeze, but Charlotte took a cape which she folded into the basket on the front of her bicycle. Then she waved goodbye to her aunt and set off to cycle the ten kilometres into Paris.

As Charlotte got closer to the centre of Paris, she could see more of the emptiness she had witnessed when she stepped of the train and stood by the empty taxi rank. There were still signs of black smoke drifting across the city, but nowhere near as much as on that first day. The absence of birds was another unexplainable sadness, and she hadn't seen any cars other than the occasional police car. She did see some motorcycles, but not too many.

She cycled up to the Rue du Faubourg Honoré where she knew the British Embassy was situated and dismounted. She had never been to the embassy before and had no idea what kind of welcome she would receive. The building was an imposing looking edifice set back with the main entrance at the end of a long path that was between two wings of the building. Two British soldiers were standing on sentry duty either side of the ornate gates that were open.

Charlotte wheeled her bicycle up to the gates. One of the soldiers turned towards her.

"Can I help you?" he asked in English.

Charlotte answered him in that language. "I want to see somebody about sending a letter back to England," she told him.

"Do you have identification?" he asked.

Charlotte knew she would be asked that question,

which was why she'd brought her passport with her. She took it out of her shoulder bag and showed it to him. He opened it up, looked through it and handed it back.

"Can you open your jacket please? I need to see you aren't carrying any weapons."

Charlotte couldn't help smiling to herself. She pulled open her waist length jacket and held her arms out. She could see the young man was looking quite uncomfortable, but he made a cursory check and told her he would walk her up to the main door. He said she could leave her bicycle behind the railings.

Once Charlotte was inside the main entrance, she went over to the reception desk and explained what it was she wanted.

"It's for a Mister Jefson — he works for the government," she said, pointing at Jefson's name on the envelope.

The woman took the letter from her. "Well, if its government business," she said, "It should be okay to go in the diplomatic bag." She dropped the letter into a tray on the counter. "It might take a while to get there though. Does it matter?"

Charlotte shook her head. "No, not at all."

The woman smiled. "Anything else?"

Charlotte shook her head. "No, that's it. Thank you." She walked away, surprised it had been so easy.

She went back for her bicycle and thanked the soldier as she wheeled it out on to the pavement, but as she was about to get on the bicycle, she saw Jacques Garnier, the man who had taken her to her aunt's place.

He was leaning up against the carriage. He was wearing the same faded blue denim coat that he wore when she saw him last. His cap with the peak sat at an angle on his head and he was smoking a cigarette. The horse had its head in a nosebag and was busily tucking into the whatever was in there. She pushed her bicycle across the road and came up alongside him.

"Hello, Jacques. Fancy seeing you here."

Jacques pushed himself away from the carriage and tapped his forehead with his finger. "*Bonjour*, Charlotte. How are you? And what are you doing here?"

She pointed back towards the embassy. "I've asked them to take a letter for me. It's for my mother. She'll be worried about me, especially now that the ferries had stopped."

"So, you couldn't persuade your aunt to go back to England?" Charlotte shook her head. "And now you are trapped here?"

She puffed her cheeks out. "It looks that way. But at least I'm home; it isn't as if I've been trapped in a foreign country."

"So, what will you do?"

Charlotte looked at him, puzzled. "What do you mean?"

He leaned back against the carriage. "When the Germans arrive, which they surely will, there will be a demand for French workers." He studied her for a few moments. "It might pay to be in some kind of employment, rather than let them find you at a loose end."

"I hadn't thought of that," she admitted. "At the moment I wouldn't know where to start — looking for work, I mean."

"I know there are some vacancies at the Hotel Metropole. It's near the Place Saint-Michel."

"I know where it is, Jacques," she told him.

"I know the *Concierge* there. His name is Armand. If you're interested, tell him I told you. That's if you want a job."

Charlotte pursed her lips and nodded her head slowly. "I could do with earning something," she admitted thoughtfully. "At least I would be able to pay my aunt some rent."

"Then I wish you luck," he said. He dropped his cigarette on the road and stubbed it out with his foot. "I have to get Charles back to his stable, get him cleaned up and then back on the road." He went to the horse and pulled its nosebag away. He hung it on a brass hook and then clambered up on to the carriage. "Au revoir, Charlotte. Maybe I'll see you at the Metropole one day."

He touched his forehead again with the tip of his finger and flicked the reins. The horse responded and strained momentarily before dragging the carriage away.

Charlotte watched him go thinking how fortuitous it would be if she could get some kind of employment. She got on her bicycle. "Right, Hotel Metropole it is then," she said and started peddling in the direction of the Place Saint-Michel.

Chapter 4

Pierre Baudet stepped out of the French Embassy into the warm sunshine; his mind on his own problems rather than the disappointing news coming out of France. Despite hearing that the French Army was in disarray and already retreating, and that the French Administration was falling apart, none of that mattered to Baudet because he had more pressing things on his mind. The money he'd won earlier in the week, coupled with the amazing night he'd had with the woman he'd met, had helped, but he'd been back at the tables the following night and lost everything. The fact that France was falling apart meant less to him than his own situation. He'd even managed to have suicidal thoughts but was too much of a coward to take that option. News was trickling in as well that Marechal Petain was to become Vice President at the Council of Ministers in Paris; an appointment that simply confirmed his country was about to concede defeat against the Germans.

One thing that Baudet disliked was weakness, despite his own addiction to gambling, and he felt a sneaking admiration for the strength of the German assault and the dominance they displayed against what was supposed to be an overwhelming French army. He even got to a point in his mind where he wished he'd been born a German; such was his growing dislike with the way his life was crumbling.

He heard a voice call him as he hurried along the street, his head down, heading for a favourite café where he often had lunch. He stopped and looked round. He saw a familiar face.

"Havertz?"

The Swiss held his hand up. "Yes. How are you?" He walked up to Baudet. "How did you get on the other night?" he asked.

"Remarkably well as a matter of fact."

"A winning streak?"

Baudet nodded. "You could say that. In more ways than one."

Havertz looked intrigued. "Really? Tell me about it."

Baudet glanced up the street. "Well, I'm just on my way to lunch. Why not join me if you have time?"

Havertz looked at his watch and shook his head. "I'm sorry, but I have an appointment." He touched Baudet on the shoulder. "What about tonight? I'm going to the club. Why not meet me there?"

Baudet wanted to say no because he had precious little money left, and the thought of risking it on the tables was difficult to contemplate. But the invitation was planted in his mind, and he thought he might even be able to coax some money out of the friendly Havertz.

"Why not?" he said after a few moment's thought. "I'll be there this evening."

Havertz grinned and nodded firmly. "Good. I look forward to it."

He strode off leaving Baudet wondering if he could make something out of this burgeoning friendship. At least it made him feel a little better about himself, which meant he would probably enjoy his short lunch break for a change.

***

The Hotel Metropole was one of the most elegant hotels in Paris, and had been a popular place for many years, particularly among the wealthy and people of significance, including high profile celebrities. Top acts like Josephine Baker and Maurice Chevalier had performed there, and the majority of shows there were constant sell-outs.

Charlotte knew precious little of the hotel's history because it was never of any consequence to her in her earlier years; her youth having been spent in more prosaic pursuits and never belonged to that particular culture. She turned into the road beneath the Monument at Place Saint Michel and cycled up to the colonnaded entrance to the Metropole. The relatively short ride from where she'd left Jacques had been through empty streets, virtually no traffic other than a few cyclists and the occasional horse and cart. It was eery to see a city emptying itself of life, and she wondered if there would be sufficient clientele at the hotel to warrant it remaining open.

She found a metal loop set into the wall where she was able to lock her bicycle. Then she brushed her hands down her skirt and fussed with her hair a little before walking into the grand foyer. Her time in Oxford among the old spires and architecture of the city had always left her in awe of such splendour. She recalled those moments as she gazed at the magnificent décor in front of her. She stood transfixed for a while, then sighed and made her way over to the reception desk.

There were two people behind it, both wearing the distinctive purple uniforms with gold edging on the jackets. One of them, a young woman looked at Charlotte.

"Can I help you?" she asked.

"Yes. I'm looking for Armand, the concierge," she said. She tried to make it sound as natural as possible.

"He will be in his office. If you tell me your name, I'll call him."

She picked up the phone and punched in a single number. After a few seconds, her face brightened. "Oh, it's Claudette here. A young lady here wishes to speak with you."

Charlotte watched the young woman's face, trying to read the expression.

"What is your name and why do you want to see the concierge?" Claudette asked.

Charlotte couldn't invent anything, so she told the truth.

"My name is Charlotte de la Cour, and I'm looking for a job. Armand's friend, Jacques, suggested I try here."

Claudette passed that on and then put the phone down. "Wait there," she said, and pointed over to a table and velvet covered chairs on the opposite side of the foyer.

Charlotte did as she was asked and went over to the chairs and sat down. Within a few minutes, she saw the man she assumed to be Armand coming towards her. He stopped by the table. He was big, overweight and it was obvious that his waistcoat was struggling against his rotund girth. He had a pleasant face though. A dark moustache adorned his upper lip.

"Charlotte de la Cour?"

Charlotte nodded and took the hand he was offering. "Yes."

Armand sat down. "How do you know Jacques?" he asked. When Charlotte told him how they had met, he laughed softly. "Yes, Jacques will not let the Germans drive him out of Paris. But why are you here?"

Charlotte told him of her dilemma now that the ferries had stopped running. "It's as I told Jacques: I am not trapped in a foreign country; this is my home. I am French. And because I cannot go back to my mother in England, I need to earn money so I can live and support myself."

"Do you have any skills you can offer the Metropole?"

"I speak French, German and English fluently, which means I should be able to talk to any of your clients —"

"Guests!" he interrupted smoothly. "Guests."

She apologised. "Sorry — guests. I could speak to them in their own language." She stopped because he was holding his hand up.

"You are aware of what is happening and how this could impact on the hotel?"

Charlotte shrugged. "I think we all know that France is losing the war."

"The army is in retreat. Already the British are heading for the coast. It is said they will be at Dunkirk even as the Germans arrive."

He leaned back away from the table. "But let's not talk of war, Charlotte; let's talk of work. I can offer you a job here as a waitress. You would be expected to wait on tables, serve drinks, be here for important functions and always, always be clean, polite and dressed in the Metropole uniform. Do you think you can manage that?"

Charlotte said she could. Armand seemed satisfied.

"Come in tomorrow first thing and we will find you something to wear and show you what your duties are. You'll get 2500 francs a month in wages. It isn't much, I admit, but you will get tips, I'm sure."

It wasn't a good wage, but Charlotte knew she was lucky to have found a job, and, like Armand said, her money would be boosted by tips. She thanked him, shook his hand and wished him good day. Then she walked out of the hotel with a spring in her step and looking forward to telling her aunt that she had a job.

She was so pleased with herself that she didn't see Jacques who was standing by his carriage watching for her.

Jacques slapped his horse on the side of its neck. "Time to go home, Charles," he said with a satisfied smile on his face. "Time to go home."

***

Baudet's mind was in turmoil as the news poured in about the capitulation of the French Army and that the British Expeditionary Force were scrambling in retreat and gathering near the coastal town of Dunkirk. Soon it would be over: the Germans would have completely routed all forces against them and would be in Paris within days. He wished he had the security of being neutral like Havertz. He even considered that there might be a way of strengthening their friendship in the hope that some of that neutrality would rub off. It was complete nonsense of course, but so was the way his miserable life was turning out. He was desperate to find a way of resolving his problems and hoped Havertz would be the answer.

He walked through the club entrance with a cursory nod to the uniformed man at the door and went straight over to the bar where he ordered a cognac. Once he had the drink in his hand he turned round and looked over at the gaming tables. All he could see were happy, smiling faces, which in reality was simply not true; it was how he imagined those people would be feeling, but the truth was, he was envious of them, and this gave him a jaundiced view of life at the tables.

He saw Havertz sitting in a corner booth. The man was on his own. Baudet pushed himself away from the bar and went over to him. Havertz saw him coming over and immediately straightened and smiled brightly. He stood up and held out his hand.

Baudet shook it. "Good evening, Rudolf. On your own?"

Havertz released Baudet's hand and sat down. "For the moment, yes. How are you?"

"Not so good," Baudet admitted. "The news coming out of France is depressing. Quite like my luck, it seems."

"But you won the other night, did you not?"

Baudet sat down and put his brandy on the table.

"Luck has a habit of deserting me as soon as it looks like I'm doing well. I came back the following day and…" he shrugged. "Let's say I should have stayed at home."

Havertz caught the eye of a waiter and called him over. "Another brandy, Pierre?" When Baudet nodded, he ordered two drinks. "Perhaps we can change your luck for you tonight," he said with a lift in his voice."

"I think what little money I have would soon disappear." He raised his head and looked around the club. "And my credit here is like the French Army — finished."

"But your credit with me could be different."

Baudet looked at him. "Really? How?"

At that moment he was distracted as a woman slid into the sear next to Havertz.

"Hello, Rudolf," she said and kissed him on the cheek.

Baudet frowned. It was the woman he'd spent the night with. "Clementine?"

She smiled at him. "Pierre, how are you?"

He switched his gaze from her to Havertz and back again. "You two know each other?"

"I'm Rudolf's sister," she said.

Baudet relaxed immediately; for a moment he'd thought the worst. But his mind instantly switched to the thought of another night with the gorgeous Clementine, and he felt a lot happier at the prospect.

"Will you be playing tonight?" He hoped the double meaning would be picked up.

"I think so. It was such fun the other night."

He looked at Havertz. "We were talking about, erm, credit. How would that work?"

Havertz turned towards Clementine. "Do you have them?"

She opened her purse and took out a paper tube of gaming chips which she handed to him. He took the tube in his hand and ran his thumbnail around the centre. Then he snapped the tube in half and handed one half to Baudet.

"You give me back that half and half of what you win."

Baudet felt the weight of the tube and compared that to the weight on his mind. "But what if I ..."

"Lose?" Havertz answered for him. "We'll see, but I think you could be lucky again." He stood up. "Let's go play Baccarat."

***

When Baudet woke up the following morning in his apartment overlooking the River Thames in Putney, it took him a while to figure out what had happened the night before. He threw back the covers and swung his legs out of bed, then staggered over to the window and swept the curtain back. He looked out over the river flowing by effortlessly and silently, then turned away and went through to the bathroom.

He was still trying to process what he'd been up to and what he'd done, or drunk, to render his mind an almost complete blank, and set about making himself a cup of coffee, hoping that would revive his memory. He took his cup over to the small table by the window, sat down and sipped the strong black coffee.

He remembered Havertz laughing. Then Clementine. He looked over at the bed and wondered if she'd slept there. And that's when he spotted a small package lying on top of the Victorian dresser on the far side of the room. He frowned and went over to the dresser and took the package back to the window. He tore it open and emptied the contents on to the woven table cloth.

His mouth opened in shock; a pile of banknotes covered a small, manilla envelope. He picked up the money and flicked through it. Two hundred pounds. He frowned and checked it again wondering if that was his winnings. Then he picked up the envelope, put his finger in the flap and ripped it open. He held it upside down and shook it. Several photographs fell out. He picked one up and his whole world came crashing down when he saw the images displayed.

He slumped into the chair and put his hand on his forehead. Then he scattered the other photographs over the table. They were of the same people: himself, Clementine and two others: a man and a woman he neither knew or remembered. Their nakedness and positions left nothing to the imagination, but the killer was the Swastika flag hanging in the background.

His phone burst into life. The sound of the double ringing repeating itself frightened the life out of him. He stared over at the black instrument, then shook his head, got up and with a heavy heart, he wandered sluggishly to the dresser and picked the phone up.

"Pierre Baudet."

"Morning, Pierre," Clementine's voice came singing

down the phone. "Lovely photographs, don't you think?"

He pulled the phone away from his ear and stared at it as though it was an alien. "What have you done, Clementine? I thought we…"

"Silly boy," she said with a chuckle. "We'll be waiting for you downstairs — in the car. Fifteen minutes."

The phone went dead.

Baudet put the receiver back and started shaking all over. He guessed the 'we' she mentioned was her and Havertz. He knew it was a sting, but there was nothing they could get from him in return for the photographs because he had no money. So, what else could they be after, he wondered?

And that was when it hit him, and he knew exactly what it was they wanted.

Chapter 5

Charlotte had been working at the Metropole for a week now, and what fascinated her about the place was the number of well-known people who used the hotel, mainly the restaurant which was where Charlotte worked. It wasn't just senior government officials, what was left of the government, but entertainers, artists, and celebrated journalists. There were never that many, simply because of those who had left Paris from fear of the advancing German Army. Quite a few Americans used the hotel too, which surprised Charlotte. But they had no reason to leave Paris because America was not at war with Germany; consequently, they moved around Paris, and France for that matter, free from the concerns that were undermining the sanity of the French people.

Because there was no longer any public transport running in Paris, the number of people forced to use bicycles was growing, and Charlotte was no exception. But she found the ten-kilometre ride to the hotel was not a problem. It was all reasonably flat and allowed her to take in those elements of Paris that had escaped her as a young girl.

She had been horrified at the concrete blockhouses that had sprung up in various parts of the city. These were guarded, so it seemed to Charlotte, by the police rather than soldiers. She thought the concrete structures were a hideous addition to the old elegance of the city streets.

She had made one good friend in the few days she'd

worked at the hotel. Like Charlotte, she was a waitress. Her name was Camille Chalamet. Camille was in her early twenties and was a mine of information and advice. She was very pretty, dark hair, small frame; petite was the word. She laughed easily and enjoyed teasing Charlotte on occasions.

She made sure that Charlotte understood Armand, the Concierge, in that although he was a stickler for style, politeness, quality service and deference to the guests, he was always ready to listen, give advice and share a joke or two. He'd made little comment to any of the staff about the prospect of Paris falling into German hands and the consequences but had advised them all to consider seriously leaving Paris before the Germans arrived. This had reduced the number on his payroll by half and literally doubled the workload of those who chose to remain.

One permanent guest who Camille had pointed out as a real gem was the Russian Countess, Rosa Lipovsky. Camille admitted she didn't know whether a Countess was a real title in Russia, but everyone seemed to be happy to refer to the lady as Countess, but when speaking to her, she was to be addressed as 'Madame'.

Charlotte's first encounter with her was memorable. The Countess had swept into the dining room in a display of regal elegance and immediately asked Charlotte her name as she looked at the breakfast menu.

"Charlotte, Madame."

"Your name, young lady, your full name!" the Countess snapped sharply.

"Charlotte de la Cour," Charlotte answered awkwardly.

The Countess put her hand on Charlotte's arm. "That's better my dear; there are many Charlottes in Paris. Now I know which one you are." She patted Charlotte's arm and ordered toast and coffee.

Charlotte spun away and saw Camille smiling broadly at her. She guessed Camille had been through the unusual introduction too.

When the Countess had finished her breakfast, Charlotte came over to clear the plates away.

"Would you like more coffee, Madame," she asked.

The Countess put her hand on Charlotte's arm. "Are you afraid, my dear?"

Charlotte couldn't answer the question immediately because she wasn't sure what the Countess was referring to.

"I'm sorry, Madam," she started to say, but the Countess stopped her.

"A lot of staff have left the hotel, but you and Camille are still here."

"This is my home," Charlotte told her. "I am French; it's where I belong. I can't speak for Camille."

The Countess chuckled. "I am Russian, but Russia is not where I belong." She made a sweeping motion with her free hand. "My friends are here. My life is here. And I have nowhere to go. But you my dear Charlotte…"

She left the statement there.

"I am looking after my aunt," Charlotte lied. "I can't leave her." She managed to pull her arm away. "Now, if you'll excuse me Madame, I have to get on."

The Countess moved away from the table, waved at someone sitting on their own in the corner of the dining room and made her way over.

Charlotte started piling the debris from the table on to a tray when Camille came over.

"Strange, isn't she?"

Charlotte frowned. "How do you get on with her?"

Camille lowered her voice to a conspiratorial whisper. "She's a sweetie really; she just acts regal. Word is she doesn't have two Francs to rub together."

"So how can she afford to stay at the Metropole?"

Camille shrugged. "Your guess is as good as mine, but she must have friends in very high places; that's all I can say."

***

Eugene Bayard walked into the breakfast room at his Chateau yawning deeply. He put his hand to his mouth, mumbled an apology and kissed his wife, Marcella, on the cheek. Bayard had purchased the Chateau several years earlier when it became clear to him that his wife wanted to live in her beloved France. He spent a prodigious amount of money on the Chateau, turning it into a sumptuous home, which he gave to his wife once all the refurbishment and landscaping had been completed. But when war was declared between France and Germany, Marcella suggested leasing part of the Chateau and the extensive grounds to the American government so that it could be used as the temporary home of the American Embassy. It was a favourable union for both parties. It meant that the Chateau would be under diplomatic American protection and could not be requisitioned by the Germans should they occupy Paris. The lease was a peppercorn rent, which Bayard was happy to go along with.

"Morning my darling," he said, and went over to the buffet and helped himself to a cup of coffee. He brought it over to the table and sat down facing her.

She smiled sweetly at him. "And what did you and the Ambassador get up to last night?" she asked with a knowing expression on her face.

Bayard grimaced. "Drank too much Bourbon, I think."

"Celebrating something?"

He tipped his head to one side briefly. "Well, Petain has been confirmed as Vice President of the Council of Ministers, and Charles de Gaulle has been promoted to Brigadier General."

Marcella frowned and the brightness in her eyes became dulled. "And that is something to celebrate, is it? Will that win the war for France?"

He gave her a piercing look. "Unlikely. I think it is simply accelerating the outcome. We believe de Gaulle is on his way to England."

"What on earth for?"

"Perhaps he thinks he'll do better over there," he said unkindly. "I'm afraid, my darling Marcella, your brave French Army are done for."

Marcella was French. She'd met Bayard in America thirty years earlier. She fallen in love with him almost immediately. He was an imposing figure of a man. Well over six feet tall, broad shoulders on a towering frame. He had a rich, baritone voice that commanded attention when he spoke, and piercing blue eyes that contrasted sharply to his blond hair. A whirlwind courtship followed that first meeting, and they were married within six months. She loved him as much now as she did when they married. Probably more so.

Bayard had been scratching a living in scrap metal when they met, but his intelligence, fierce determination and sheer will to win helped him forge a career that brought him unimaginable wealth and power as owner of a global network of manufacturing companies. And as the German Wehrmacht was breaking all before it, Bayard was making an awful lot of money selling them the arms and weaponry they needed.

"People are leaving the country in their droves, Eugene," she said. "There will be no-one left."

"There will be plenty of Germans here to fill the gaps," he answered. "It's as well that America have refused to get involved, which makes you and I both neutral."

"In name only. For me that is," she added.

He smiled. "At least you have my protection as my wife."

Just then one of the kitchen staff came through.

"Would you like breakfast, Monsieur Bayard?"

He looked up. "Yes please, Marie. The usual." She was about to walk away when he stopped her. "Marie, why haven't you left France? Why are you staying?"

"My mother is stubborn; she won't leave," Marie explained. "And I have a duty to her and to France. So no, I will not leave either."

Marcella was looking directly at her seeing a brave but frightened young woman.

"Marie," she said. "If you feel the need, you can bring your mother here to the Chateau for protection. Things might become uncomfortable, but I believe we can keep you safe here."

Marie bobbed in a little curtsey. "Thank you, Madam; I will tell my mother." She turned away and walked out of the breakfast room.

Marcella turned and looked at her husband. "What do you think she meant by having a duty to France?"

He held his hands out, palms upwards. "There will be a lot of brave French people who will fight the Germans with whatever they can and are willing to die for their cause."

"Resistance?"

He nodded. "And they will need some powerful friends."

Marcella knew the kind of friends her husband was referring to, but they were unlikely to find them in France.

"Is Bobby up yet?" he asked, looking over the top of his cup as he took a mouthful of coffee.

She gave him a peculiar look. "I shouldn't think so; he was out with Nicolas last night, and you know what those two can get up to."

He made a grumpy sound. "Hmm. I worry about that boy at times, especially now that France is at war with Germany. There's precious little of anything for him to get his teeth into, and I doubt if the Sorbonne will remain open." He put his cup down. "I think it might be in his best interest if we pack him off to America. He can go to university over there."

"Oh, Eugene," she said sternly, "you can be quite dense at times. Bobby is practically French. He's been brought up here; he's a native in all but name."

"But he's still American."

"And he wouldn't thank you for packing him off to the States. He wouldn't go anyway."

The subject of their conversation walked into the breakfast room. "Hi, Mom, hi Dad." He came over to the table and kissed them both, then helped himself to a coffee. Bobby was a smaller version of his father and, although he lacked his father's charisma, he possessed the kind of charm and affability that attracted the ladies.

"So, what did you get up to last night?"

He shot his father a knowing look. "Girls, dad. What else?"

Marcela affected a deep sigh. "Bobby!"

"Just joking, Mom. We went to a movie, then grabbed a nightcap at the Moulin Rouge."

Marcela shook her head, knowing he was playing with her.

He came over and sat down. "We talked about the way the war is going. Nicolas is a bit concerned of course, being French. He doesn't think his job with the Ministry is going to last and expects to get called up into the Army."

"What army?" his dad muttered. "He can't sign up for something that's unlikely to exist. He should leave France."

"And go where, Dad?"

His father acknowledged the dilemma by nodding his head.

Marie came in carrying a tray. She put Bayard's breakfast in front of him and placed another in front of Bobby.

"Will there be anything else, sir?"

Bayard shook his head. "No thank you, Marie."

She glanced at Bobby and gave him a smile, then hurried out of the breakfast room.

"That was quick," his father said to him.

"I popped into the kitchen, dad."

"Did you get a lovely smile in there too?" his mother asked.

Bobby winked at her. "Always."

Bayard picked up his napkin and tucked a corner into the neck of his shirt and picked up his knife and fork but paused before starting on the food.

"Your mother and I have been talking about sending you to the States."

Marcela looked shocked. "Eugene!"

"Well, I thought it was a sensible thing for you, judging by the state of France and the advances the Germans are making."

Bobby frowned. "I'm not going anywhere, Dad. I might be a neutral American, but France is my home and this is where I'm staying."

"If America enters the war, Bobby, you will no longer be a neutral and will have a decision to make."

"Then I'll do that if and when America takes sides against the Germans." He pointed his knife towards his mother. "And what about Mom?"

Bayard gave Marcela a quick look. "Your mother would have to return to the States."

Marcela glared at him. He shrugged.

"What do you know that you're not telling us, Dad?" Bobby asked.

"Your father was with the Ambassador last night," Marcela told him. "He has a far better insight into what's going on and what's likely to happen."

Bobby switched to his dad. "So how long before it happens?"

Bayard shook his head. "No-one can say. It depends on how long the British can hold the Germans at bay. Churchill will make sure their factories will be burning the midnight oil building arms and aeroplanes."

"And until our President declares war on the Nazis, you'll be making a ton of money building weapons for them."

"It's business, Bobby," was Bayard's lame answer. "Business."

"But some French hotheads may not see it that way, dad. Perhaps it would be better if you hightailed it back to the States instead of me."

Bayard leaned forward. "I am technically a friend of the Germans, and the Ambassador sees an advantage in that should it come to negotiating some kind of agreement that would suit France."

Bobby shovelled the remains of his breakfast into his mouth, drained his cup and dropped his napkin on his empty plate.

"I take it all this is classified stuff you're talking about, Dad?"

Bayard nodded. "Well, not to be mentioned outside these four walls of course, but until any of us can see which way the war is going, we just have to hope it will end soon."

Bobby got up from the table. "I'm off to work then." He gave them both a kiss and left them.

Marcela looked at her husband. "Will it end soon, do you think?"

He shook his head. "The Ambassador thinks it's going to get a whole lot worse. Much worse," he added solemnly.

Chapter 6

Charlotte was sitting with Camille in the small rest room attached to the kitchen where the staff were allowed to take their short rest breaks. She had been listening to Camille with interest, capturing images in her mind of the real Paris; the one rarely seen in the reports of how the city was stoutly maintaining its defiance in the face of the German threat. Camille was smoking a cigarette, which she would draw on quickly, blowing out the smoke and waving it away with a flutter of her hand.

"I live in the 16th Arrondissement," she was saying. "Have you been there?"

Charlotte nodded. "My father's Ministry work often took him over there."

"I live in what used to be a hill village years ago," Camille went on. "It's called Auteuil. Lot of embassies and consulates there and in Passy, another old village. You probably know them if your father worked over there. It's often described as a prestigious place to live because of all the high rollers and influential people who have homes there." She sucked on the cigarette again and waved the smoke away. Her gaze was now firmly fixed on the floor beneath her feet. "Well, not anymore; they're all packing up and leaving." She glanced up quickly and looked at Charlotte. "The chauffeured limos have been seen driving south. The word is they are heading towards Porte d'Orléans."

"Why there?" Charlotte asked.

"I asked my mother," Camille answered, stubbing her cigarette out in an ashtray. "She knows a Lieutenant in the police. He said that since the Germans attacked Belgium two weeks ago, those who are 'In the know'," she fluttered quote marks in the air with her fingers either side of her head, "have been told that Paris is in danger and, despite what the newspapers and radio are saying, the Battle of France is over, and for some reason, Porte d'Orléans is the safest place to be."

Charlotte felt a tiny frisson of fear ripple through her body. Her stomach knotted briefly; just long enough for her to understand that what she'd agreed to do for Jefson while in the relatively safe environment back in England bore no resemblance to the reality of the commitment she'd taken on here in France. The risk level had now risen a notch and was set to climb further each day.

"Are you okay?" Camille asked, her face showing concern.

Charlotte snapped out of it. "Sure, I'm fine." She sat up straight in the velvet cushioned dining chair. "Just lost myself there for a while."

"My mother said I should move south," Camille went on. "but I told her I'm not going anywhere. You're staying, aren't you, Charlotte?" Camille asked, her voice lifting a little with the question.

Charlotte nodded. "I have to look after my Aunt," she lied.

"But what about your mother; won't she be worried for you?"

Charlotte shook her head. "She thinks I'm lodging

in London at a secret address."

Camille drew her head into her shoulders and gave a conspiratorial laugh. "If only she knew the truth," she said. "She'd have a fit."

"I would have thought so," Charlotte agreed.

"She won't find out though, will she?" Camille asked.

"No," Charlotte answered, her voice lowered in a long denial. "I shouldn't think so. And I don't think this war will go on much longer anyway; I'll be back in England by the end of the year, you'll see."

***

At that moment, Charlotte's mother was having a chat over a cup of tea with her neighbour, Agatha Weston who everyone knew as Aggie. The talk had been about the war and Aggie's husband who was a key worker, which meant he had avoided being called up, and of Charlotte who, her mother assumed, was tucked up somewhere safe in London. She also mentioned the upcoming 'Bring and Buy' sale the village council was holding in the Village Hall.

"I'm helping with a couple of the ladies. It's to support our lads." The soldiers were often referred to in that way because it reflected the closeness people felt about their menfolk going to war. "Will you be bringing anything, Connie?"

"Of course; it's just a case of deciding what I want to get rid of and whether it would be the kind of thing someone would want to buy."

Connie heard the letterbox rattle at the front door and the sound of letters falling to the floor. She stood up.

"That will be the post," she said. "I'll just get it."

She went out into the hallway and picked up several letters. One of them was a brown Manilla envelope. She went back into the front room and dropped the letters onto the coffee table but held on to the Manilla envelope.

"This looks official," she said. "Perhaps I'm being called up," she added with an ironic smile.

Aggie got up from the armchair. "I'll let you get on," she said, "you'll want to read your mail. Thanks for the tea. I'll let myself out."

Connie watched her leave and opened the envelope with a paperknife that always resided in the fruit bowl for some reason. She opened the letter, which was typed, and then a broad smile crossed her face when she saw it was from Charlotte. She sat down and read the very uninteresting and unexciting things her daughter had been up to in London, most of which were with her roommates at the secret location where they were billeted. She read it through twice and folded it back into the envelope, then took it over to a bureau and slipped it into a small drawer along with the other two letters she'd received from Charlotte. She thought the letter had been a bit bland, but at least her daughter was okay and keeping in touch. And that was all that mattered. But the truth was, she was concerned that she hadn't been able to see Charlotte, so she decided to give it a couple more weeks and, if nothing changed, she would risk the bombing in London and go up there to the Inter-Service Bureau where she knew Charlotte had been interviewed and find out where her daughter was.

***

Charlotte and Camille's break time was interrupted when the door flew open, and Armand poked his head round the door.

"Chop, chop ladies," he said, clapping his hands together. "The American Ambassador has just come in with Monsieur Bayard. "Out you go. Oh, and one thing, Charlotte: Monsieur Bayard owns the hotel, so be extra courteous." He smiled when he saw the expression on Charlotte's face.

The two women got to their feet. Camille pointed to the toilet and indicated to Charlotte she needed to go. Consequently, Charlotte was first into the lounge area where she guessed she would find the Ambassador and Monsieur Bayard.

The two men were sitting by a low coffee table. Charlotte didn't know either of them and had never seen them before. Armand had stopped her as she left the kitchen area and was heading towards the lounge. It took him about two seconds to point out who the American Ambassador was.

"He's the smallest of the two," he said.

Charlotte came up to the table, smiled at the two men, and asked them if they would like to order.

The Ambassador, William Bullitt, smiled up at her. He had a very smooth face and a receding hairline that effectively left half of his head bald. She judged him to be well into his fifties, possibly older. He looked reasonably slim. The other gentleman, Eugene Bayard was the opposite: he looked very tall to her even though he was sitting, and he had a full head of hair. They ordered coffees with a cognac on the side.

The two men started talking; still small talk, not wanting to discuss anything too deep until the waitress had returned with their coffees and brandy. Once they had them, Bullitt switched the conversation from small talk to something far more serious.

"Belgium has capitulated."

Bayard almost choked on his coffee. "What?"

Bullit nodded his head slowly. "News came in this morning that Belgium surrendered to the Germans to avoid complete annihilation."

"Fuck!"

Bullitt grinned. "My sentiments entirely, Eugene."

Bayard put his cup down. "The Germans will be in France within days now their attention isn't being diverted by the Belgians."

"And you realise what that means?"

"It won't be long before they reach Paris."

Bullitt shook his head. "It's a little more complicated than that, I'm afraid. The French are about to concede defeat. Their soldiers are already laying down their arms. It's beyond belief, Eugene, but the largest army in the world is being humiliated. The Germans have met precious little resistance."

"Is this why you asked me here, to tell me this?" Bayard asked.

Bullitt moved a little closer. "We believe the French will offer a surrender in exchange for being allowed some form of National government here in France."

Bayard looked shocked. "My God, that's

embarrassing."

"The point is, I will be…" He stopped and struggled to find the words. "As I will be the highest ranking, legal entity in the city; I will be asked to act as *de facto* Mayor of Paris."

Bayard tried to suppress a laugh. "Bullshit, William. How can you be a government official when there will be no government?"

"Well, that's the point; the Germans will want to negotiate with a legal authority once they arrive in Paris. The French will have no authority here, apart from the police I should think. I could appoint you as an aide. And you are American, which means they have a double reason to be happy with you."

"But I can't negotiate on America's behalf, can I?"

Bullitt grinned and lifted his cognac glass. He raised with a subtle gesture. "No, but your manufacturing outlets are still selling weapons to the Germans." He held his hand up a little. "I know — it's legal and perfectly legitimate, which means you are effectively their ally. You can socialise with them, put them at their ease, and let me know anything that could be useful to us and to Winston Churchill. Your health," he added and downed the cognac.

Charlotte had been standing across the other side of the lounge. She had been told by Armand to make sure she was near enough in case the Ambassador needed anything else. As a result of that, she was able to follow their conversation with her lip-reading skill. And what she understood of the conversation between the two men made her feel weak and trembly all over.

Chapter 7

The light was fading, bringing a mood of melancholy to the empty streets when Jacques Garnier settled his horse into the stable for the night. He'd seen very little to change that feeling such was the paucity of people wanting a ride in his beautifully maintained carriage. Tourism was certainly not going to pay him enough to live on, and relying on the occasional taxi fare didn't alter that either. Not that Jacques was too disappointed; he was a philosophical man and accepted the unwanted changes in his life. He left Charles chewing away at the fresh hay hanging from the feeding crate in the stall and went back to the house to get his bicycle. He'd already eaten supper, but now he needed something else.

Lillie Garnier was the owner of probably the most expensive brothel in Paris, which meant her clientele were mostly high rollers in the city and carried much influence in places that mattered. But now trade was low and many of her girls had fled despite Lillie's pleas for them to remain until she knew for certain Paris would not fall. Jacques was not a high roller in the city though; he was Lillie's brother.

The ride through the quiet streets took Jacques about twenty minutes or so. There was no traffic, just the occasional car. He used the time to process his thoughts about the threat posed by the Germans now that Belgium had surrendered. He was confident in his assumption that they would be marching into Paris very soon which could be beneficial to his sister's business and a prime source of information from the inevitable pillow talk he was sure would occur.

Jacques wheeled his bicycle in through the rear entrance and left it propped up against the corridor wall. Lilie's office was through a door in the passage. He knew she would be in there because the light was on, lighting up the dappled glass. He tapped on the glass and pushed the door open.

"Evening, Lillie."

She was sitting at a desk writing. She looked up and her face brightened when she saw her brother. She got up immediately and gave him a hug.

"Hello, Jacques. Here for a quickie?"

He laughed and kissed her on the cheek. "Too old for that," he said as he flopped into a well-worn leather chair. "How are your girls?"

Lillie shook her head and sat down. "Not good; some of them are thinking of leaving Paris."

"I think they should all leave."

"And that would be bad for business, wouldn't it?"

"But safer, don't you think?"

She smiled and closed the ledger she'd been working on. "Would you like a drink?"

"I'll have a cognac please."

She pushed a button on a box in front of her and waited until she had a response.

"Yes?"

"My brother's here, Rose. Can you bring him a cognac please?" She released the button and sat back in the chair. "So, what brings you here?" she asked.

"Belgium has surrendered."

As a statement, it had no intensity, but as a fact in the current situation, it was hugely important. Lillie looked up at the ceiling.

"Mon Dieu." She turned and looked at him. "What happens now?"

He sighed heavily, blowing his cheeks out. "France will be next, no doubt. The British army is at Dunkirk, so there's little hope we can survive now. It won't be long before the Germans are in Paris."

Lillie's expression was grim. "I worry for my girls; they haven't all gone yet."

The door opened and Rose came in with Jacques' cognac. She handed it to him. "You want to see me tonight, Jaques?"

He gave her a winning smile. "I'm broke."

She flicked a knowing look at Lillie and left the office, pulling the door closed behind her.

Jacques took a sip of the cognac. "If the Germans occupy Paris, which I'm sure they will, you could be in for a lot of business."

Lillie's expression changed as she raised her eyebrows. Jacques thought she looked thoughtful.

"What's on your mind?" he asked.

"We will either be shut down or allowed to remain open." She answered. "My guess is we'll be allowed to carry on under certain conditions."

"Such as?"

"It could be Germans only. If they agree to let our French regulars use us, we will have to bar the Jews."

He sighed heavily, puffing out his cheeks. "Sad bastards."

"Who? The Jews?"

He shook his head. "No, the Germans."

She stretched her arm out and put her hand on his knee. "What will you do, Jacques? Where will you go?"

He pulled a face and tipped his head to one side. "Me? You forget I have Charles to look after. I can't leave him, can I?"

She scoffed. "You and that bloody horse," she said, pulling her hand away. "I think you love him more than you loved Giselle."

Jacques laughed at that. His wife, Giselle, had died a few years earlier. They'd been married nearly fifty years, and he mourned her every day.

"Charles helps keep the wolves from the door. If the Germans do take up residence in Paris, I'm sure my tourism business will grow."

Lillie affected a surprised look. "Collaboration, Jacques? Surely not."

He gave a short nod. "I can listen in on the passengers I take round Paris: learn secrets from them."

"You wish. I'll get more from them here if the girls are clever enough."

Jacques straightened a little in his chair. "You serious?"

She sat back. "I've been thinking about it for some time now. If we can stay open, there's a good chance some of the more..." She paused for a moment. "Effusive clients may start talking when they get to know the girls better."

"When they've had a few drinks, you mean?"

"It happens, Jacques. You wouldn't believe some of

the stories our girls hear." She lifted her hand and pointed at him. "And that's from men working in important government positions."

"How would you get anything relevant to the right people?"

She shrugged. "Who are the right people?"

"That's a point," he agreed. "We'll have no government in Paris. The police would be the only people you could talk to, but you wouldn't be able to trust them. You'd be arrested very quickly if you talked to the wrong policeman."

"It would have to be London," she said deliberately. "And someone who we know can get the information through."

"Do you know anyone?"

She shook her head. "No."

"Me neither."

"Well, that's it then, Jacques. Unless a resistance movement starts up, we'll have no one we can trust."

"And in any conflict, it's difficult to find someone who you can trust."

She sighed and stood up. "I have to go, Jacques. Clients will start coming in and they like to see me."

He looked at his sister. Even in her late sixties, she managed to look beautiful. She was always elegantly dressed when she was overseeing the girls and their clients. He knew she'd been offered some very serious money to spend a night with whoever was making the offer, but she had always kept her clients at arm's length.

He finished his cognac and got up from the chair.

"I'll catch up with you later, Lillie. Thanks for the drink."

He put the glass down and kissed her on the cheek, giving her a warm hug in the process. Then he turned and walked out of the office feeling very pleased with himself; he'd wondered how he was going to persuade his sister to use her girls in the battle against the Germans. Now he didn't have to.

And he knew someone who was already in place and in contact with London.

Chapter 8

Charlotte came down earlier than usual for her breakfast before cycling off to her job at the Metropole. She was surprised to see her Aunt Matilde still in her dressing gown and listening intently to the radio broadcast from London. She turned the moment she heard Charlotte come into the kitchen and switched the radio off.

"Morning, Matilde," Charlotte called out as she made her way over to the stove and the coffee pot. "Any news?" Matilde's expression and the fact that she was shaking her head told Charlotte everything. She poured her coffee and came over to sit beside her aunt. "Bad news then?"

"The evacuation at Dunkirk is over," she said solemnly. "And they've made that fool, de Gaulle a Brigadier General."

Charlotte frowned. "Why is that such a bad thing?"

Matilde stood up and walked over to the stove. "Over one and half million French soldiers have been captured by the Germans, Charlotte. The Army no longer exists, but we can sleep safe in our beds because we have a Brigadier General fighting for us in London." She lifted her jaw and yelled at the wall. "*Merde!* What colossal fools we have made of ourselves." She spun round. "De Gaulle has been named as under-secretary for war and national defence." She slapped her hands on her chest. "How in Heaven's name is he going to defend France while he's run off to London? What with?"

Charlotte had never seen her aunt so angry. Sure, there were times when she'd lost her temper, but this was a vitriolic display of anger and contempt.

"I'm sure there was nothing he could do," Charlotte said lamely.

Matilde turned back to the stove and poured a coffee for herself. "My God, if they had let us women join the army, none of this would have happened."

"And who would have looked after the families while the mothers were away fighting? The men?" Charlotte put to her.

Matilde grinned. It was a fact that women in France had no station in life other than to look after the family and the home. Service in the army was forbidden. She couldn't imagine how the men would cope looking after the children, shopping, cooking and being the perfect housewife and mother. She sighed, rant over and walked over to the table. She sat down and put her hand on Charlotte's.

"When Germany invaded Poland, we thought nothing would come of it. They were saying it wouldn't last long; it would be over by Christmas. We believed them." She took a sip of coffee and put her cup down, looking at Charlotte with a lightened expression on her face. "Less than a year ago, France was celebrating the storming of the Bastille. There were parties, balls, circuses, marching bands, parades." She breathed deeply. "It was such fun." She shook her head slowly. "Now look at us. And who is let to defend us?" She snorted. "Hmmph — the women."

"And how can we do that?" Charlotte asked affecting an innocence while recalling much of Jefson's words to her back in London.

"How can we do that?" Matilde repeated. "By going to war, Charlotte; by going to war."

***

Charlotte set out for the bicycle ride into Paris with Matilde's words still ringing in her ears. She had never told her aunt the real reason for her being back in France, but her aunt's last statement about going to war had a ring of truth that her aunt was probably not aware of. Charlotte was part of the secret war that had already started with agents like her in place in Paris and elsewhere in the country. She didn't like to think of herself as an agent; it was a 'catch-all' word that implied shadowy creatures and secret meetings in dark places, but the truth was, she was working for the British government's secret service, which meant she was an agent — a spy. But despite accepting that, she had no idea who she was supposed to be reporting to — who was her handler? And there was precious little she could do about that other than to wait until, as Jefson told her, someone would be in touch.

Charlotte was ruminating on those thoughts when she saw a group of men, about five in all, walking towards her. Two of the men were walking in the road. She frowned and felt apprehensive because it was most unusual to see more than just one man on his own in the empty streets. Then she remembered the distressing news that there were French army deserters wandering aimlessly away from the harrowing defeat and capitulation against the Germans and heading for Paris. The men all looked like they were wearing the same clothes, which could only have been army uniforms, but none of them appeared to be smartly dressed.

She slowed down as the two men in the road moved over to her side of the road, looking as though they intended to stop her. For a brief moment, Charlotte started to panic, unsure what she should do. But before she could get her thoughts straight, the two men reached her. They stood with their arms stretched out, effectively blocking her way in the narrow street. She stopped and put one foot on the ground. One of the men lowered his arms and took hold of the handlebars.

"What are you doing?" she asked him, trying to show some assertiveness in her voice.

"Do you have any cigarettes, mademoiselle?"

Charlotte shook her head. "No; I don't smoke."

The other came stepped up beside her. "Do you have any money?"

"No." She tried to pull the bike away from the man holding the handlebars, but it made no difference.

"What can you give us?" he asked as he looked briefly at his companion and grinned.

"I don't know what you mean?" She was beginning to get quite scared now. "Now, please let me pass."

"What about a kiss?"

Charlotte started struggling to get the bike free, but the man standing beside her put his arm around her waist and held her tight.

"One kiss," he said.

Charlotte swung her arm and elbowed him in the

face. He swore and put his hand to his cheek. His friend started laughing.

"A fighter, eh?"

"More than you by the looks of it," Charlotte snapped back at him. "Bloody deserters!"

He was about to put his hands up to her when he was suddenly grabbed from behind by one of the men who had been walking on the pavement.

"Enough, Henri!," he said, and pulled him away making him release his hands from the handlebars. "Leave the woman alone."

It seemed to be enough for the two men. They walked away, ambling over to the pavement where the rest of the men were standing. They were muttering and gesticulating. Their friends were laughing at them.

"I apologise for their behaviour, mademoiselle," her rescuer said to her, "but a pretty woman like you should not be unaccompanied. Next time you may not be so lucky." He smiled, touched his forehead with the tip of his forefinger and waved his hand forward indicating that it was safe for her to go on.

Charlotte felt her body relaxing and mumbled her thanks but was now anxious to get away and into the relative safety of the hotel.

And as she cycled away she was immediately troubled by the prospect of travelling each day to work and hoping that she would not have an encounter like that again. But she knew that soon it would not have to be French Army stragglers she would be concerned about, but the invading, German army.

***

Charlotte arrived at the hotel with no more incidents involving French soldiers. She felt desperately sorry for those men because of the total capitulation of what had been described as the biggest army in the world. Three million soldiers put to the metaphorical sword by a triumphant German army. She, like most people left in Paris, knew it wouldn't be long before the Germans reached the city; after all, there was no-one to stop them. Most people suspected they would be there by the end of the month, just three weeks away. The last newspaper to be printed was about to suspend publication, which meant most news was verbal and completely unreliable. Not that it mattered who got the timing right; the German occupation would soon be a fact of life.

She wheeled her bicycle into the back yard of the hotel, padlocked it and hurried into the kitchen. Her friend, Camille saw her come in and went to greet her. As they touched cheeks, Camille thought she could feel tension in Charlotte's hug.

"*Mon Dieu*, you are tense, Charlotte. Something wrong?"

Charlotte sighed deeply and told Camille of the unhappy bunch of soldiers she had run into. "We've all heard of women being attacked," she said as they walked into the locker room to get changed. "I thought I was in real trouble." She shook her head and wiped the back of her hand over her eyes. It was shaking. "Look at this," she said, showing Camille.

Camille took her hand. "You need a coffee," she said.

"I need more than that," Charlotte said, laughing softly. "A large cognac would be better."

Camille tutted. "If Armand sees you quaffing cognacs on duty, he'll have a fit."

Charlotte finished tying her apron on. "I'll have a coffee then," she said and glanced at her watch. "We've got ten minutes."

She closed her locker door and followed Camille into the kitchen. Armand was in there. He took a fob watch from his waistcoat pocket, looked at it and slipped it back into his pocket. He beckoned the two girls over.

"Bring your coffee to my office," he said, and walked away. When they reached the office, Armand turned to them. He looked downbeat.

"Charlotte, Camille, our illustrious Premier has declared Paris an open city." He flopped down into the chair by his desk. "He made the announcement thirty minutes ago."

They waited for him to say something else, but he appeared to be lost for words.

"What does that mean, Armand?"

He looked up at her. "Paris will not be defended. It's a complete surrender. Reynaud believes it will save Paris from Hitler's bombs." He shook his head despairingly. "I have to ask if you wish to leave Paris before the Germans arrive."

Charlotte knew she couldn't do that; her situation meant she had little choice. "I can't do that, Armand," she told him.

He looked at Camille, the question forming on his

face as he raised his eyebrows.

"I'm staying," she said.

He waited for an explanation, but when he saw none was forthcoming, he visibly relaxed. "I had to ask you both." He shrugged his ample shoulders. "You two were the only ones left of the staff I hadn't asked." He chuckled. "I have some brave people working for me; no-one will be leaving." He paused there for a moment, lowering his gaze to the floor as he rubbed his chin. Then he puffed out his cheeks and lifted his head. "Monsieur Bayard has asked me to be prepared for a large influx of clientele; mainly Germans, which means there will be opportunities for more staff, so, it's good that you are staying."

"And what about you, Armand?" Camille asked. "Are you staying?"

He leaned back in his chair. "Well, we expect the hotel will be busier than ever once the Germans arrive. So yes; I'm staying."

He flapped his hands at them, shooing them away. They went back to the kitchen taking their empty cups with them. Two minutes later they were standing by the restaurant buffet both wondering what life would be like once the Germans arrived.

***

There were no guests in the restaurant for dinner that evening other than William Bullit and Eugene Bayard. Bullit had been made Mayor of Paris the previous day, the 12th, by the French government. His first unenviable duty would be to welcome the Germans into Paris the following day. The reason for the absence of guests was simply down to the fact that a deep uncertainty haunted the minds of those citizens who had not fled along with the estimated three million souls who had, and the last thing on their minds was to dine at the Metropole as if that day was just another normal day, not the precursor to the German shadow that was enclosing the city.

Earlier that evening, Charlotte had waited on Countess Lipovsky who had chosen not to linger but retired to her room before the two men arrived. She had asked Charlotte why she hadn't left Paris like most people.

"I have my Aunt Matilde to think of," she told the Countess. "She wouldn't leave because she has no news of her husband." She picked up the Countess's empty plate. "She's waiting for him to come home." It was a simple statement that summed up the dilemma facing wives who had no news of their husbands. Do they go or do they stay?

As the evening wore on, most of the staff had been dismissed until there was just Charlotte and Camile plus a few left in the kitchen. Armand came through and beckoned Charlotte. She walked over to him thinking he may be letting her go home early.

"Jacques is in the kitchen. He wants to see you."

She frowned and went through to the kitchen where Jacques was waiting. His face brightened when he saw her.

"You want to see me, Jacques?"

"I hear you had a difficult ride in to work today."

She nodded. "Yes, but how did you know?"

"Armand." He was leaning up against the kitchen

worksurface. He straightened. "He told me you refused to stay here in one of the staff rooms because of getting home to Matilde. So, for your safety, I will be happy to escort you home tonight."

Charlotte opened her mouth in surprise. "Well, erm, thank you, Jacques. Are you sure?"

"That's a silly question, Charlotte. I wouldn't have offered if I didn't want to do it."

"But it will be late and dark. And what about your horse?"

He grinned. "Charles says he is quite happy to escort mademoiselle home."

She put her hand on his shoulder. "Thank you, Jacques." She looked at her watch. "I finish at eleven." She looked back over her shoulder. "Although there it's unlikely anyone will be here. Except maybe the Mayor and Monsieur Bayard," she added.

"In that case I will see you at eleven."

Charlotte had been trying not to think too much about her bike ride home, but her encounter that morning with the French soldiers had frightened her, and the prospect of cycling through the dark, empty streets did not fill her with enthusiasm.

Jacques was waiting outside the front of the Metropole when Charlotte came round with her bicycle. He lifted it into the back of the carriage and helped Charlotte up on to the front seat. He clambered up beside her and said nothing for a moment or two. Then he looked at her.

"Have you ever known Paris to be this quiet?" he said. The question was rhetorical, but it had a point. All around them was nothing but emptiness. There were no sounds of the usual nightlife that would normally echo around the streets. Above them the moon shone from a cloudless night sky, but no longer did the smoke from the fires that had once smothered Paris hide the stars, although the government had ordered the burning of the oil storage depts around the city. This had led to plumes of black smoke again, but mercifully the wind was blowing the smoke away from the city centre.

There was no music filtering from the night clubs because all their doors had been closed and the shutters locked. No streetlights were lit, which left the dark corners devoid of life — places normally inhabited by the hookers, the lowlifes and the kind of people who populated those darker places. The smell that had once polluted every nook and cranny, clamped in by the black smoke of the burning oil and papers, was no longer present. But now dwelt a different Paris. No longer the city of light, love and fashion. No longer the *'Gay Paree'* where one could drink in the *'Joie de vivre'* for which Paris was renowned. No longer the essence of warmth, of laughter and hope. Paris was now dead, and into her lifeless soul would sweep the all-conquering Germans to despoil its charm and rip out its heart.

Jacques tugged briefly at the reins and released the foot brake. The carriage jerked and then moved smoothly and quietly, and only the sound of the horse's hoofs broke the silence as they moved through the deserted streets.

"You chose to stay, Charlotte?" Jacques said after a

while. "Are you not afraid?"

Charlotte wanted to admit that she was but fear was something she had to consign to the back of her mind. She simply muttered, "Of course."

Jacques nodded in the darkness. "I am too, *Cherie*. But we must not break; we have to face them."

"Will you be there tomorrow?" she asked. "When they come?"

"Yes. I will stand there, look into their faces and show defiance." He shrugged. "What else can we do?"

"We can resist," Charlotte said unwittingly. "If we knew how."

He turned his face to her. "That will come, Charlotte, make no mistake." Then he looked back towards the empty road. "Make no mistake."

They lapsed into silence then, each with their own thoughts until Jacques brought the carriage to a halt outside Matilde's smallholding.

"What will you do now, Jacques? Go back?"

He shook his head. "I think I will stay here. Charles will be fine, and I can always sleep in my carriage." He looked at her and grinned. "I've slept out many times in the past, Charlotte, so it's something I'm quite used to."

Charlotte looked up at the night sky, then at her aunt's cottage. There were no lights showing. She sighed deeply. "She'll be waiting up for me; she always does."

She got down from the carriage seat. "Thank you, Jacques. Good night."

"Don't forget your bicycle," he said as he clambered

down and retrieved it from the back.

She smiled and took the bike from him. "I might see you tomorrow, Jacques; if Armand lets us watch them."

"Then show your defiance, brave girl. I will see you soon."

Charlotte turned away and wheeled the bicycle up to the small shed where she always kept it. But the shed was locked, which was unusual. She frowned and propped the bike against the front door. Then she shook her head and wondered why Matilde had done that.

She gave up thinking about it and hurried back across the yard to the small farmhouse. But there too, the front door was locked. Curiosity and a frisson of concern flooded her mind before she realised just how late she was coming home from work. She figured her aunt must have locked up because of the lateness of the hour. All she could hope for now was that her aunt hadn't gone to bed. Then she admonished herself for overthinking everything. She rattled her knuckles on the door several times.

"Matilde?" she called. "It's Charlotte."

She heard the sound of footsteps. Then a key turned in the lock and the door swung open.

"I'm sorry, Charlotte; I didn't mean to lock you out, but I have a visitor."

She turned away and let Charlotte in, closing and locking the door behind her. Charlotte waited until her aunt had finished and then followed her into the kitchen.

Sitting at the table was a young woman. She was wearing what looked like a FANY uniform, the like of which she'd seen on the women she spoke to on the train some months ago. The woman looked up and as she smiled, the small sliver of a scar across her lip distorted the smile slightly but did nothing to detract from her beauty.

She was the woman Charlotte had seen leaving Jefson's office in London.

Chapter 9

It was dawn on the morning of June 14th and the sky in the East was giving way to early morning light as two French Officers met with German delegates under a flag of truce at Sarcelles, north of Paris. The two officers were there simply to acknowledge the declaration that Paris was now officially an 'Open city', which meant Paris would not be defended but handed over according to international convention. It was an embarrassing ceremony for the two officers, and something of a humiliation. And from that moment, small columns of German infantry began marching to selected key points in the city, including the railway station and government ministries.

The two officers watched as German motorcyclists wearing leather topcoats motored past them, leading a column of marching soldiers led by a German officer, replete in a smart uniform carrying a Nazi flag. One of the French officers closed his eyes unable to watch the humiliating spectacle. Then he turned to his companion and quoted the phrase that had so often been used by French politicians, the newspapers and many of the intellectual hierarchy that dominated the hedonistic lifestyle of the beautiful city of Paris.

"So much for the *drôle de guerre,"* he muttered bitterly. *So much for the phoney war.*

***

A few hours later, as German units were taking over various strategic posts around the city, Charlotte was on her way to work. She had been asked by Armand to get in early because he was expecting a lot of activity at the hotel. As she got closer to the Metropole, she could see small groups of people gathered together on the pavements approaching the Place de la Concorde. There were several French police officers in view at strategic points around the streets. And something she never believed possible, German military vehicles parked outside some of the ministry buildings.

When she reached the hotel, Charlotte dismounted. She stayed where she was for a while watching some German soldiers putting up an enormous Nazi banner over the entrance to the hotel. She saw the *Préfet* of the police, Roger Langeron, talking to a German officer. She learned later that the officer was General Bogislav von Studnitz who had been appointed temporary military governor of Paris. She saw him point up to the Nazi banner with the dominant Swastika cross in its centre and clapped his hands together. Then he ushered Langeron into the hotel.

As she was about to turn round and take her bike to the rear of the hotel, she saw Armand come hurrying out on to the pavement. He glanced up and down the street and was about to rush back inside when he saw Charlotte. He came running over to her.

"Thank goodness you're here, Charlotte," he said a little breathlessly. "We've been ordered to prepare a champagne reception for this afternoon."

Charlotte looked at him with a frown deepening on her forehead. "You haven't been waiting for me, Armand, have you? Surely not."

He shook his head quickly. "No, I'm waiting for Monsieur Bayard. He stayed overnight. He was asked if someone of high rank could be here when the Germans arrived, so he asked Monsieur Bullit. They are supposed to be on their way over." He pointed across the road to the American Embassy. "I called the embassy to let them know that Monsieur Langeron is here with the German military governor. We have no-one here of sufficient rank to meet the General, which would be a poor show for the hotel."

Charlotte put her hand on his shoulder. "No-one said it was going to go smoothly, Armand. Calm down; I'm sure they will be here soon, but they will not be in a hurry to lick the boots of any Nazi."

He smiled. "You're right." He flapped his arm towards the main entrance. "Right, get yourself in there and see Camille. I've put her in charge of the restaurant staff, so she'll want your help."

"I've got to take my bike round the back."

He shook his head. "Bugger protocol for now, bring it through the front entrance."

She raised her eyebrows and laughed. "Resistance already, Armand. I'm proud of you."

He looked at her and a strange expression flashed across his face. Charlotte wondered if she had touched a nerve.

"I'm going," she said, and wheeled her bicycle triumphantly beneath the Nazi banner and into the hotel.

***

It was as though the world had gone mad. Armand had

miraculously procured about thirty more staff to wait on those who would be attending the champagne reception that afternoon. There was a sense of apprehension in the air, a tension that tugged at their nerves. And all that could be heard was just the murmur of quiet conversation between a small group of German officers who had arrived earlier. One of them was General von Studnitz, the military governor. He was talking to General Kurt von Briesen who was there to take the salute as the Werhmacht marched triumphantly into the open city. The third officer was an aide to Von Studnitz.

Suddenly there was movement as William Bullit walked into the room. Eugene Bayard was with him as were two American Embassy staff. They acknowledged Von Studnitz who bowed his head formally. His heels clicked together, but not with the snap associated with the usual formal Nazi greeting. He then introduced von Briesen. The two Americans shook hands with the two men. It was a very brief handshake. As neutral Americans, there was no reason for the two men to react as any Frenchman might under the circumstances. Their own, personal feelings needed to be kept at bay though, but they resonated with all those who detested and despised the Nazi Occupation, for that was what this was: nothing more than an Occupation.

A young German officer came through from the entrance and walked up to the group. He spoke to Von Briesen.

"Fifteen minutes, General."

Von Briesen lifted his head a little. "Ah, thank you. He turned to the others. "Duty calls. The moment has arrived." He bowed his head in a short movement, clicked his heels together and walked out of the hotel. Within minutes there was a sudden movement as Bullit, and his embassy officials followed them out. Bayard turned round and signalled Armand to come over.

"Armand, the parade is about to begin. I suggest you and some of your staff assemble outside the front of the hotel if they wish to witness what is an historical but tragically regrettable occasion for France. Don't force anyone though; it must be their own choice."

Armand acknowledged Bayard's instruction and went in search of those who wanted to watch the triumphant entry into Paris of the all-conquering Werhmacht.

Charlotte felt compelled to watch, but instead of going out into the street, she went upstairs to a vacant room overlooking the Place de la Concorde. Camille went with her and followed her out on to a small balcony overlooking the street.

They could see Von Briesen, who was mounted on a horse, riding towards a dais that had been erected at the Arc de Triomphe. He dismounted and walked up on to the platform. Behind him, hanging from the famous arch, a huge Nazi banner dominated the scene. They could hear the sound of a marching band in the distance beating out a steady rhythm. Then slowly, the sound got closer as the band reached the Champs Elysee and led the following lines of infantry up the long avenue towards Von Briesen.

When the columns reached the dais, Von Briesen threw his arm up in a Nazi salute as the soldiers goose-stepped past him. They all turned their heads towards him, backs erect, rifles at the slope to give an imposing show of military discipline and power.

As the band moved further away from Charlotte's position, the music faded to be replaced by the noise of military vehicles and half-tracks, some with machine gun barrels pointing skyward, slowly making their way into the heart of the city and belching out stinking diesel fumes in clouds of dirty grey smoke.

Nazi Germany had arrived.

Chapter 10

Charlotte arrived home a little before midnight after a hurried ride through the empty streets. Her mind was still full of the images from a day she never imagined she would ever see in Paris. Shortly after the humiliating spectacle of Von Briesen taking the salute as the German Army marched past the Arc de Triomphe, he had returned to the hotel where other senior Nazis had gathered for the champagne reception, which had transformed the atmosphere in a most unexpected way.

"It was like a party," she explained to her aunt who had been worried about her and was anxious to learn how the day had gone once Charlotte had settled herself at the kitchen table. She was still a little breathless from her ride home. "The Germans have commandeered the hotel."

"Commandeered?" Matilde repeated, a puzzled look on her face.

"General von Studnitz — he's the military governor," Charlotte explained, "has taken the Presidential Suite. Armand was furious, but he calmed down when Monsieur Bayard told him that the Germans would be paying guests. Can you believe that?"

She took a mouthful of coffee that Matilde had made for her.

"So, when you say it was like a party," Matilde said. "What do you mean?"

"Well, once they all got stuck into the champagne and canapes, it was as though they were celebrating something other than a victory. There must have been over a hundred of them there. Not just Germans: there were senior French officials, Americans too. I must say it was very civilised; nothing like I thought it would be. There was a lot of laughter. I even saw one of von Studnitz's staff officers greet one of the Americans like an old friend." Charlotte didn't tell her aunt that because of her lip-reading skills she learned that the two men were at university together in Bavaria. "It was bizarre."

"Were the any soldiers there?"

Charlotte shook her head. "Not in the hotel, but by about five o'clock there were hundreds of them just milling around the Champs Elysee, the Jardin de Tuileries." She flapped her hands. "They were everywhere. They were like tourists." She looked down at her coffee. "It was incredible, but it seemed to bring life back into the streets."

What about when you cycled home; were there many about?"

Charlotte shook her head. "No, the streets were still empty. I think the obvious attraction was the city centre. But I'm sure that will change."

Matilde was about to say something, but Charlotte stopped her. "Matilde, I have to ask, but who was that woman who was here last night?"

For a brief moment, her aunt's expression changed. The she relaxed. "Oh, you mean Agata."

"Agata? Is she a friend of yours?"

Matilde shook her head. "Goodness, no. She is a member of FANY — the nurses."

"What was she doing here?"

Matilde looked away. "Oh, I heard they were passing through the village." She turned her face back towards Charlotte. "As silly as it may seem, I wanted to know about Pierre." She waved her hands rapidly over the table. "Oh, I know she wouldn't be able to tell me, but I wanted to know if they had any information on wounded French soldiers." She shrugged. "It was a mad moment, that was all; to think she would know anything about your Uncle."

Charlotte reached over and laid her hand on her aunt's arm. "I'm so sorry, Matilde. A bit futile, don't you think?"

Matilde managed a smile. "Yes, a bit. But at least I was able to give her a cup of coffee."

"So where is she now?"

Matilde shook her head. "I don't know. I think they have been busy helping the refugees running from Paris, so I guess that's where she went."

Charlotte didn't believe a word of it, but she couldn't challenge her aunt's statement because it would reveal the fact that she'd seen the woman in London, and that would mean Charlotte owning up to the reason she was in France.

She stifled a yawn. "Sorry, Matilde; I'm so tired. Time for bed, I think."

Matilde got up from the table and took Charlotte's empty cup away. "I presume you're back at work in the morning?" she said. "The Germans haven't sacked you yet?"

Charlotte managed a chuckle. "No. In fact, Armand says he will need to recruit more staff, and because Paris is technically an open, free city, there is no prejudice against French citizens returning to their homes and picking up from where they left off."

Matilde came over had kissed her on the cheek. "I hope you're right, *ma petite*. Goodnight."

Charlotte took herself off to bed feeling quite pleased with the way things looked to be going. She had been able to lip read a conversation between two senior German officers, and as she laid her head on the pillow, she recalled that moment.

"It shouldn't take long," the officer said to his companion. "I believe Churchill will see the futility of continuing any aggression. Once the armistice with the French government is signed, I believe he will be willing to sue for peace. After all, we have Europe in our hands. The British have nothing to gain now. And let's face it, they have been beaten." Charlotte could see the two men raising their glasses. "By the end of the year," he said, "the war will be over."

And with these thoughts in her mind, Charlotte drifted off into a peaceful sleep.

***

Liliane Garnier had watched the day unfolding from the windows of her brothel. She felt torn between the utter despair most Parisiennes were feeling and the prospect of a wave of new clientele now that most of her regulars had fled. But coupled with that she was afraid the Germans would commandeer the brothel or, even worse, shut her business down permanently. On the last count, not that Liliane was counting, there were two hundred brothels in Paris; a number passed on to her by one of her girls. It was pillow talk, but when the whisperings came from a high-ranking officer in the Prefecture, she knew it had some basis in truth.

It was the day following the triumphant entry into Paris by the Wermacht. The rumour mill was working as efficiently as ever, despite the few French citizens remaining in Paris, and Lilianne had been surprised to learn that the expected pompous declarations by the Nazis were more or less subdued, to be replaced by assertions of good-will and *bonhomie*. People had braved the once empty city centre to see German soldiers walking around like sightseers. Stories circulated about the champagne reception that definitely had a party atmosphere. The whole thing had changed the metric in less than twenty-four hours. It gave some kind of hope to the metaphorically beleaguered Parisiennes.

Those thoughts were on her mind when the sound of a soft knocking broke them, and her office door opened. It was one of her girls, Giselle. She had wide expression on her pretty face.

"There's a German officer to see you, Liliane. He has two soldiers with him." She stepped into the office and closed the door gently.

Liliane frowned and felt sudden disappointment flood her mind. "Where are they?"

Giselle pointed back over her shoulder. "I've left them in the front lounge."

Liliane stood up and let out a deep sigh. "Okay, Giselle, let's see what they want."

She followed the girl out into the passageway and into the beautifully decorated lounge where she saw the officer browsing the artwork on the walls. He had his arms clasped behind his back. The two soldiers were standing away from him, their rifles hanging from their shoulders.

The officer turned when he heard Liliane and Giselle come into the room. He straightened up, a look of pleasant surprise on his face.

"Ah, good morning, Madame." His heels came smartly together with a robust click. "Allow me to introduce myself. I am Colonel Otto Junger, Staff officer to General von Studnitz."

Liliane walked over to him. She held her hand out. "Good morning, Colonel, how can I help you?"

He shook her hand, barely a touch, and then made a slow movement with his arm. "What a charming place you have here." He pointed at several of the paintings, some of which were pure erotica, but even to an amateur, they looked like they'd been painted by talented artists. "They look like they may be worth a great deal of money."

Liliane's heart slumped. "Do you intend taking them?" she asked.

He looked back at her. "Goodness me, no; I'm here to ask you about your intentions for the…" He seemed to struggle to find the right word. "House," he said eventually.

"My intentions?"

"Yes, do you intend remaining open?"

"Well, I would like to," she told him, "but I didn't think…"

He laughed. "That we wouldn't allow it?"

She smiled. "Something like that."

"And your staff, are there any left? Or have they all run away?"

"They had good reason too, Colonel, but I do have a few girls still here."

He pointed to the two soldiers who were showing little interest in the conversation between the Colonel and Liliane. "That's good. So would you prepare a list of the girls' names that you have and pass it on to one of my men."

Liliane turned to Giselle and called her over. She passed on the instruction and then turned back to Junger. "Would you like a tour of our…" She paused. "Our house?"

He shook his head. "I don't think that will be necessary," he told her.

"So, you're familiar with bordellos, are you?"

He laughed out loud. "Heavens no, Madame. I'm a happily married man. I love my wife dearly. We have three sons, and I've never wanted or needed to experience the so called pleasures found in houses of ill repute."

Liliane was warming to him already despite the stories and rumours she'd heard of the invading German army and the awfulness of the Nazi machine. She began to feel at ease standing there talking to him, seeing him laugh and showing no signs of arrogance at all.

His laughter slowly died away, but his eyes sparkled a little as the humour was retained in his expression. He pulled a small card from his pocket and handed it to Liliane.

"You can contact me at the Hotel Metropole." He pointed to the card. "That's my official title and the position I hold on the General's staff. It will help you should you encounter any difficulties or hold-ups in acquiring provisions or whatever it is you may need."

Liliane looked at the card. "Well, I think we are sufficiently prepared," she said. "I can't imagine we'll be that busy for a while though."

He laughed softly at that. "I think maybe you are underestimating the numbers, Madam, and you may need more girls for what I can only describe as another kind of invasion." He clicked his heels and bowed slightly. "I do hope you understand my meaning."

Liliane pocketed the card and thanked him as he took his leave. She watched him go with a warm feeling running through her and hoped that all the Germans could be like Colonel Otto Junger.

Chapter 11

As one day followed another, Charlotte found herself in a far more relaxed mood than when the Germans marched into Paris just one week earlier. There had been no sudden change in the relative freedoms enjoyed by those citizens who had chosen not to flee Paris, but to remain behind. The news that the Armistice between France and Germany was to be signed the following day brought some relief to the French, so much so that those who had fled were even beginning to trickle back as news reached out to them about the calm that had settled on Paris.

The Germans were more like tourists than conquerors and were enjoying the goods that the shops had to offer, much of which was literally unobtainable in Germany. This all contributed to a *laissez faire* sense of life and lifted the mood in the city. And incredibly, the news that Hitler would be visiting Paris was received in many places almost like the homecoming of a celebrated champion. As tension dropped and more people returned, Charlotte found herself wondering exactly what she was supposed to do as an agent of the SOE and decided that the task was withering on the vine, and she would soon be free of her obligation.

Until she arrived home from work that evening and found Agata Stasiak waiting for her at Matilde's.

Agata was not dressed in the uniform of a FANY nurse but was wearing a dull grey jacket in the style of an army blouson, and trousers. She was sitting in the same chair she had occupied when Charlotte saw her last. Matilde was with her. As always, Charlotte tended to hurry into the kitchen when she got back from the Metropole, but on seeing Agata, she literally stopped in her tracks.

"You," she said, pointing her finger at the SOE agent. "I saw you in London." She sat down slowly. "So why are you here?" She turned her head towards Matilde, her expression opening up as she realised that her aunt must have known about her connection with the SOE. "You knew. That's why my room was ready when I arrived from England."

Matilde smiled and put her hand on Charlotte's arm. "Agata will explain. And yes, you are right; I did know."

Charlotte turned back towards Agata. "Mister Jefson did this?"

Agata nodded her head slowly. "Who else could have contrived all this?"

"But…" For a moment, Charlotte was lost for words. Then she recovered her composure. "I'd decided it was over; that my work was, well, pointless now that the Germans had won. I've never been contacted by anyone for information. I've never been told who my contact is in Paris. In fact, I'm simply a waitress who works at the Hotel Metropole."

"Then you are being naïve, Charlotte; your work has just begun," Agata told her.

"And how am I supposed to know what my work consists of? I have no contact."

"I am your contact for now, but someone else will

be in touch soon, I promise."

"You're not British," Charlotte said to her.

Agata shook her head. "I'm Polish," she said. "And you are French, but we are both fighting for the same cause."

Charlotte stared at her for a few seconds, then looked at Matilde as if she was asking for assurance.

"Would you like a coffee?" Matilde asked suddenly. "Or perhaps a cognac?"

This simple question made Charlotte relax, and she felt her body sink into the hard kitchen chair. "I think a cognac would be good, Matilde; a large one."

No-one spoke while Matilde was fetching the cognac. She put the glasses on the table, poured a generous helping into Charlotte's glass, but just a shot into hers and Agata's. She sat down and lifted her glass.

"Vive La France."

The three empty glasses clattered on to the table in unison. Charlotte gave a little shudder as the cognac went down. "I've never been a fan of cognac really," she said with a soft chuckle, "but on this occasion, I think I probably needed it." She looked over at Agata. "So, what next?"

"Unfortunately, that is something we don't know," Agata answered. "At the moment anyway. We have to acquaint ourselves with the kind of knowledge and information that will help build a response to the German invasion and make it extremely difficult for them to win this war."

"And how do we do that?"

"We have to support the resistance that will

inevitably come in whatever way we can."

Charlotte pulled a face. "How, by waiting on tables?"

"No; we do that by supplying them with intelligence and arms."

Charlotte's questioning expression hadn't left her face. "Oh, I see, I'm supposed to find guns and ammunition and —"

Agata held her hand up and stopped her. "No; that's my job. Yours will be to feed me any information you can from those so-called tables you're waiting on. Even the smallest piece of gossip could be based on an element of truth. And whether you feel it's relevant or not, you let me decide that."

"But how can you do that when you're here…" she made a sweeping movement with her hand, "… and not waiting on tables with me?"

Agata gave a short nod of her head. "I know it sounds amateurish, but at the moment it's all we have." She laid the flat of her hand on the table. "It might sound subjective, Charlotte, but until we have more information it will be the only way we can operate. Hopefully we'll become a vital link between London and the Resistance. And we are not the only SOE agents in France, believe me."

Charlotte picked up her empty glass and twisted it back and forth in her hand. Before her aunt could ask he if she wanted another cognac, Charlotte shook her head and waved her aunt away. Then she looked at Agata.

"I must say it sounded much easier in London.

There's a big difference between talking and doing."

Agata stood up. "I need to go. I'll be back, hopefully, in one week. All you need to do, Charlotte, is to keep your eyes and ears open, gauge the mood of the Germans and don't write anything down; keep it in here." She tapped the side of her head with her forefinger. "And always bear in mind that you are now entering very dangerous territory. Don't trust anyone, not even your closest friends; you will never know if they've been compromised in some way by the Germans. And remember, they have had their spies in place both here and in London for a long time. You and I are just novices compared to that. Never forget it." She moved away from the table. "Until next week," she said and left without another word.

Charlotte waited until her aunt came back from locking the door. She blew her cheeks out. "Phew! I think maybe I could do with another cognac, Matilde," she said.

Her aunt shrugged her shoulders and reached for the cognac, pouring a more sensible measure into Charlotte's glass. She sat down, lifted her glass and touched Charlotte's.

"To a successful outcome and remembering not to trust anyone."

Charlotte laughed and drained her glass. "Not even you, Matilde, if we are to believe Agata."

Matilde stood up. "No, Charlotte, not even me. Goodnight my love." She walked round the table and kissed Charlotte on the cheek. "Not even me."

***

Charlotte returned to work the following morning with a great deal on her mind, particularly the revelation that her Aunt Matilde was connected to the SOE. She couldn't imagine how Jefson would have recruited her aunt but could only think it was because of some vague link between her late father and the fact she was studying at Oxford. It was a solid truth that Universities were breeding grounds for reactionaries of all colours, and it wasn't uncommon for the 'right' students to be nurtured and primed by national security services. Somehow, Jefson had joined up the dots on hers and Matilde's recruitment long before her student days were over. But it was all speculation, and Charlotte needed to remember Agata's warnings about not trusting anyone, which put a different slant on how she expected her day to turn out.

Charlotte started her morning in the usual way, an update on the day's business from Armand and a quick chat with Camille, mainly just girlie talk. She walked into the dining room and took up station by the buffet when Armand came over and directed her to a table where Eugene Bayard was about to sit down with his wife and their son and another young man. She reached the table as a German officer approached and came to attention, clicking his heels together.

"Herr Bayard, good morning."

Bayard glanced up and got to his feet as recognition dawned on him, he smiled and offered his hand. "Good morning, Colonel Junger. I hope you are well."

Junger nodded. "As ever." He turned and beckoned to another German officer who was standing just a few feet away. "Allow me to introduce Major Felix Heller. Staff officer with our security service."

Bayard shook Heller's hand who responded with the now familiar click of the heels. "Good day to you, Major. I do hope you are able to enjoy Paris despite the situation." He pointed to his wife and son. "My wife, Marcela, my son, Bobby and his friend, Nicolas."

Heller nodded. "Good day to you all. I'm sure I will enjoy Paris, and I hope to get to know you all a little better in the fullness of time, but for now I will leave you to enjoy your meal." He glanced at Bayard's son and his companion, Nicolas, then at Bayard's wife and backed away.

"Cochon visqueux" Nicolas muttered.

Marcela looked at him sternly. "Slimy pig? Really?"

"He's SD, the *Sicherheitsdienste:,* Nicolas answered with a grim expression. "Himmler's security people. They are all pigs."

"Better not let them hear you say it young man," Bayard warned him. "They can be pretty touchy about their image, don't you think?"

Before Nicolas could answer, Charlotte stepped up to the table.

"Good morning, Monsieur Bayard." She looked at Marcela. "Madame. Can I bring you a drink before you order?"

Marcela looked at her son. "Would you order for us, Robert?" She pronounced his name in accented French.

He picked up the wine menu, but before ordering, he asked Charlotte for her name.

"Charlotte, sir," she answered.

He smiled at her. "I'm Bobby. Please don't call me sir."

Charlotte felt herself blushing a little. Bobby pointed to his friend. "And this is Nicolas Escoffier."

Nicolas hadn't taken his eyes off Charlotte from the second she reached the table. "Mademoiselle, you are French" he asked.

"*Oui.*"

He smiled. "*Moi aussi* — Me too."

Charlotte liked the sound of his voice. She could tell from his accent he wasn't a Parisian. "You are from the South."

He nodded. "Antibes."

Charlotte was about to respond when Bobby put his hand on Nicolas's arm. "Will you stop chatting the young lady up so I can order the wine?" He had an impish expression on his face.

Nicolas apologised. "I got carried away. I'm sorry." He looked up at Charlotte. "*Autant pour moi* — my fault." He sat back in his chair but didn't take his eyes off Charlotte while Bobby ordered the wine, asking for the House red.

Charlotte walked away, a smile tugging at the corners of her mouth. She thought Nicolas was nice and was amused by the way he got into trouble from his friend.

***

As Charlotte went about her work serving the growing number of German Officers using the Hotel, she kept glancing over at Eugene Bayard's table, and from time to time she caught Nicolas's eye. When he was in the middle of a conversation, she was able to lip read a little of what he was saying. She caught references to the fact that Adolf Hitler would be visiting Paris within a couple of days. Charlotte assumed that was supposed to be a secret, but the rumour had been circulating for some time, and judging by the way in which the German Officers were behaving, it was fairly obvious the Führer's visit was imminent. Charlotte thought about the lack of discipline shown by those garrulous mouths, but they all appeared to be in such high spirits, it was little wonder they felt confident enough for the Führer's security.

She saw the American Ambassador, William Bullit walk in and make his way over to Bayard's table. She watched as he acknowledged everyone there. Then he stooped and spoke into Bayard's ear. Charlotte was unable to read his lips. She saw Bayard say something to his wife who put her hand on his arm and nodded. He kissed her briefly on the cheek and got up from the table. His wife turned and spoke to her son, nodded towards Nicolas and left the table. This gave Charlotte the opportunity to go over there, clear away their plates and ask if there was anything else they needed.

"No; we're finished, Charlotte, thank you," Bobby answered. He stood up and looked at Nicolas. "You coming?"

Nicolas shook his head and held his hand up. "I'll see you tomorrow. Be good."

Bobby glanced quickly at Charlotte who was standing by waiting to clear the table, then took his leave. And as Charlotte started clearing away, Nicolas spoke to her.

"What time to you finish your shift?"

Charlotte paused. "Oh, well, I'm here until dinner is finished. I'm on late shift so it will be about ten o'clock. Why?"

"I would like a chance to talk to you. If you wouldn't mind," he added.

Charlotte thought he had a pleasant way about him — the way he spoke, how polite he was. Nice looking too, which helped. She figured he was about the same age as her and thought it would be nice to get to know him, even as only a friend.

"I have to get home to my aunt," she told him. "It wouldn't be fair to her if I didn't get home until late. She would worry. But I'm back in on the early shift tomorrow. I finish at three o'clock."

"Would it be okay to meet you for coffee after your shift?"

She smiled, gathered the remains of the dirty plates and nodded. "That would be nice. I'll meet you out the back, where my bicycle is locked up. For an hour, no more."

He beamed and a broad smile broke out on his face. "I'll see you tomorrow then," he said, and got up from the table.

Charlotte finished putting the debris on her tray and watched as he left the dining room, hoping that some good might come of gaining the friendship of the young Nicolas Escoffier.

***

The following morning, Charlotte arrived at the hotel

for the start of her seven o'clock shift. There was a buzz about the place; one which made her think this was the pre-cursor to Hitler's planned visit. Or maybe the reaction, a consummate sigh of relief as it were, that the Armistice had been signed the previous day, which meant there would be no further hostilities between the two countries — for France the war was over. As she locked her bicycle away, she thought ahead to her meeting with Nicolas, and found herself humming a tune; something she hadn't done for a long, long time.

Shortly after Charlotte had started, she saw Countess Lipovsky walk up to the small table that had been set apart from the main area of the dining room and shielded with a screen — at her request — because she didn't want to become associated with the German officers who, in her opinion, were cluttering up the hotel with their air of conquering soldiers lauding it over the vanquished enemy.

Charlotte hurried over to the Countess and greeted her with a lovely smile.

"Good morning, Countess. How are you today?"

The Countess glared at her. "How do you think I am, Charlotte." She picked up her napkin and laid it on her lap. "I couldn't sleep, which means I shall be irritable for the rest of the day. There will be no conversation that has any merit because the hotel is overrun with the Bosch."

"But there are no problems between Russia and Germany, "Charlotte pointed out, "which means you should be able to talk as equals, surely?"

The Countess arched her eyebrows. "You mean that

so-called non-aggression pact between Hitler and Stalin?" She shook her head. "My dear Charlotte, please don't be fooled; the ink is barely dry on their so-called pact and I can tell you it will not last. Russia is Communist, Nazi Germany is Fascist: two bedfellows who will hate one another before the year is out. Mark my words. I'll have coffee and toast," she then said to bring the discussion to an end. "And bring me some of that delicious Seville marmalade."

Charlotte grinned. Marmalade from a Fascist country for the Countess Lipovsky who, Charlotte reasoned, was probably not a Communist and never was.

***

At the end of her shift, Charlotte made her way out to where she'd left her bicycle and expected to see Nicolas Escoffier. It was a warm, pleasant day, which meant the journey home later that afternoon would be good. She'd promised Nicolas one hour and intended to stick to that. She'd told her aunt about her planned meeting with him. She didn't like to call it a date because that would have been a presumption, but she did wonder if there might be more.

Nicolas came round the corner of the building on his bicycle and pulled up beside her.

"Hello, Charlotte. Sorry I'm late."

Charlotte glanced at her watch. "Not too bad though," she said. "Where do you want to go?"

"Let's go down to the Latin Quarter," he suggested. "We'll just have to put up with the Germans."

They cycled away together, and as they turned on to

the Place de la Concorde, Charlotte was surprised to see so many German soldiers milling about like tourists. Many of them were in groups of four or five. It didn't surprise her because she believed they may have been instructed to stick together in groups because of the possible reaction of the French to any soldier brave enough to risk wandering around on his own. The Nazi banners seemed to have proliferated overnight, adding a glaring statement to the city. Many buildings were sporting the long, curtain-like banners hanging vertically on their frontage, blazoned in red with the black Swastika encircled on a white background. The Metropole had a huge Nazi flag jutting out like a phallic symbol almost. It revolted Charlotte.

It didn't take long for them to reach the Latin Quarter, and they soon found a café that had reopened. They propped their cycles against the wall and sat down in the sunshine. Nicolas looked over at Charlotte and smiled.

"So, I have you to myself for a while," he said.

Charlotte looked at the few tables that were unoccupied. "For now," she said. "The place will be full of Germans soon." She surprised herself because she had lowered her voice to a conspiratorial whisper.

A waiter came up and took their order for coffee and a slice of cake. Nicolas asked him if he had served many Germans.

"They are our only customers," he told him. "You two are the first French people today." He nodded and walked away.

Nicolas turned to Charlotte. "So, tell me about

yourself. Why are you here?"

"I live here. This is my home."

He leaned forward against the table. "I have to confess to being that curious about you, so I made some discreet enquiries."

"Camille?"

He laughed and leaned back into his chair. "You came back to Paris for your Aunt and got trapped: couldn't get back to England where you were living with your mother."

Jefson's words came into her head. *Say as little as possible and reveal nothing, however innocent the questions may seem.* "I'd finished my studies at Oxford and was coming back anyway." It was the truth, part truth anyway, but only insofar as she had planned to go back to England with her aunt, return to France and not get trapped by the German advance. "And what about you, Nicolas? How come you didn't join the army?"

"I was working in a key role for the government. I volunteered but you don't always get the choice. Now I'm unemployed but on balance I have to say I'm happy they wouldn't let me join."

"You got lucky," Charlotte told him with a grin on her face. "I would be happy too."

He frowned and shook his head. "Not really; no-one can be happy with the situation." He glowered as he looked up and down the street. "Nazi invaders walking among us as though it was the most natural thing in the world."

"But what about now? What will you do for a job?"

"I have a job with the Communist Party."

"Paid?"

"Not yet. I've been a member of the PPF for a few years now, so maybe they will offer me a position. I don't know; we'll have to see. I hope one day I will hold a senior position in the party, but until we get these scum out of here, that ambition will have to wait."

The waiter arrived at that moment with their order. Charlotte waited for him to go before returning to their conversation.

"You see your future with them then?"

He nodded. "Yes. *Vive la Republique*."

"A revolutionary?"

He picked up his cup. "I wouldn't call it that," he told her and took a sip of coffee. "But I would love to become the first Communist President of France." He put his cup down. "But that is in the future, and this is now. I should be getting to know you better, Charlotte, and not talking about my political ambitions."

Charlotte could imagine him fired up and shouting the odds about whatever President was ruining the country and how much better it would be under Communist rule. But it was a pipedream for him at the moment particularly as another strident regime had moved in.

Their conversation inevitably drifted into more prosaic things like what kind of music they liked; what kind of films; hobbies; favourite places etc. Charlotte found herself enjoying his company and was sure that he would want to see her again. But for Charlotte there was the added complication of her reason for being in France, which meant a close relationship with someone like Nicolas could only work if it was beneficial to her work with the SOE. She decided to ask Agata Stasiak if she got the opportunity.

Eventually, Charlotte told him it was time for her to leave. He said he would pay the bill, then stepped up and kissed her lightly on both cheeks.

She waved at him as he went into the café and cycled away with a great deal running through her mind. Uppermost though was Nicolas Escoffier and how she might enjoy a closer relationship with him.

Chapter 12

Charlotte's mother thought the event at her local village hall to support the war effort would be interesting and, in some way, inspire her to make some kind of contribution; although at that moment she had no idea what she would be encouraged to do.

She was on her own and had walked the short distance to the hall in the warm sunshine. It felt good on her back and teased some humorous thoughts about her daughter, Charlotte, working in in some stuffy office in London. But one thought that often dominated her thinking was how much she would love to see Charlotte but had been warned that it might not be for some time yet.

She walked in through the open door of the hall past the hand drawn and painted posters asking for all manner of contributions as well as calling for volunteers to throw themselves into the task of sorting and categorizing whatever was contributed during the length of the campaign, which at that time was one week.

Inside the hall were several tables on which were displayed the samples of what was needed, what could be important and, at some tables, a demonstration of how to produce something like a knitted scarf or woolly hat, but not necessarily for the soldiers who had been evacuated from the shores of Dunkirk and were now billeted somewhere waiting to be moved on. Many of them had arrived on the shores of England in an armada of small boats, many of which were little more than privately owned pleasure craft. But it was the spirit that dominated the news bulletins, and it was that which inspired villages and communities all over the United Kingdom to play their part.

The majority of people in the hall were women, which was to be expected, but there were a few elderly men, one or two who looked as if they had served in the First World War. Some other men looked young and fit enough to be serving in the armed forces, but she understood that was not necessarily the case.

She stood just inside the hall and studied the room, picking out any familiar faces she knew. She noticed one or two women who she had spoken to a few times: mostly when she was standing in a meat queue at the local butcher, or in the grocer shop with her shopping list and her ration book. It was the same for everyone of course, although most people guessed there would be those who were well connected enough to defy the rationing and not suffer any deprivation.

She came to one stall where one of the familiar faces was presenting — a Mrs Lilly Dartnell. Connie had spoken to her several times at the library; a place she often liked to frequent.

"Good morning, Lilly," she said with a short wave of her hand.

Lilly Dartnell beamed at her. "Connie, how are you? Looking to do something for the war effort."

"Yes, trying to support my Charlotte's attempts in a way."

"Oh, of course. She's working in London, isn't she?

For one of the ministries was it?"

Connie looked around quickly. "Well, I'm not supposed to say, but I think she's working as a translator or something with one of the government departments."

"Do you see her much?"

Connie shook her head. "Not at all, but she writes regularly. I get a letter once a fortnight."

"Does she tell you much about London?"

Again, Connie shook her head. "No, but at least she's keeping in touch."

There was an elderly gentleman sitting behind the table. Connie thought he looked quite frail and judged him to be about sixty or so years old. He had a walking stick propped up against the chair, and he showed some interest in the conversation between the two women.

"Oh, this is my father," Lilly said when she saw Connie glance at him. "Edward." She turned to him. "Dad, this is my friend, Connie. Her daughter works in London. One of the ministries."

He looked at Connie and nodded. "Good day to you. Your daughter is doing her bit, is she?"

Connie shrugged. "Well, she tells me she is, so yes, I hope so."

He smiled and looked away.

"Don't forget to get yourself a cup of tea, Connie," Lilly said to her. "Once you've looked around and decided what you'll contribute.

Connie thanked and moved away from the table unaware that the old man's eyes followed her as she moved around the room.

She spent about thirty minutes looking around the tables. Although she wasn't a knitter, she thought she might be inclined to sign up for an instruction class, thinking it might be fun to spend time knitting and talking.

After looking round the tables, she moved over to the where tea and coffee were available. She did wonder how they managed to get hold of the coffee but chose not to dwell on it too much. And with that she sat down on a vacant chair just as Lilly Dartnell's father came over. He was stooping and needed the walking stick to help him.

"May I?" he asked Connie, pointing to the empty chair beside her.

"Of course," she said, moving aside.

"Edward," he reminded her as he sat down.

"Yes, I remember," she told him. "Can I get you a cup of tea?"

"Thank you, no; I think I've had my daily quota." He looked across the room. "My daughter makes sure I don't go without."

Connie smiled. "I'm sure."

"You may wonder why I've come over." He looked at her with an enquiring expression on his face.

She shook her head. "No, I suppose you just wanted someone to talk to?"

"I couldn't help overhearing the conversation you had with Lilly about your daughter. Charlotte is it?"

"Yes, Charlotte." She frowned as she wondered why he mentioned it.

"I used to work for 'one of the ministries' as you so

eloquently put it," he said.

"It's what my daughter tells me. When she writes. Well, not every time, but she did make sure that I understood she wasn't at liberty to divulge anything else."

He nodded briefly. "That's the way they work."

Connie wasn't sure what he meant by that. "What way?"

"There's a war on, so no-one is at liberty to explain their job if they are working for…" He bobbed his head from side to side. "One of the ministries. It's a euphemism. A useful one too; covers a multitude of sins."

"Well, Charlotte is simply a translator, so she could be working anywhere that require her skills."

He looked at her sharply. "What language apart from English does she speak?"

Connie took a mouthful of tea and put her cup down. "My daughter is French. She was born and brought up in France. She studied English and German at Oxford. We came here after my husband, Charlotte's father died, otherwise she would have been studying at the Sorbonne I imagine."

He looked away briefly, lost in thought. "Does your daughter write to you much?" he asked, turning his head back towards her.

Connie nodded. "Of course: every fortnight."

"And you write back, I presume?"

"Naturally. I think she would be disappointed if I didn't. Wouldn't you?"

"I would, but are you sure it's your daughter who is

writing to you?"

Connie's mouth fell open in astonishment. "What on earth…"

He stopped her. "Let me ask you something else. "Was Charlotte's first letter written by hand?"

Connie had to think for a moment. "Yes. Why?"

"And all her letters are hand written too?"

Connie's eyes glazed over as she dragged the images into her mind. "Well, no, actually; they're typed. She said it was easier to type a letter while there was a quiet moment in the office. She signs them by hand of course."

"And all her letters arrive promptly each fortnight?"

"On a Monday, yes."

He was about to say something else, but Connie stopped him. "Edward, let me stop you there. Why are you asking these questions? And has it really got anything to do with you, how me and my daughter correspond?"

He offered both hands, palm upwards. "I apologise for any apparent and unwanted intrusion into your private life, but I worked for the Security Service for a good many years. I know how they work, how they obfuscate and deceive, and not just to our enemies. I believe the letters you receive from your daughter are written by an agent in the Security Service. If you have kept the letters, study them and a pattern will emerge, I promise."

Now Connie started feeling trembly inside, and a state of confusion began to settle in her mind. "But why?" she asked. "Charlotte is a translator, nothing else, so why be underhand about her job?"

He sighed deeply. "Your Charlotte sounds like a gift to the secret service with her language skills and the fact that she was born and raised in France." He paused and studied Connie, a look of sadness clouding his face. "It's possible she may not be working in London; she could be in France."

***

Connie felt physically sick as she hurried out of the village hall desperate to get home. The nausea was so bad, she thought she would throw up in the street. Edward's words were still ringing in her ears, which frightened her to death. She simply couldn't believe that Charlotte was working for the government as an agent in France. She refused to believe it and was determined to find out the truth.

She opened the front door of the cottage and dropped her shoulder bag on the hall table along with the keys, and then went through to the small front room and over to a bureau against the far wall. She opened a drawer and pulled out the letters she had received from Charlotte: all neatly kept in a pretty box that her daughter had made as a small girl.

There were several letters, all of which were in rectangular manilla envelopes except one, which was in a white envelope. She took them through to the kitchen and opened them on the old wooden table, laying them out so she could see them all at a glance.

The letter in the white envelope was the first one she'd received from Charlotte after she'd taken the job in London. It was handwritten in her recognisable script, finishing with the rather archaic phrase '*Toodle pip*'. Charlotte had come across the phrase while she was at Oxford. She loved the Englishness about it; a kind of overarching farewell used by toffs and dandies that filtered down to the lower classes. She finished all the letters she'd written from Oxford in the same fashion.

Now Connie was seeing a rather formulaic pattern emerging as she looked quickly at the remaining letters that had been sent in the manilla envelopes. None of them had used the phrase; and she knew they hadn't been written by her daughter. The old man at the village hall was right: Charlotte had to be in France.

She slumped down on to a hard wooden chair and buried her face in her hands trying to fight back the tears but didn't succeed. Soon she was sobbing uncontrollably as all kinds of horrors forced their way into her imagination, and the worst one was that she would never see Charlotte again.

***

Another letter dropped onto the doormat — a brown, manila envelope with a London postmark. Charlotte's mother picked it up, turned it over to see if there was a return address there, and knew it had to be one of her daughter's regular letters. She frowned and shook her head slowly, then walked through to the lounge and took the paperknife from the fruit bowl. She slit the envelope open and pulled out the letter. It had been typed, just like the others. The words had no life to them; they were droll and uninteresting. She went to the drawer where she'd put the others and dropped it in with them, disappointment written all over her face.

The thoughts on her mind were not good; she was becoming increasingly convinced that Charlotte was not the one sending those letters, but someone working for the Inter-Service Bureau. She decided the only way to find out the truth was to travel up to London and ask.

Connie knew that the bombing in London was getting worse, but much of it was over the docks in the East End, so she figured a trip up to the city would not be too risky. She vaguely recalled her daughter mentioning the name of someone called Jefson, so she decided this would be the best person to speak to. She decided not to drive up to London but to get the train. She did think of maybe phoning but thought the direct approach was probably the best. She made up her mind to travel up early the following day and caught the early train which got her into London by eight o'clock.

Connie knew that Charlotte had an interview with the Inter-Service Bureau in Baker Street and made her way there by tube. She felt strange knowing that she was retracing Charlotte's footsteps, but somehow it made her feel closer to her daughter. And as she rattled the brass knocker on the same wooden door, she half expected Charlotte to open it.

The door swung back noiselessly and the same man who had spoken to Charlotte regarded Connie with a curious look.

"Yes?"

Connie hadn't exactly planned how she would approach this, it was all a bit *ad hoc* really, but she'd made her bed and had to lie in it.

"I would like to see Mr Jefson."

He frowned. "Do you have an appointment?"

She shook her head. "No, but I'm Charlotte de la Cour's mother and I would like to speak to him about my daughter."

She heard the sounds of far-off explosions and felt tremors beneath her feet. She glanced back along the alleyway and wondered how close the bombing was getting. The drone of aircraft, although a long way off, was a frightening backdrop to what was happening. The peace and quiet of her farm cottage suddenly became very desirable, and she hoped it wouldn't be too long before she could see Charlotte and be on her way home.

"Wait there please, Mrs de la Cour." He closed the door, leaving her standing there.

It seemed like an age before the door swung open. He pulled it back and beckoned Connie inside, taking her to Jefson's office and showing her in.

Jefson looked up from behind his desk. He stood up. "Good morning, Mrs de la Cour." He pointed to the same chair Charlotte had occupied several weeks earlier. "Please, sit down."

Connie did as she was asked and waited for him to speak.

Jefson lit his pipe and shook the match, dropping the dead ember into the ashtray. "I understand you are here about your daughter, Charlotte?"

She nodded. "Yes, I need to know where she lives so I can go and see her."

"Why is that? Is it an emergency; a family problem or something?"

"No, but I'm her mother. I shouldn't need a reason to see my own daughter."

"Have you communicated with her at all?"

"I wrote a letter to her, but I had to address it to the Ministry of Information. She hasn't replied. I'm worried about her."

"Isn't she writing to you then?"

"Well yes," Connie answered a little irritably, "but she hasn't responded to my letter."

He made a gesture with his hand. "I'm sorry to hear that, but there's nothing I can do about it."

"You could tell me where I can find her."

He shook his head. "I'm afraid that information is classified because of the war. Your daughter holds a significant position and would be of interest to any German spies in London. I'm sure you'll understand the need for caution, Mrs de la Cour." He sighed softly. "I'm sorry, but I'm afraid I can't help you. My hands are tied."

Connie glared at him. She thought he was like a snake: slippery and slimy. And she didn't believe a word he said. She started getting angry inside but knew it wouldn't achieve anything.

"Is my daughter in France?" she asked him suddenly. She could see by his reaction that the question was unexpected. For a very brief moment his austere, patronising countenance altered significantly, but almost as quickly it was restored.

"I'm afraid I cannot answer any more questions; I really can't." He stood up. "All I can suggest is that you write to your daughter and address it to me here. I will see that she gets it; that's all I can offer." He walked around the desk and came up beside her. "I have to ask you to leave now Mrs de la Cour; I have work to do."

He moved his hand nearer to Connie's elbow as she started getting up from the chair. She felt it was about as close as he dared get to physically throwing her out. He smiled at her, said goodbye, and closed the door as she walked out into the dimly lit corridor.

Two minutes later, standing at the beginning of the alleyway and doing her best to control her temper, Connie decided there was only one other person who might be able to help, and that was Pierre Baudet who she knew was working at the French Embassy here in London.

***

Connie managed to hail a taxi which took her to the French Embassy at the Albert Gate entrance to Hyde Park. When she got out of the taxi, she looked up at the tall building and thought how eloquent it must have looked in its prime, but now it was surrounded by sandbags around the lower windows, all of which were covered with a crisscrossing of tape to reduce damage in the event of a bomb explosion. The main entrance porch was surrounded by sandbags, and a French soldier stood guard there together with a London policeman.

Connie walked up to the two men and stopped. Then she opened her bag and took out her passport, told them who she was and that she wanted to speak to Pierre Baudet. The police constable nodded to the soldier and took Connie through into the main hall and across to the

Reception desk. He explained to the woman behind the desk the reason for Connie's visit, and she was asked to take a seat.

Pierre Baudet's brow furrowed when he was told that Constance de la Cour wanted to see him. It was quite some time since he had last seen the family, and that was at her husband's funeral. She never spoke to him then but had simply nodded her acceptance of his condolences as the line of mourners passed the family. He knew why of course, but now he was intrigued.

He got up from his desk and slipped his jacket on, then hurried down the stairs to the front entrance. Connie stood up as soon as she saw him and came over. He brushed her cheek lightly with his in the usual, courteous way of greeting, then pointed back to the chairs and suggested they sit down.

Connie could tell by the look on his face that seeing her was most unexpected, which didn't surprise her, and it made her wonder if she'd done the right thing by coming.

"Hello, Pierre," she began. "I suppose you're wondering why I'm here."

He nodded. "Yes, of course."

"It's about Charlotte," she said and told him everything that had happened and how worried she was about where her daughter was. "I think she may be in France."

Baudet's face lightened in surprise. "And this man, Jefson, won't tell you whether she is or not."

"No." She looked down at her hands which were gripped together. "I want to send her a letter, Pierre, but

Jefson has suggested I send it to him, and he will pass it on to her."

He raised his eyebrows. "And if she is in France, he won't be able to do that, unless he sends it through diplomatic channels. The Swiss maybe, but they're hardly likely to be impressed with delivering personal mail."

She lifted her chin. "Could you do it, Pierre?"

He shook his head quite sharply. "I'm sorry, no. And I cannot go into any reasons why, although I would have thought that would have been obvious to you."

She nodded briefly. Bloody secrecy, she thought to herself. "Are you sure there is no way I can find out?"

He sighed heavily. "I'm afraid you will have to rely on your Mr. Jefson my dear Constance. I cannot help you."

Connie understood the reason why and had to admit defeat. She decided to find a stationer, buy paper and envelopes, and write a letter to Charlotte. Then she would go back to Jefson and hand it to him in person. It did make her feel just a little more comfortable, but only just.

She stood up. "Thank you, Pierre, for seeing me. I'll be off; let you get on with saving France."

Baudet got up. They hugged briefly. He watched her walk out of the door, his mind working overtime. Constance de la Cour had innocently told him that her daughter was now embedded in France as an agent for British military intelligence.

It was a gem he could sell to Rudolf Havertz.

Chapter 13

Major Felix Heller lit a cigarette, inhaled deeply, looked at the clock on his desk and blew the smoke noisily from his mouth. In front of him was a pile of folders. He'd been at his desk since six o'clock that morning. It was now eight o'clock and he had managed to read through just one of the folders. It had been tedious but necessary work. The documents were the result of an enormous effort by the German security service, the SD, before the war to infiltrate spies into Paris and to learn as much as they could about those people who occupied important positions within the heart of the French government — positions that were permanent and not likely to change as a result of an election.

But the names of those people were not the only thing that interested the SicherheitsDienste; it was their political leanings, their histories and whether they were Jews or not. The SD had also listed the names of those occupying the elegant homes that could be used by high-ranking Nazis once the occupation of Paris had become a *fait accompli*.

Also listed in Heller's folders were the names of the academics, the art connoisseurs, authors, entertainers and people who inhabited the higher strata of Paris's cultural life. It was essential from the Nazi viewpoint that they could eliminate the difficult, preliminary work and filter out those people who could essentially work against the autonomy that the Germans had planned to impose on the French people.

Many of the names on the list now had a line drawn through them because they were known to have left Paris. The most notable among them was the Duke and Duchess of Windsor who had fled to Portugal just four weeks previously as it became clear that their presence in Paris would be a major problem for the British government. Heller was disappointed by that because the Duke had become an asset to Hitler due to his visit to the Führer a year earlier. He sniffed loudly and moved his pen down the list.

By mid-morning, Heller had completed three folders. He leaned back in his chair and stretched, raising his arms high in the air. He called out loudly to his aide, Sergeant Wilhelm Witborg, and then opened a gold-plated cigarette case emblazoned with the German Eagle and removed a cigarette. Witborg came into the office, snapped to attention and raised his arm in the Nazi salute.

"Ja, Herr Major?"

"Coffee, Sergeant, and something savoury."

Witborg snapped another salute and left hurriedly. Heller chuckled to himself at the deference shown by his aide, but it was early days; Witborg had been assigned to Heller's office just a day earlier. No doubt he was trying to make an impression, Heller reasoned.

He lit his cigarette and pulled another folder towards him. It was different to the others; quite slim but contained several sheets of paper. They had been marked as 'Secret', although Heller wasn't too impressed by the delineation; to him, everything had to be secret as far as he was concerned. He lifted the files out and thumbed through them until he came to one with the Hotel Metropole printed boldly at the top. He dropped the other files and looked intently at the list of names typed beneath the heading. He was billeted at the hotel, which gave him a good reason to take note of what was written.

What Heller was looking at were the names of the hotel staff, their roles, addresses, length of service, political affiliation if any, and, naturally, whether they were Jewish or not. He took time over each entry because he wanted to ensure he had the full measure of their importance and value to the hotel, and whether there was anything he thought was important to know of them in the course of his job. And the one name that seemed to leap off the page at him was that of Charlotte de la Cour.

He closed the slim folder and laid the Metropole paper on the desk as Witborg came in with his coffee and a few biscuits. Heller grunted but didn't look up as Witborg withdrew. He lifted the cigarette to his lips and drew in a deep lungful, expelling the smoke above his head with a quick lift of his jaw, then started reading the detail about Charlotte.

She was French, raised in Paris, studied German and English at Oxford university in England. He frowned and asked himself the question why this girl had not studied at the Sorbonne, which would have made sense to him seeing as she lived in Paris. Her father was deceased, and her mother lived in England. The next question on his lips was why she came back to France in… He ran his finger through her details… In May this year, shortly before Paris was occupied. Why? He noted that she started working at the Metropole barely four weeks earlier, so how did she manage to find work in a hotel that would soon be housing senior German officers? He frowned again as he tossed a few thoughts around in his mind, the most bizarre of which was the notion that the French Intelligence service knew that the Metropole would be singled out as the most likely place for senior officers to be domiciled while in Paris. He grimaced and shook his head. No, impossible; no-one was that prescient except God almighty, so he dismissed the thought as nonsense.

He put the paper back into the folder, promising to come back to it another time. And although there were many others on the staff of the hotel that could be there simply to pass on information to the French Security people — if there were any left — he thought it would make sense to find out more about this Charlotte de la Cour.

***

Charlotte's Aunt Matilde came hurrying out of her cottage and sprinted across the yard to the wooden garage that housed her beloved Citroen 15CV Traction Avant car. She had received news that names were now available of some of the 1.8 million French soldiers who had been taken prisoner by the Nazis. It was barely a month since the Germans had occupied Paris, and the list of names had been hurriedly produced as a gesture of goodwill and an attempt to curry favour with the families whose loved ones were missing.

Matilde rolled the dust cover off the car and let it fall to the floor. She then retrieved the starting handle from the boot and pushed it carefully through the small opening in the front bumper and turned the engine slowly. It was hard work, but her husband always did this if the car had been standing a long time. They'd bought the car just two years earlier; one of the first models off the production line. They loved driving out into the countryside when they could and enjoying a picnic. Heady times indeed for Matilde and Pierre, but that was then, and this was now.

She clambered into the front seat and started the car, silently offering up a prayer that there was enough life in the battery. The engine fired and popped a little. Matilde blipped the throttle and drove slowly out of the garage. Then she hopped out, closed and locked the garage doors. Fifteen minutes after hearing the news that the lists were available along the Rue de Rivoli, Matilde was on her way into central Paris in the dire hope that she might learn of her husband's fate, although she was aware that the lists might not be complete, and likely to be haphazard.

She turned into the Rue de Rivoli and could immediately see a crowd gathered around what appeared to be a hastily constructed hoarding. There were three German soldiers there attaching sheets of paper to the wooden hoarding. Watching over the crowd were two French policemen. Matilde stopped at the side of the road and ran along the pavement, reaching the women who were almost fighting to grab the lists as the German soldiers were attempting to pin them up on the board. One man was holding a small notice with the headline *Prisonniers et Blessés Francaise* (French prisoners and wounded). Several women were in tears as they struggled in the commotion.

Matilde, anxious just like those who were there hoping for news of their loved ones, was desperate to find her husband's name, but it was obvious that the struggling women were impeding the process and causing real problems for the two policemen. She hurried over to the board where she could see the names were being posted up in alphabetical order, but despite the fact that her surname began with the letter A, there was no Auroy, and she could see that it could be hours before the German soldiers had even reached the end of the letter A. She stepped back from the board and shook her head wearily and wondered if it was worth waiting. Then she realised she was just a few hundred metres from the Metropole where Charlotte was working.

She ran back to her car and drove up to the hotel, going round the back and parking in the staff car park. She frowned as she pulled into what appeared to be the last vacant slot; most of the other bays were occupied by German military cars and some very high-end Mercedes cars.

She got out of the car and walked to the rear entrance where two armed German soldiers were standing, obviously on guard duty. When she reached them, one of them put his hand up and stopped her. Then, in excellent French, he asked her for some identification.

Matilde took her passport from her handbag and

showed it to him. He flicked through the pages, handed it back to her and asked her to wait there. He said something to the other soldier, which Matilde didn't understand, and went into the hotel.

The soldier returned about five minutes later. He had Armand, the concierge, with him.

"Madame Auroy," he said, pointing to Matilde.

Armand came up to her. "How can I help you?" he asked.

"Oh, I thought I would call in and speak to my niece, Charlotte de la Cour. I was in town unexpectedly…" she pointed back over her shoulder. "I came up to see the list of missing soldiers."

He stopped her. "You are Aunt Matilde?"

Her face brightened. "Oh, you know who I am?"

He looked at the German soldier. "I can vouch for Madame Auroy," he said. Then he put his hand on Matilde's elbow and ushered her into the hotel and into his office. Once inside, he asked her to wait while he went to find Charlotte.

Armand had seen Charlotte talking to Major Felix Heller earlier. He guessed she would be happy to be given an excuse to detach herself from the Major. He found them still in conversation at the table where the Major had eaten lunch.

Charlotte looked up as Armand came up to the table. He glanced at Heller. "Excuse me, Major." Then he turned to Charlotte.

"Your Aunt Matilde is here; she wants a word with you."

Charlotte frowned. "Matilde? I wonder what she

wants." She turned to Heller. "I'm sorry, but my aunt is here; it could be urgent."

Heller's face brightened a little. "Your aunt?" He stood up. "I would like to meet her," he said as he dropped his napkin on to the table. He held his hand out indicating that Charlotte should lead the way.

Charlotte didn't know what to do at first. She might have felt flattered that a German officer wanted to meet her aunt, but she also understood that she had no alternative but to go along with his request.

The three of them walked out of the dining room and along the corridor to Armand's office. Matilde sprung to her feet when she saw them but was surprised to see a German officer with her niece.

"Charlotte…"

"Aunt Matilde, what are you doing here? Is there something wrong?" Charlotte asked.

Matilde shook her head. "No, nothing wrong. I came into town because I heard they were posting lists of our missing soldiers. I'd hoped to find your uncle's name there, but the list is still short."

Charlotte stopped her and turned towards the Major. "Matilde, this is Major Felix Heller of the SD. He would like to say hello."

Matilde looked at Heller, seeing a tall, elegant and handsome young officer, but at the same time seeing a Nazi. She didn't want to show any pleasantness but had no option; she took the officer's hand briefly and nodded.

"Major Heller."

Heller bowed his head and clicked his heels

together. "Madame. I've just had five minutes in conversation with your charming niece. It would have been a shame to have passed up the opportunity to meet a member of her family."

He sounded smooth and urbane: polite and friendly. Matilde felt revolted. She looked hesitantly at Charlotte.

"I won't keep you, Charlotte, but I wondered if you could check the list for me when you've finished your shift. You have to pass it on your way. It's in the Rue de Rivoli. They've started posting the names alphabetically. They haven't got as far as our surname yet."

Heller leaned forward a little and spoke. "Perhaps I can help," he said. "If you let me have your husband's name? I presume it's your husband," he added. "I will find out what I can for you." He smiled. "I'm in a better position than you are of course. It shouldn't take long."

Matilde felt an overwhelming relief for his offer, but at the same time she felt she was guilty of betrayal by simply being connected in such a personal way.

"Oh, no; I can always come up and check the list myself," she said hesitantly. "And Charlotte can check on her way home.as well."

He shook his head gently. "Believe me, it will not be a problem." He put his hand up to his breast pocket and opened it. Then he pulled out a small notebook and pen. "Now, what is your husband's full name and age?"

"Pierre Phillipe Auroy. He's forty-eight."

Heller wrote down the details and slipped the notebook back in his pocket. "There, all done." He bowed his head. "I will let your niece know as soon as I have any news." He clicked his heels together. "Good day to you Madame Auroy."

He turned and walked away leaving both Matilde and Charlotte stunned, Matilde more than Charlotte; she felt she had unwittingly walked into a trap from which there would be no escape.

***

Matilde walked out of the hotel with a whole raft of emotions running through her body, not the least that she had actually shaken the hand of a Nazi. She shuddered at the thought as she opened the car door and slid into the front seat. She sat there for a while thinking of the brief and unfortunate meeting with Heller, and despite the fact that he was willing to use his position to find out where her husband was, she wished she'd never met him.

She started the car and pulled out of the parking area into the Place da la Concorde and was immediately struck by the number of German soldiers that were milling around in the street as though it was the most natural thing in the world. She hadn't noticed this on her way to the hotel, but now she was seeing, virtually for the first time, the results of opening Paris to the Hun.

She turned towards the Champs Elysees and motored up to the Arc de Triomphe, slowly becoming more appalled as she saw the hated Swastika adorning important buildings. The Arc had an enormous German banner draped on it, declaring the complete subservience of the French government and its people.

She began to feel sick to her stomach as she drove

through the city centre, eventually passing the Eiffel Tower on her way home. For the first time in her life, Matilde felt utter shame and horror at what had befallen the city. And as she left the visual reminders of Germany's supreme power, she thanked God that she had agreed to help the British by providing a safe house for Agata Stasiak, and vowed to do everything she could to help the British agent in whatever endeavour in which she was involved.

She arrived home, her state of mind still at a low level, and put the car in the garage. When she got indoors, she found Agata sitting there. It shook her for a moment because her front door had been locked, which meant Agata would have locked it after letting herself in with the key that was always under a flower pot by the front door.

Matilde put her hand on her chest. "Oh, my goodness! Sorry, Agata; I didn't expect to see you."

Agata smiled. "I couldn't leave a warning note pinned to your door, could I?"

Matilde sighed and chuckled to herself as she took off her coat and dropped it over the back of a chair. Then she lifted the coffee pot off the stove and walked over to the sink. She filled it with water and put it back on the stove.

"Coffee?" she asked Agata.

"No thank you Matilde. I don't want to be here too long, but I have something to ask you."

"Ask away," she said.

"I need to borrow your car."

Matilde frowned. "Borrow my car?"

The total surprise at the unexpected request was clearly evident in Matilde's response; Agata could see that. "And there is something else: I need some help."

Matilde leaned up against the sink. "What kind of help?"

Agata had to choose her words carefully. "I have to be somewhere at midnight to pick up a transmitter and some weapons."

Matilde's mouth fell open. She stepped forward and dropped into a chair at the table. "I don't understand," she said after a few seconds. "Weapons?"

"Hand guns," she said. "They will be in the same crate as the transmitter which will need two people to lift it. The British anticipated the Occupation and believe there will be resistance groups getting together, but they will be useless without weapons. And they will need help and guidance, which is where the SOE agents will be doing their best work." She shrugged. "It is war, Matilde, and we are part of it."

The coffee pot started whistling away as it came to the boil. It broke the moment, dragging Matilde back from her shock to her present need for caffeine.

"Excuse me, Agata. Are you sure you wouldn't like a coffee?"

Agata shook her head. "No thank you."

Matilde made herself a coffee, and while she was doing that, her mind went back to that moment as she was driving away from the city centre when she vowed to help Agata in whatever endeavour in which she was involved. She thought too of her husband, Pierre, and his commitment. She went back to the table and sat down.

"I will help you, Agata; it's the least I can do."

Agata reached forward and grabbed Matilde's forearm. "Thank you. I will let you know where we're going when I get back." She stood up. "I'll be here by ten thirty."

Matilde watched her go. Then she picked up her coffee and was surprised to see how badly she was shaking. She managed to drink some before putting the cup down and heading for the cognac. Now, it seemed, her real war had started.

Chapter 14

Charlotte didn't arrive back at her aunt's place until late afternoon. As usual she hurried into the house a little flushed from her cycle ride from the hotel. She was a little breathless as she came into the kitchen where she knew she would find her aunt. Matilde rarely sat in the lounge until later. During the winter months she would be curled up in front of the fire either reading a book or listening to something on the radio. Her husband would be there as well. In the summer evenings they were often sitting in the garden relaxing or chatting to a neighbour. Before the war Matilde and her Pierre had an idyllic life, but now how much their circumstances had changed.

Charlotte pulled her scarf from her head and leaned forward to kiss Matilde on both cheeks. As she did this, she thought she noticed something different about her. She straightened up.

"Are you okay, Matilde? You look different."

Matilde had been reading an old magazine, which she let drop on to the table. "Yes," she said brightly but with affectation. "I'm fine. Miles away." She closed the magazine. "You're late. Have you been with Nicolas?"

This had become the norm for Charlotte for a few days now. After finishing her shift, she would meet Nicolas Escoffier and spend a pleasant hour or so with him, often by the River Seine. They were no longer fazed by the presence of the German soldiers, some of whom had managed to attract local French girls, and it helped to see how the couples laughed and teased each other as if it was the most natural thing in the world and not forced.

Although Charlotte enjoyed Nicolas's company, she wasn't quite ready to commit to a more permanent relationship. She was beginning to get feelings for him that she knew were being reciprocated, but she had to put those feelings aside in view of the uncertainty that the German Occupation could bring. Although judging from the way those young French girls were behaving, they had little of that uncertainty to bother them.

So, when her aunt asked her about Nicolas, Charlotte smiled a little coyly.

"He's nice. We spend an hour or so by the Seine." She walked over to the coffee pot which was on the stove. "I see the local girls are getting on fine with some of the German boys." She poured herself a cup of coffee. "You wouldn't think we were enemies," she said. "Well, not from what me and Nicolas have seen." She sat down at the table. "Oh, I haven't seen anything of Major Heller since we spoke," she told her aunt. "I thought that was nice of him to find out what he could about Uncle Pierre though, don't you?"

Matilde nodded briefly. "Yes." Her voice was too quiet to carry any meaning.

Charlotte put the cup to her mouth and looked over the rim at her aunt. She took a mouthful and put the cup down.

"Something is bothering you, Matilde. What is it?"

Matilde knew there was no way she could avoid telling Charlotte about her promise to Agata Stasiak, so she told her.

Charlotte's expression widened in horror. "You cannot do that," she told her aunt, her voice raised. "You simply cannot."

Matilde touched her arm. "I can and I will."

"What if you get caught?"

Matilde shrugged. "We will be careful. We don't intend to get caught."

"Neither did Uncle Pierre!"

Matilde's eyes hooded over at the mention of her husband. "Charlotte, it's because of Pierre that I have promised to help Agata."

"But that's her job, not yours. Yours is simply to provide a … "she stammered for a moment trying to find the right words. "… a staging post, a safe house; not to go off during the night against German patrols. You simply cannot do it."

Matilde fixed her eyes on her niece, a smile tugging at the edges of her lips. "Charlotte, my darling, the moment I shook hands with that German Nazi, I knew I had betrayed your uncle. It wasn't until I'd left the hotel and seen how they were strutting round our streets, adorning everything with their awful banners as though they were preparing for a street party that I knew I had to metaphorically cleanse myself of the filth and do everything in my power, whatever it took, to help Agata and France in whatever way I could. That is why I'll be going tonight."

Charlotte bridled at that. She stood up and went over to the kitchen window, her arms folded across her chest and stared thoughtfully through the small panes of glass out on to the yard which was now beginning to lose the sunlight. Evening was coming and soon it would be night.

"I'll go," she said suddenly and spun round. "I will go with Agata."

Matilde looked shocked. "No, Charlotte; that's impossible. You have work. You cannot risk it."

"I can. It will be far better if you remain in the house. If anyone came asking for you, what would I tell them? You've gone out?" She came back to the table. "But me? If anyone asks, you can tell them I have an assignation with a boy, which is a secret. People will believe that."

"And what about the German patrols?"

"The Germans do not believe women have anything beyond their natural homely instincts to even contemplate anything so outrageous as fighting a war against them. Even the French government don't believe that otherwise they would allow women to join the Army. We can talk our way out of any meeting with the patrols."

"What makes you think they have nothing to fear from women?" Matilde asked, her voice lifted in surprise at such a statement.

"I've heard them talking," Charlotte answered. "They believe women have a place, but it isn't outside of the home." She leaned forward, her hands flat on the table. "I have even heard them say we do not have the mental capacity or ability that men have, so they have nothing to fear from us." She straightened up. "They are unbelievably arrogant, Matilde."

What Charlotte hadn't revealed to her aunt was that most of the comments and remarks she was relating, were what she'd learned from her ability to lip read.

Matilde, reluctantly, had to agree that young women like Charlotte were better equipped physically and mentally to be very proactive in the fight against the Germans. But at the same time, it was difficult for her to agree that Charlotte would be better suited to the task.

"We will ask Agata," she said eventually, drawing in a deep breath and expelling the air quietly. If she agrees, I will remain here."

The die had been cast, and the mood was tense between the two women as they waited for Agata. Matilde made a point of checking the car for petrol. She had two full jerry cans in the garage, so was able to top the tank up. Charlotte tried to settle down and read a book, but with the distraction of what was to come, she found it particularly difficult. Few words were exchanged between them, not because of any animosity, but because they were both aware of what could go disastrously wrong for them. Matilde did understand that Charlotte was better equipped because of her brief period of training in England, and the fact that she had been experiencing contact with the Germans. It was flimsy but a marginal gain for Charlotte as far as Matilde was concerned.

***

It was late evening, about ten o'clock when the sound of knocking came at the door. Matilde hurried out of the lounge and let Agata in, her anxiety levels rising a notch or too now that the moment had arrived.

"We have something to ask you," Matilde told her as she walked with her into the kitchen where Charlotte was waiting.

Agata looked at Matilde and then at Charlotte as though she expected bad news. "What is it?"

Charlotte spoke first, not letting her aunt say anything.

"I want to take my aunt's place," she said without preamble. "I think it would be better if you let me help you."

She was standing up straight, and despite her attempt to appear relaxed and calm, Charlotte felt as though her whole body was rigid like a piece of timber.

Agata was not given to prevarication; she had been selected by London because of her mental and physical abilities and the way in which she could make decisions under stress.

"You know what we have to do?" she asked Charlotte.

Charlotte glanced quickly at her aunt. "Matilde has told me. We will be picking up a heavy package and some weapons."

Agata looked at her steadily, assessing the odds of Charlotte's youth over Matilde's advancing years. "What about your work?"

"If we don't get back in time, Matilde will phone the hotel and tell them I am sick." Her heart thudded beneath her ribcage. "And if we don't get back, then it won't matter, will it?"

Agata nodded. "Good." She made a point of

studying the clothes Charlotte had on. "Make sure you wear everything dark. Go and change now."

Charlotte hesitated for a moment, then hurried away to her room to change. And as she was pulling off her brightly coloured garments, she started to tremble as the realisation sank in that she was about to go on a mission against the Germans.

When Charlotte appeared again, Agata and Matilde were in earnest conversation. As son as Charlotte entered the room, Agata got to her feet.

"We go now, Charlotte. I will brief you in the car, but it's all about being sensible, remaining calm and to do everything I tell you.

Matilde handed Agata the car keys. Charlotte kissed her aunt but said nothing; words were not necessary. She followed Agata across the yard and helped her pull open the garage doors. Then Agata drove the car out into the yard and waited until Charlotte had closed the doors and climbed into the seat beside her. Within ten minutes of walking into the kitchen dressed in black, Charlotte was listening to Agata's instructions as she drove into the countryside without lights and relying on the moonlight to light their way.

Mercifully they saw no-one on the road. Agata explained that the Germans did not have enough manpower to provide extensive patrols, but she did not expect that situation to last.

"Once they know the threat they face from the Resistance, they will up their game, believe me. At the moment I think they all have their head in the clouds because of their success in subjugating France."

Their journey continued in silence after Charlotte had been briefed. She had no idea where they were going, only that they were heading in a northerly direction and deep into German Occupied France. She had asked Agata where they were going, but Agata wouldn't say; she simply told Charlotte she didn't need to know.

Charlotte then decided it was best not to ask questions but to leave well enough alone and let Agata do her thing. It was close to midnight when Agata turned the car into a farm track that bordered a line of trees. She continued down the track for about two hundred yards before stopping. As soon as she had turned the engine off, Agata got out and went round to the boot, which she opened. She then took out a small lantern and handed it to Charlotte.

"I will show you where to stand. You'll be out of sight, but when you see my lantern come on, turn yours on also. You'll hear the aeroplane come into land. Once it's down, turn your lantern off and run to the aeroplane. Once it has stopped, someone will bring out a crate and possibly a small case. I will be handing something over as well. Don't go near the propellor because the engine will still be running. They expect to be on the ground no longer than five minutes. If we don't get to them, they will not stop." She touched Charlotte's arm. "Are we clear?"

Charlotte nodded. "Yes."

"Good. And don't forget, don't turn your lantern on until you see mine."

She ran off, leaving Charlotte standing beneath the

trees and feeling totally alone.

It wasn't long before Charlotte heard the unmistakable sound of an aircraft. She instinctively looked up into the sky, but them remembered what Agata had told her. She lowered her head and stood facing towards somewhere invisible where she expected to see the lantern come on.

Suddenly, she saw the yellow light and immediately turned her lantern on, spinning to face the sound of the aircraft. Then she saw the silhouette of the aeroplane dropping out of the empty sky. She couldn't see the point at which it landed, but once she saw it go trundling past, she turned her lantern off and ran as fast as she could, following the plane.

She reached it as the side door was flung open, and two men carried a small wooden crate out and dropped it on the grass. Then they ducked inside the plane and produced another small crate. Agata handed them something that Charlotte couldn't identify, and then turned to Charlotte. But before Agata could say anything, Charlotte pulled a folded envelope from her pocket and shoved it into the hand of one of the airmen.

"Please, make sure my mother gets this."

Agata looked mortified. "Charlotte, what are you doing? Take it back. Now!"

A loud voice suddenly came from the cockpit. "Are we done?"

The airman looked at Charlotte and winked as he shoved the folded envelope into his tunic pocket. "We're done." He pulled the door shut and the aeroplane started moving away.

Agata shoved her annoyance to the back of her mind. "Grab the handle," she said, pointing to one end of the crate.

Charlotte put her hands through the course rope loop and lifted as Agata did the same at the other end. The plane was some distance away as the two women carried the case into a safe area. Then they sprinted back and lifted the other case as the aircraft was roaring towards them with a noise that was loud enough to wake the dead. They were not more than thirty feet away when the aeroplane rushed past them. They felt the thrust of air from the propellor, which almost blew Charlotte off her feet.

Within ten minutes of sighting the aircraft for the first time, the two women were loading their cargo into the Citroen. Five minutes later and Agata turned on to the main road and headed for home.

Chapter 15

Charlotte came into the kitchen where Matilde was making breakfast. She grabbed a cup of coffee and sat down at the table.

Matilde looked over her shoulder at her. "Well?"

Charlotte took a mouthful of coffee and shook her head. "God, I never want to do that again."

Matilde managed a hint of a smile. "Why, what did you expect?"

"I was terrified." She glanced round the room. "Where's Agata?"

"No idea."

"She must have nerves of steel," Charlotte muttered, blowing air out of her mouth in a rush. "So calm, you would have thought we were on a jolly night out in the countryside."

"So, you won't be helping her again?"

Charlotte closed her eyes and, for a brief moment, relived the sound of the aircraft, felt the weight of the heavy crates and the relief the moment they arrived back. She also recalled the rollicking she got from Agata about security and not handing unsecured letters to the aircrew.

"I just hope she doesn't ask me again," she said, shaking her head.

"Well, she will ask me instead, I guess." Matlde couldn't help the wry smile on her face, which she kept turned away so Charlotte couldn't see it.

Charlotte gave her a withering look. "Don't tease

me, Matilde."

Matilde came over to the table and put an omelette down that she had cooked for her niece. "Eat that, settle yourself down and then go to work. There will be that many Germans around you'll get used to hiding in plain sight."

"Matilde," she said. "It was unbelievable. It was a lovely night, not a soul in sight. Quiet. Then when I heard the plane, I thought the noise would bring people from all over the place, especially the Germans. The plane was only on the ground five or six minutes, no more, and then it was gone. But no-one came. I think I would have wet myself if anyone had shown up."

Matilde sat down. "It will get worse, Charlotte. Many people will be risking their lives for their freedom, and fate will decide who lives and who dies. We have to decide if we will gamble and let fate make the choice or become submissive and know that we have failed France. Become collaborators if you like."

Charlotte's expression changed at her aunt's dissertation, but she understood the ramifications. "Uncle Pierre didn't have a choice, did he, Matilde?"

"Nor did three million other men," Matilde said softly. "Now finish your omelette and get yourself off to work. Let your bike ride clear your mind; give you a fresh perspective." She stood up. "I've got work to do," she said and walked away from the table.

Charlotte finished her breakfast and took her plate and cup over to the sink where she left them. She hoped her aunt was right; that she would expunge all nerve-jangling thoughts as she rode to the hotel and resumed the ingenuous countenance she had managed to maintain since arriving in France.

***

Charlotte was only feeling marginally better when she walked into the rear entrance to the hotel. Her lack of sleep didn't help. Neither did the nervous anticipation she felt, knowing she would be metaphorically walking into the Lions' den, despite knowing she was virtually safe and foolproof, and nothing was likely to change that.

She was able to spend ten minutes with Camille without telling her about her adventure the previous evening, and the adrenaline rush and fear she'd experienced. As much as she wanted to, she had to learn to button her lip, so much of what she told Camille was just boring, everyday events that seemed to repeat themselves in the telling. Camille was much the same as well, but she did have a slightly more relaxed view of life now.

Her morning went well. She picked up a lot of irrelevant chat with her lip reading skill, none of which was worth reporting. And because it was only Agata she reported to, she had no idea when she would see her again, and how much of the German chatter was worth hanging on to. There were times when Charlotte wished she could make notes: something that always brought a smile to her lips.

There was one occasion when this almost got her into trouble. One of the German officers she was serving saw her smiling and asked her what she was smiling about. She tried to brush it off with a throwaway remark about a joke she'd heard in the kitchen, but naturally the German asked what the joke was. Charlotte had to come up something, so she dragged out a feeble one liner she heard while in Oxford. Then she made a hurried exit from the table, but it was a scary moment for her when she realised how she could easily be caught out by lack of forethought and caution.

It was lunchtime when Charlotte was in the staff rest room with Camille and Armand came hurrying in.

"Ah, Charlotte!"

Charlotte turned her head as he came up to their table. "Major Felix Heller wants a word with you." He pointed away from the rest room. "He's in my office."

Charlotte felt her thighs weaken and a gentle shaking began to affect her hands. She dropped her napkin on to the table and pushed her chair back. For a moment she thought she was going to topple forward but took a deep breath and straightened up.

Camille looked startled. "Charlotte, are you okay?"

She nodded and brushed her apron with her hands. "Yes, I'm fine. I've had a good morning so far and I'm in no mood for a chat with bloody Major Heller."

Armand touched her briefly on the arm. "Don't tell him that," he said with a chuckle. "Be good."

Major Heller was sitting in Armand's chair when Charlotte walked in. He immediately got to his feet, bowed his head a little and clicked his heels together.

"Mademoiselle, good morning." He came round to the front of the desk and leaned back against it; his arms folded across his chest. "How are you?"

Charlotte nodded her head briefly, not wishing to say anything. She had this inordinate fear running through her that her secret excursion the previous night had been discovered, and that was the reason Major Heller wanted to speak to her.

"I'm fine," she said and managed a thin smile.

"That's good." He looked down at his highly polished jack boots. "I have some news of your uncle, Pierre Auroy." He looked up and smiled. "He is currently in Oflag 17A in Austria waiting to be processed. He is unharmed and is with most of his unit."

Charlotte felt herself relaxing, so much so that she had to sit down on the chair that was beside her. Tears came to her eyes.

"Oh my God, thank goodness for that; my aunt will be so relieved." She brushed the back of her hands over her face, then lifted her apron and dried her tears. "Thank you so much, Major."

He straightened up. "It was the least I could do. Now, I will let you get back to your work. Please give my best wishes to your aunt."

He clicked his heels together and walked out of the office.

Charlotte slumped bodily into the chair. It was as though her spine had dissolved and there was little to support her. But it was more of the overwhelming relief that those demons that had plagued her were simply figments of her imagination. The tension drained from her, and she felt wonderfully calm now. She drew in a couple of deep breaths and got up from the chair. Time now to get back to work and look forward to meeting Nicolas later that afternoon and enjoy spending time in his company.

***

Charlotte reached the spot by the river where they normally met, but there was no sign of Nicolas. She propped her bicycle up against the wall overlooking the river bank and beside an open-air café. She locked it and sat down at an empty table. She felt calm now and content. The sun was shining, there was very little wind, which made for a pleasant afternoon. She even found herself glancing round at the soldiers who were more like tourists than troops in an occupying army. Some were with French girls who seemed to be quite happy being seen with them. It helped Charlotte to feel optimistic about the future and how long the war would last before they could feel free again.

She thought about the letter she'd written to her mother and the way she had embellished the story of how and why she was in France. She hoped her mother would understand; she had taken pains to paint a happy consequence of her current life in Paris.

She saw Nicolas walking along the embankment with his bicycle. There was a woman with him. Charlotte frowned and a brief moment of discomfort settled in her chest. It past quickly as Nicolas saw her and waved his hand. He said something to the woman as he propped his bicycle on top of Charlotte's and locked it. Then he came over to her with the woman. He reached down to Charlotte and kissed her on both cheeks.

"Hello, Charlotte, how are you today?"

Charlotte smiled. "I'm fine," she lied.

He held his hand out towards the woman. "Allow me to introduce my friend, Margot Aveline."

Margot was dressed fashionably as was the way with many women in Paris, despite the problems of the Occupation. The newspapers had campaigned for a continuance of the elegance so popular in French society that many women endeavoured to comply and affect the notion that haute couture could not be crushed, and as a consequence, neither could their spirit.

Margot was not too attractive, which, selfishly, pleased Charlotte. She inclined her head and held her hand forward. "So pleased to meet you, Charlotte. Nicolas hasn't stopped talking about you."

Nicolas laughed softly and blushed. He and Margot sat down at the table as a waiter came over and took their order for coffee, which was starting to become scarce, but still available. Margot declined because she was on her way to work and didn't want to linger too long.

"I met Margot at art school," Nicolas began.

Charlotte raised her eyebrows and looked at her. "You was a student there?"

Margot shook her head. "No; I was a teacher. Still am in fact, although my classes are not so full these days."

"Margot works at the Louvre and the Musée de l'Homme

"Oh, is that your profession?" Charlotte asked her.

"I'm a curator."

Charlotte looked surprised. "I thought all museums and art galleries were closed. Or supposed to be closing," she added.

Margot's expression changed. It transformed her whole countenance.

"So many people were fleeing Paris that the Director and myself decided to remain in the city and keep the museum open. It was our way of demonstrating our refusal to capitulate to the Nazis."

Charlotte thought that was either extremely brave or extremely foolish. And then she recalled the night before when she herself could have been accused of bravery or foolishness.

"And the Louvre?" she asked.

Margot pulled a face. "No. My work there is to catalogue the art and help put the most valuable pieces into storage. Many of the masterpieces have been shipped out to Lyon thankfully."

Charlotte frowned. "Why do you say 'thankfully'?"

"It was done to preserve them in the event of Paris being bombed."

"Now they are in danger of being stolen by the Bosch," Nicolas said with a snarl.

Charlotte looked at him. "Stolen?"

"Herman Goering is very keen on moving as many treasures as possible to Berlin," Margot answered for him. "They will turn Paris into an artistic wasteland, I'm afraid."

Charlotte was horrified. "That is such a shame," she said. "And you cannot stop them?"

Margot shrugged. "No; they will do as they please. They are in charge now. They will take what they want."

The sound of some people laughing broke the afternoon atmosphere. Charlotte looked round and saw a group of young people sharing something funny. It seemed impossible to believe there was any malice in the intentions of the people they represented, but much of what the Nazis had done to the countries they had overwhelmed was common knowledge. It beggared belief, but sadly it was true.

"They started on the Jews, particularly those whose homes are empty. The galleries too." Nicolas said. "They knew which families had important works of art in their big homes." He opened his hands up in an empty gesture. "All gone now."

Charlotte looked at Margot for confirmation.

Margot nodded. "I have already been tasked with identifying and cataloguing their provenance ready for shipment."

"That must be awful for you," Charlotte said. "And you can't refuse, can you?"

Margot put her hand on Charlote's arm. "I think we are venturing into dangerous territory, Charlotte, so why don't we change the subject? Tell me about yourself."

Charlotte gave Margot a sanitised version of her life, avoiding too much detail. She said she'd come over to France when she'd finished her degree to take her Aunt Matilde back to England, but managed to get trapped in France, which was why she was now working as a waitress at the Hotel Metropole.

Margot suddenly looked at her watch. "Oh, time for me to go," she said, and touched Charlotte's arm. "Sorry to run away like this, Charlotte, but perhaps we can meet up again sometime." She looked over at Nicolas. "You'll manage that for us, won't you?"

Nicolas said he would. Margot got to her feet and kissed Charlotte on the cheek. "Goodbye."

Charlotte watched her walk away until she disappeared from view.

"What a nice woman, Nicolas," she said without looking at him.

Nicolas nodded his head quite slowly. "Clever, brave and resourceful," he said. "Amazing woman."

The two of them were quiet for a while, just letting the moment fade away. Nicolas turned towards Charlotte suddenly.

"Would you like to come to a meeting with me?" he asked.

Charlotte looked at him, surprise registering on her face. "What kind of a meeting?"

"What you might call a clandestine one," he told her. "Some of us younger members of the Communist party want to consider how best to deal with what's to come."

It sounded ominous to Charlotte, and scary. "Won't that be risky? After all, the Germans won't allow secret meetings, surely?"

He reached across the table and laid his hand on hers. "My dear, Charlotte, we are not stupid, but at the moment, because Hitler has agreed a non-aggression pact with Stalin, Communists are treated with a certain amount of caution and respect." He grinned as he said that. "And we would be extremely careful."

Charlotte couldn't see any point of attending what would be a political meeting, but then she remembered she had been sent over to France as an agent of the SOE, and it would make sense to learn what she could about the Communist's intentions. She thought it best to show reluctance but had made up her mind to go.

"I'm not sure I'm brave enough for that," she told him, which was partly truthful. "What if we're caught?"

He laughed softly. "They would break up the meeting and maybe hand out some sort of prohibition order on the group, but we wouldn't let that happen; it will look more like a bunch of young people have got together for booze up, nothing more."

"Would I be the only woman?"

He grinned and shook his head. "No; Margot will be there."

Chapter 16

Charlotte's mother was sitting in her front room reading. It was late afternoon, and sunlight was streaming through the net curtains adding warmth and cosiness. The radio was on quietly in the background and a sense of peace and tranquillity had settled itself on her troubled shoulders when she heard the sound of a motorbike in the distance. She lifted her head and listened briefly but then returned her attention to her book,

The sound of the motorbike got louder until it suddenly came to a stop. Connie put her book down and went over to the window. She looked through the net and could see the rider getting off the motorbike, which was now parked outside her front gate.

The rider was wearing a uniform and Connie immediately thought he would be a dispatch rider. Suddenly an overwhelming sense of panic rippled through her veins and Charlotte came into her mind. She could see the rider making his way up the footpath, so she hurried round to the front door and pulled it open just as he was about to knock.

"Ah, good morning. Are you Mrs De la Cour by any chance?" he asked with a lightness in his voice. He was wearing an RAF uniform with a half brevet on his tunic, sewn just above his breast pocket. He was a sergeant.

Connie hesitated briefly before answering as the question registered. "Er, yes, I'm Mrs De la Cour."

He had an envelope in his hand which he offered up

to her. "Good. This is for you," he said. "It's from your daughter."

Connie's mouth fell open. "My daughter?" she stammered. "Where is she? Is she okay?"

"Read the letter," he said as he handed it to her.

Connie took it from him and stared at it. Then she looked at the sergeant. "I don't understand…"

"Just read the letter," he said again.

She stood away from the open door. Would you like to come in?"

He made a point of looking at his watch.

"I'd better not," he told her. "I have to be back at camp." He put his arm down. "Best I was away. I wouldn't be able to answer any of your questions anyway, so…" he shrugged. "I hope it's good news." He raised his hand in a salute.

"Goodbye."

Connie watched open mouthed as he made his way down to the road and climbed on to his motorbike. He kickstarted it into life, turned and waved at her and roared away, soon disappearing into the into the distance, barely five minutes after arriving at her gate.

She closed the door and hurried into the front room She didn't bother looking for the letter opener but started ripping the envelope open with her finger as she ran.

She dropped into the armchair, her heart beating loudly in her ear, and pulled the letter from the torn envelope, her hands shaking, and started to read.

Dear mother

By now I think you will have guessed that I'm in France. I have to tell you I am fine, so please don't worry about me. I'm living with Aunt Matilde and working as a waitress in the city. This was never my plan; I intended returning with Matilde, but she refused to come with me, and by then it was too late because the ferries had stopped running. I have to tell you that Paris is quite safe now. You wouldn't have thought it would be like this, but because it's an open city, life is returning to normal (if normal is possible during a war). The atmosphere seemed a little strained at first, but the Germans are behaving superbly. In fact, many of those people who fled are now making their way back. We all believe the war will be over by Christmas. It's called the phoney war here, just as it was in England, so in that respect I believe I'll be able to come home by the end of the year. I cannot say too much but once again please don't worry about me; I'll be fine. Aunt Matilde sends her love. We'll share a glass of champagne at Christmas and laugh about this.

I love you

Toodle pip.

Charlotte.

xx

Connie finished reading and folded the letter into her

lap, still holding on to it and trying to work out if there was some hidden message in there. She read through the letter again and then took it over to the drawer where she'd kept all of the letters she'd received from her daughter. Tears came to her eyes as she slipped it into the pile and retied the ribbon. Now, more than ever, she knew that Charlotte had been sent to France as a secret agent by Jefson in London.

***

Charlotte had a great deal on her mind, not the least her mother and the hope that her letter had been delivered. There was nothing she could do about it anyway, so worrying was futile. Another thought on her mind was Nicolas Escoffier and his invitation to attend a clandestine meeting; one he tried to persuade her was safe. There was another element to their association and that was her growing feelings for him. She found him fun to be with although he did get a little too political at times, but that was small beer and made little difference to their growing friendship.

Charlotte explained to her aunt that she would be staying in Paris after work that day but would be home before the curfew which had been extended to midnight earlier that month. It was another indication that Paris was returning to normal. Matilde suggested she took the Metro as it was back in service, but Charlotte said she would enjoy the ride home in the pleasant July evening to avoid the general stuffiness of the underground train.

And so, Charlotte unwittingly took another step into a world that was destined to become a struggle for survival and one of unimaginable horror, which no-one knew was to come.

Chapter 17

They met at their usual watering hole alongside the River Seine. Nicolas gave Charlotte a kiss on the cheek and a warm embrace. She liked the feel of his arms around her, even though it was fleeting.

"What time is the meeting?" she asked once they'd ordered their coffee.

"Six o'clock."

"That's early," Charlotte said. Then she leaned forward a little, her shoulders hunched in a conspiratorial fashion and arched her eyebrows. "I thought it was a clandestine meeting. You know; somewhere dark and hidden away in a back street."

He laughed. "You've been reading too many spy stories." He shook his head. "No, but we don't want to make it obvious, do we, so we have only advertised it by word of mouth."

Their coffee arrived along with a couple of small biscuits. Charlotte thought of the lavish meals she'd been serving to the German officers at the Metropole and wondered idly if there was a widening gap between the lifestyle the French enjoyed (if that was the right word) and the Germans in Paris.

"Six o'clock?" Charlotte said, leaning back in her chair. She looked at her watch. "So, what shall we do in the meantime?"

"I have some things to pick up at my apartment. It's on the way, so we could go there now and…"

Charlotte's questioning expression disappeared

rapidly. "Nicolas!"

He laughed and shook his head. "No, Charlotte, not that. But it will give you a chance to see how I live." He shrugged. "I could make us a snack before we go to the meeting. And maybe have a cognac or two," he added.

"For Dutch courage?" she said, grinning slightly.

"For me? No. But for you? Maybe."

"Is it far?" she asked.

He shook his head and pointed. "I live in the Rue de la Huchette. It's in the Latin Quarter."

Charlotte turned her head and looked in the direction in which Nicolas was pointing.

"I used to love going there with my father," she told him. "My mother and I would come up to meet him from work sometimes. We would wander along the banks of the Seine until we came to the Notre Dame. Sometimes we would stop there, but more often than not, we would head towards the bookshop in the Rue de l'Odéon. My father loved browsing there."

"The Shakespeare?"

Nicolas was referring to the bookshop, *Shakespeare and Company*,. It was often frequented by great writers like Ernest Hemingway and William Joyce among others.

She looked back at him and smiled winsomely. "Happy memories, Nicolas." She shrugged. "But that's all in the past now unfortunately."

"It will happen again," he said reassuringly. "I'm sure." He stood up. "Shall we go then?"

They gathered up their belongings and made their way into the labyrinthian streets of the Latin Quarter but did not ride their bicycles; they simply wheeled the bikes and wandered deeper into the streets until Nicolas stopped.

"Here we are."

Charlotte stared up at the old building standing shoulder to shoulder with others as though pressed in there by some giant hand. A few German soldiers had ventured this deep, none of whom took any notice of them. Nicolas told her that the Germans avoided the Quarter at night because of the risks, but in daylight hours they had little to be worried about although they were usually in groups of three or four.

Nicolas opened the front door and wheeled his bicycle in. Charlotte followed suit and left her bike alongside Nicolas's in the poorly lit passageway. He put a leather loop around both bikes and padlocked them together, then looked at Charlotte.

"Can't leave them without padlocking," he told her. "But no-one minds; they all understand." He pointed to the stairs. "I'm up there on the first floor," he said and started climbing the stairs, his shoes thumping noisily on the bare wood.

Charlotte followed, peering up like someone venturing into the unknown. There were no lights, which made it all very gloomy. Unlike Nicolas, she was careful to tread softly.

He stopped at a door and unlocked it. Then he pushed it open and stood aside to let Charlotte in first. There was little inside to suggest that Nicolas enjoyed the luxury of a well-appointed apartment. It had the look of single man's lifestyle: basic furniture, an escritoire which had a scattering of papers on the desktop surface, and a settee that had seen better days and had probably been used as a bed by his friends.

The front room was surprisingly well lit through the two full length sash windows that looked out over the street. The drapes, which were open, showed signs of sunlight damage. But it was serviceable and ideally situated for a man like Nicolas.

"Bathroom's through there," Nicolas said and pointed to a doorway. "You go through the kitchen to get to it. Have a look round if you want, Charlotte. It will be brief and there is very little to see. I have two bedrooms, but I only use one. The other is where I put things that I plan to put somewhere else in time."

Charlotte smiled at this. "I know the feeling," she said and sat down on a soft armchair that looked and felt well used. But at least it was padded.

"Would you like a drink? Coffee, cognac, water?" He arched his eyebrows. "And maybe a croissant?"

She shook her head. "No thanks. We can get something later though, can't we?"

"Yes. We're meeting in a back room, but we can get something at the bar."

"Where is this place, anyway?"

"Not far." He pointed towards the window. "Couple of streets from here. We meet there regularly." He paused and snorted. "Well, we used to, but the Germans buggered that up for us."

"So will it be safe to go there if the Germans have stopped it?" She was beginning to get a bad feeling about it.

"It was only temporary," he reassured her. "We thought we were going to be attacked, remember? But once Paris was declared an open city, it meant we could return to normality. More or less," he added sourly. "We try not to be too obvious though," he said. "We need some discretion. No-one brings anything…" He stopped and looked thoughtful for a moment or two. "Well, nothing that would give the Germans any reason to think we were planning some kind of a resistance movement."

"Which you are, of course."

He laughed. "You are so gauche," he told her with a shake of his head and sat down in the only other armchair in the room. "I hope you retain your innocence longer than I've been able to, Charlotte. It won't be long before we will need to fight them by whatever means we can."

"I hope you're wrong," she countered. "People are coming back to the city. Things are returning to normal." She shrugged. "Well, within reason. But I believe it will be over by the end of the year. Churchill will sue for peace and the war will fizzle out."

He chuckled and shook his head slowly. "Churchill will not let that happen; I promise." He was about to say something else when they heard the sound of the front door opening and footsteps thumping up the stairs, then a rapid knocking at the door of the apartment. Nicolas jumped up and went to the door. He pulled it open and threw his arms up in the air when he saw who was standing there.

"Bobby!"

It was his American friend, Bobby Bayard, the son of Eugene Bayard who owned the Metropole. Charlotte remembered serving the family some weeks ago, before the Germans arrived.

He swept into the room, his eyes brightened by seeing Charlotte sitting there. "I didn't know you had company, Nicolas, you rogue."

Nicolas came up beside him. "This is my friend, Charlotte de la Cour." He looked at her. "Charlotte, allow me to introduce my noisy American friend, Robert Bayard; known as Bobby to those foolish enough to make friends with him."

Bobby shook Charlotte's hand. "We've met, but any excuse to hold your hand again will do. I'm pleased to meet you, Charlotte. You can call me Robert or Bobby; I don't mind which."

Charlotte smiled at him. "I will call you Bobby, but only when we are away from the hotel, otherwise I will have to call you monsieur. Or sir if you prefer the English."

"From someone as pretty as you, anything."

Nicolas tugged him away. "Come on, Romeo, leave my friend alone." He brought an upright kitchen chair over to him. "Now, sit your bum down and tell me why you are still in France. I thought your parents wanted you to return to America."

Bobby sat down and beamed it Nicolas. "No. I am now officially a correspondent for the New York Post. My dad managed to swing it for me. He has friends in high places over there," he explained unnecessarily, holding his hands out. "So, I now have a proper job and will be reporting on the Occupation two or three times a week, or more if things start hotting up."

Nicolas looked genuinely pleased for him. "That's amazing; I'm really pleased for you. So, tell me, why are you here?"

"I'm coming to the meeting."

Nicolas's expression changed. Gone was the happy look on his face, now it was one of complete surprise. "You won't be reporting on that, surely?"

Bobby shook his head vigorously. "Don't be daft, Nicolas; I'm not that naïve. No, I am almost as French as you and feel I should be there. I want to be there."

"But you're a Democrat, not even a Republican, which you should be if want to be French."

"Nor a Communist," Bobby said laughing softly. "But at least I can be with friends." He turned and looked over at Charlotte. "Are you a Communist?"

Charlotte pulled a face. "Absolutely not. I have no cause to hang my colours on unless it rids France of the Germans. And for now, I believe it won't be too long before they are gone."

Nicolas dropped into his chair. "Poor girl thinks it will be over by the end of the year."

Bobby looked over at Charlotte. "You do?"

She nodded. "I'm an optimist," she told him. "At least, I like to think so."

He said nothing but turned his attention back to Nicolas. "My father heard something on the grapevine."

Nicolas knew that his friend was referring to Eugene Bayard's access to the ear of the American

Ambassador, William Bullit.

"Go on," he said.

"The Vichy Government are planning to abolish anti-Semitism laws very soon. And they also plan to forbid so-called Secret Societies."

"Like Freemasonry?" Nicolas suggested.

"And the Germans will not allow Jews to re-enter the Occupied Zone."

Nicolas blew air through his pursed lips. "Phew. A lot of Jews fled Paris before the Germans came. If they can't come back, they will be trapped in Vichy France."

"Who will be singing from the same hymn sheet as the Nazis and betraying every Jewish family there."

Charlotte was aware of her own Jewishness, which made this news a little more personal than it might to people like the two boys who had no reason to like or dislike the Jewish race. Her ancestry had never been much of a talking point, but now this news brought it to the surface, which was unsettling for her, but there was nothing she could do about it, and thought it was unlikely ever to be something she needed worry about.

"If they plan to ban Secret Societies," Nicolas said, "I wouldn't put it past them to consider any clandestine meeting, like ours tonight, as something similar."

"Which means this could be the last one before they start clamping down," Bobby said.

Nicolas nodded his head thoughtfully, then he looked at Charlotte. "Will you be okay for this, Charlotte. I mean, if you think we might be sailing close to the wind, you can always back out."

Charlotte gave a short, dismissive laugh. "Why?

They haven't banned anything yet, so why should I cry off?" She grinned and tipped her head to one side. "I'm not even a fully paid-up member of your gang; just an interested onlooker."

"It isn't a gang, my girl," Nicolas scolded her softly. "It's simply a group of like-minded young Communists who care about France."

"Vive la Republique!" she said. "So, let's go the meeting."

Chapter 18

The warmth of the evening August sun pressed down into the narrow streets of the Latin Quarter and was trapped there by the closeness of the buildings and the lack of any breeze to mollify the effects of the heat. But none of this troubled the three of them as they laughed and talked without an apparent care in the world, despite the presence of armed German soldiers. Although the soldiers were generally sauntering as they made their way out of the labyrinth, they still represented the shadow that hung over the city.

Nicolas pushed open the door of a bar and held it there for Charlotte to pass through. She glanced up at the name. It was called La Chanteuse. She thought it was an odd name for a bar, but then it could have alluded to a place where singers gathered. Bobby followed them in as the door closed behind them. Walking in from sunlight to the darkness almost blinded them, forcing them to squint as they moved among the tables on their way up to the bar.

Nicolas indicated a door just a few feet away from the counter, then asked the barman for three coffees. He told Charlotte and Bobby to go through and he would bring the coffees with him once he'd paid. Charlotte pulled open the door and found herself looking into a room that was a lot larger than the bar room. There were several people in there, most of whom turned their heads as Charlotte was followed in by Bobby. Charlotte started looking round for an empty table when someone held their arm up and called over.

"Charlotte, over here!"

It was Margot Aveline, the art historian who Charlotte had met with Nicolas at the café beside the Seine. She looked back at Bobby. "This way," she said, and took him to where Margot was sitting.

"Hello, Margot. I didn't expect to see you here," she said as she sat down. "Do you know Bobby?" she asked, pointing to him.

Bobby sat down and offered his hand over the table. "Bobby Bayard," he said. "Long standing friend of Nicolas."

Margot smiled and introduced herself. "You speak excellent French," she told him. "But you are not French, are you."

"American, but I consider myself French. My father is Eugene Bayard; he owns the Metropole Hotel. I've lived here practically all my life, so my heart is in France."

Margot smiled. "I love you already," she beamed. "So refreshing."

Nicolas came up with the coffees, put them on the table and greeted Margot with a kiss on both cheeks. "Lovely to see you, Margot," he said as he sat down. "Are they still stealing our paintings?"

"As ever," she answered. "We still haven't figured out a way of delaying them without raising suspicion. Goering came to the Museum today. He made it clear that he wants the paintings shipped to Berlin as quickly as possible. And he wants the Provenance for each painting to be handed directly to a Staff Officer."

"The man's an idiot," Bobby uttered sharply.

Margot touched his arm. "Yes, but a knowledgeable and dangerous one."

At that moment a figure appeared towering over them. It was Jacques Garnier.

"Well, if the devil cast his net now," he said jovially. "How are you all?" He pulled a chair over from another table, reached over and kissed Margot and then sat down.

Charlotte couldn't help staring open-mouthed at him. He was the last person she expected to see. Not that she had any real idea of what kind of people would turn up at the meeting.

"What have you done with Charles?" she asked. "Surely you couldn't get him and your carriage down these narrow streets."

Jacques laughed. "Charles is tucked up in bed. Well, a nice warm stable. He's happy."

Charlotte, for some reason, felt herself relaxing unexpectedly. Jacques' presence made her feel safe, although she had no idea why.

The conversation level began to increase, not just at their table but throughout the room. Spontaneous laughter and sounds of glasses slamming down on the tables as the drinkers drained them. The room was in danger of becoming smoke filled too until someone thoughtfully called for the air conditioning to be turned on.

Then a strange silence filled the room as the voices were reduced to a murmur. Someone, who Charlotte didn't recognise, stood up and walked on to a small stage at the far end of the room. He waited briefly until everyone was quiet.

"Good evening everybody. I want to welcome you all here and thank you for having the good sense to know that we meet, not for a social get together, but in the knowledge that we have the future of France in our hands providing we act with purpose and decide whether it is to be cooperation or non-cooperation that drives us forward. We have to be aware now that control of Paris is not in the hands of the Germans, but that of the Prefecture, with over 250,000 policemen at their disposal, under the direct orders of the Vichy government." He paused to let the point sink in and penetrate. "Know your enemy," he said, "and trust no-one."

It suddenly hit Charlotte that he was warning them that the city would be under French control in all but name only. And by trusting no-one he meant the French police.

"We are not here to plan and plot against the Nazi Occupation, because that's what it is, but to take advantage of the Communist Party's strength and relative freedom to ensure we can influence key elements of the Prefecture."

Charlotte felt a growing sense of discomfort as the man's oratory went on, but she felt the planned direction being suggested by his speech could be of some use to Jefson back in London if only she knew who to contact apart from Agata.

Suddenly the door burst open, and the barman leaned in and shouted, "Bosch!"

For a brief moment, no-one moved. Then it was if a pre-planned strategy was put into place. The speaker jumped off the small stage as three other men from the assembly vaulted on to it. They were each carrying a musical instrument, and within a few seconds were seated like a small combo. Others in the room started rearranging the furniture into more prosaic and informal pieces so that the room started to look like an extension of the main bar beyond the door.

Nicolas grabbed Charlotte's arm. "Come with me, Bring your coffee."

Charlotte look stunned but picked up her empty cup and followed Nicolas into the bar. He immediately sat at a small table where a lonely candle fluttered its yellow flame and indicated to Charlotte that she should sit opposite him. Then Margot Aveline and Bobby pulled up a couple of chairs and sat at the table with them. Within five minutes of the barman's strident warning, there was an affected calm about the place and sounds of music in the other room.

The main door of the bar opened suddenly, and a German Officer stepped in followed by six armed soldiers. Four of the soldiers immediately spread themselves around the edges of the bar, while the other two went into the room where the meeting had taken place.

The barman walked over to the German Officer and introduced himself as Henri Le Tissier, owner of the Chanteuse.

"Papers!" the officer demanded, holding his hand out.

Le Tissier went back behind the bar and produced his passport, which the officer checked. He handed the passport back and then turned to his men.

"Check them all," he said. Then he told everyone in the room to have their IDs ready.

Charlotte watched as passports and other adequate identification was produced. She had her passport with her; something the Parisiennes had been advised to do once the German Occupation was in place.

One of the soldiers called his officer over when he checked Bobby Bayard's passport. The officer took it and looked at Bobby.

"You are American?" he asked in English.

Bobby produced his New York Post business card. "And correspondent for the New York Post," he said with a smile on his face.

"And completely neutral I trust," the officer said with a look that said otherwise. "I hope your reports are favourable and not inflammatory."

"I report only what I see," he said.

The officer clicked his heels together and handed the business card and passport back. Then he turned and called out to his men. "*Alles in ordnung!*"

Within a few minutes the Germans had left, and a collective sigh could almost be heard and felt throughout the whole of the bar.

Charlotte found herself looking at Margot for some reason who was nodding her head slowly.

"It will get worse," Margot said. "But for now they are cautious." She glanced at Bobby. "I think perhaps you made the difference."

"I would like to think so," he told her, "but for how long?"

Charlotte decided it was time for her to go home and told Nicolas because they had to go back to his apartment for her bike.

He got up and took her hand. They said goodnight to Margot and Bobby, and as they walked out of the bar, Nicolas could feel the cold sweat on Charlotte's hand. He stopped as they got out into the street.

"I'm sorry if that frightened you, Charlotte, but it's going to get worse; I think we all know that."

Charlotte felt sick and all she wanted to do was to get home and try to forget the whole unedifying experience knowing that life in Paris was getting darker.

Chapter 19

Pierre Baudet walked away from the French Embassy with a heavy heart. The Ambassador and his closest staff members had been discussing the Vichy government's decision to abolish antisemitism laws, ban secret societies, which meant Freemasonry, and forbidding Jews to re-enter the Occupied Zone. As much as he disliked the Jews, he did know that many of those who had fled Paris were now returning, and he felt an uncomfortable sense of despair for those families who would now be rendered permanently homeless.

In his moment of melancholy and sadness, Baudet made up his mind to detach himself from the clutches of Rudolf Havertz by offering him one last morsel for a price, and then no more. It was a gamble; one which he hoped he could pull off, but until he was contacted by Havertz, there was precious little he could do.

It came much earlier than Baudet had anticipated. He was enjoying a croissant and a coffee in the small café he frequented when Clementine slid into the empty chair at his table. He looked up in astonishment.

"Sorry I'm late my darling. We're snowed under at work."

He picked up on Clementine's affected manner and signalled to the waiter for another coffee.

"What on earth are you doing here?" he asked, trying not to say it through clenched teeth.

She made a fuss of opening her purse and pulling out a compact. She dusted her face and snapped the compact shut, dropped it into her purse and closed it.

"We will not be seeing Rupert again," she said.

He frowned. "Why?"

"Why is not important, but it is never wise to remain in a place where your routines can be watched over."

Baudet immediately thought of his own routines and wondered briefly if they were being watched over by French security. Or the British for that matter.

"Which means what?" he asked. Clementine's coffee arrived. He thanked the waiter.

"Someone else will contact you. Until then, you will have to deal with me."

Baudet breathed in heavily through his nose. "In that case, I have something to tell you. I will no longer work for you or any of your people. I have one piece of information that I will sell to you for five hundred pounds. Once that is done, you will get nothing more from me."

Clementine looked a little non-plussed but managed to retain a friendly countenance despite Baudet's tense manner. She lifted the cup to her lips and peered at him over the rim. Then she took a sip and put the cup down.

"You're either very stupid or very brave. I think the former."

Baudet managed to chuckle. "I have long known my failings, madame, and stupidity is one I can own. But now it is my time to be brave. So, you have my terms. Take it or leave it."

"And what is this information that will cost us a great deal of money?"

"There is an agent working for the SOE in plain sight

in the heart of Paris. This agent is a Jew, and in view of the…" He paused there and lifted his head in thought. "… future under which the Jews will find themselves, you could persuade this agent to work for you."

"And you know this so-called agent? Or is it speculation?"

He grinned and shook his head. "I know the agent, but I will not reveal anything to you until you have paid me five hundred pounds. Not counterfeit by the way."

Clementine knew why she believed him to be stupid, and this clinched it. "I will need to speak to someone."

"How long?"

She shrugged and picked up her cup. Baudet watched as she slowly drained it before putting it down. "Tomorrow, here, same time."

She got up from the table, picked up her purse and kissed him on both cheeks. "Goodbye my darling," she said brightly. "See you tomorrow."

Baudet watched her leave and had a good feeling about it. She hadn't mentioned the fact that he was dumping her and Havertz, which meant his proposition was perfectly acceptable. It made him feel a lot better, but what he didn't realise was that it simply confirmed to Clementine just how unbelievably stupid he was.

***

Detective Inspector Merril-Hyde stepped through the portals of the French Embassy after being cleared by the French policeman at the entrance to the Embassy grounds. He removed his trilby hat and walked over to the reception desk, showed his Police ID and introduced himself.

"I am here to see Inspecteur Matisse, your head of Security. He's expecting me."

The soldier at the desk wearing the rank of Sergeant on his epaulettes picked up the phone and pressed a button. He spoke briefly and then put the phone down.

"Someone will come down for you."

Merril-Hyde thanked him and stood there, looking round until a young man wearing a suit came hurrying down the stairs.

"Detective Merril-Hyde?" Merril-Hyde nodded. "This way please sir."

He followed the young man up the stairs and was shown into the Inspector's office. When the young man had gone, Matisse leaned over the desk and shook Merril-Hyde's hand.

"Good morning Detective Inspector. You have something for me?"

Merril-Hyde took a large envelope from one of the pockets in his long overcoat and laid it on the desk in front of him. He tipped the contents on to the desk.

"We pulled a chap out of the river early this morning. These were all we found in his possession. Naturally, in view of his identity and the fact that we discovered quite quickly that he was an important member of your Embassy staff, we felt it would be best, under the present circumstances, to let your Security people know. We will of course help in any investigation you wish to take up, but I believe that may not be necessary."

Matisse looked at the contents of the envelope, now splayed out on the desk. The ID card showed it to be

Pierre Baudet. There were several photographs, all water damaged, showing him naked with other men beneath a Swastika, and a Poker chip. He picked up the chip and nodded his head slowly.

"We suspected that Monsieur Baudet had a gambling problem and have been keeping a close eye on him." He tapped the photographs. "But obviously not close enough." He held the Poker chip up. "Do you know which club?"

Merril-Hyde shook his head. "No, it's a fairly standard chip, but I imagine you will know which club he frequented."

Matisse said he did. "Will you be conducting a murder investigation?" he asked.

Merril-Hyde breathed in deeply and sighed. "We should, but we have limited manpower. It would help us if you could…" He paused there, not sure how to frame the words.

"We will deal with it. Neither of us are likely to catch the perpetrators anyway; they're probably on a submarine being spirited away to the Fatherland."

Merril-Hyde liked the connotation. "D'accord," he said. "I agree."

He left the French Embassy relieved to be free of the burden of catching whoever was responsible for Baudet's murder and wondered how stupid a man had to be to get conned by a pretty face, for he was sure there would be a woman involved, and probably a gambling debt that Inspecteur Matisse had virtually admitted they knew about.

He popped his trilby hat on and made his way back

to Scotland Yard.

Chapter 20

Charlotte cycled to work wrapped up against a cold, September breeze, her mind on the short conversation she'd had with Agata Stasiak. Agata had put in a brief appearance at her Aunt's the previous evening to tell Charlotte that someone would make themselves known to her within the next twenty-four hours, and from that moment, that person would be her contact with London. When Charlotte asked how she would know, Agata simply said, "You will know."

Curiosity was her bed companion that night, which made sleep a little difficult. She felt that the relative freedom she'd enjoyed because of what was probably a false sense of security, was gradually melting away. She had sensed this after the meeting in the Latin Quarter which had been broken up by the untimely visit of the Germans. Agata had also told her that she would only put in very brief appearances because of the work she was now committed to.

The so-called 'Battle of Britain' had been raging for over a month, many believing it was a precursor to Hitler's plans to invade England once the Royal Air Force had been beaten. People had been glued to their radios, Aunt Matilde included, listening to the broadcasts from London claiming spectacular victories against the Luftwaffe. Everyone was holding their breath waiting for the outcome; some believing that if the Luftwaffe was defeated, the war would be over. But others could only see a vicious reaction from a wounded Nazi beast, and if that was the case, Charlotte knew things would get worse in Paris.

She pitched up outside the hotel where she saw a group of people standing by a notice board watching a German soldier putting a bulletin up. The Parisians were getting used to the proliferation of notices appearing like a virus, and Charlotte was no different. But she stopped anyway and straddled her bike as she read the bulletin over the shoulders of the few people there. It was an announcement that hostages would be taken and imprisoned or executed for any violence against German personnel.

She sighed deeply, shook her head and cycled round to the Metropole's rear entrance. She locked her bike and immediately thought of Nicolas. He'd been getting very vociferous about the Nazis and the need for action against them. It made her worry for him because she'd heard of attacks against German soldiers and was fairly certain that Nicolas was hot-headed enough to be involved.

She breezed into the hotel and went through to the staff rest room. The room was empty. She wondered about that and went through to Armand's office. She knocked on the door and opened it. Armand was sitting at his desk. And sitting opposite him was Jacques Garnier.

"Morning, Armand. Morning, Jacques." She showed surprise on her face seeing Jacques there, but then remembered he and Armand were old friends. "Is Camille in today, Armand?"

Armand nodded. "Yes, but she said she might be

late."

"Oh." She looked at Jacques. "Looking for a job, Jacques?" she said with a brightening expression on her face.

Jacques laughed. "Goodness no. The less I see of these Nazi vermin the better I like it."

She smiled. "That's my Jacques. I'll make a start," she said to Armand. "Anything I need to know?"

Armand gave the Gallic shrug everyone on the staff recognised. "They are not as happy as they were a month ago. The war is not going well for them, so be on your best behaviour, Charlotte."

She grinned. "Of course." She turned to open the door. "See you soon, Jacques?"

"I'm just leaving," he said and got up from the chair. He followed Charlotte out into the corridor, closing Armand's door behind him. "I'll catch up with you later, Charlotte," he said and waved at her. "Toodle-pip."

And that was the moment Agata's words came to her: "You will know."

She literally froze — Jacques has said that to her in English, which could only have meant one thing: he was her contact with London.

***

Major Felix Heller had been working at his desk for two hours when a knock came on the office door and his Sergeant stepped into the room. He threw up a Nazi salute as Heller lifted his head. He raised his hand in recognition and leaned back in his chair.

"Hauptmann Grunberg is here, Herr Major."

Heller nodded. "Show him in."

The sergeant turned and beckoned Grunberg in. He held the door open as the young officer came into the room, then stepped out and closed it behind him.

Grunberg stood erect, clicked his heels together and threw his arm up in the required Nazi salute.

"Good day, Herr Major. Hauptmann Hans Grunberg." He lowered his arm but remained at attention.

Heller studied the young Captain. He could see a typical Aryan youth: tall, handsome and probably about six feet tall. His uniform was superbly tailored, which was *de rigeur* for all German officers. Heller liked what he saw. He pointed to the visitor's chair.

"Please, Hauptmann."

Grunberg removed his cap and put it under his arm as he sat down. Heller waited until the young officer was settled.

"So, Hauptmann, when did you arrive?"

"Last night, Major. I travelled from Munich."

Heller opened a drawer and took out a slim file which he dropped on to the desk in front of him. He flipped it open.

"You enrolled eighteen months ago straight from university," he said, running his finger down the text in front of him. "And you are billeted…" He turned the page back and forth. "Where?"

"The Hotel Crillon, Herr Major."

Heller closed the file. "Not for long," he said, looking at Grunberg. "We are billeting junior officers in the homes of French citizens. As much as we expect the French to start building resistance networks, we need to have men in place like yourself to keep their eyes and ears open for any subversive activity at homes of would-be activists. We have plenty of hotheads who will take to the streets, but we can deal with those elements. A few arrests and executions will deter them if that becomes necessary. But those we have to concern ourselves with are the quiet ones."

Grunberg nodded. "I understand, Major. It makes sense."

Heller lifted a file from a tray on his desk. He flourished it briefly before opening it. "You will be billeted at..." He studied the file for a moment. "...Montrouge. It's in the 14th Arrondisement. The house, which is a smallholding, has two tenants: the owner, Matilde Auroy, and her niece, Charlotte de la Cour. It has several rooms, which means Madame Auroy will have no difficulty accommodating you." He closed the file.

"Two women," Grunberg observed.

"Yes," Heller said with a thin smile on his face. "Hardly the hotbed of espionage, I know. Women are not capable of understanding the art of spying and resistance. They serve no other purpose in France than to look after their homes and their families. They are not allowed bank accounts, or employment without their husband's consent, and to imagine them as worthy of soldiering is lamentable in the eyes of the French." He shook his head. "No, you should have no trouble there, Hauptmann, but it is necessary to establish some influence and trust within the community around you."

"French women must have some attributes," Grunberg said. "Surely?"

Heller allowed a smile to break out on his face. "Yes, fashion and making love, apparently."

Grunberg managed to smile at that but not so with Heller's misogynistic attitude to women. It smacked of Nazi arrogance, something to which Grunberg paid little respect and had the common sense not to allow his own sense of propriety to surface too readily. He believed in a woman's strength of character and feminine instinct, something he'd learned very clearly in his upbringing because of his mother.

"When will I be expected to move in?" he asked.

"Today," Heller told him. He picked up the file and handed it to Grunberg. "There's very little in there on the Auroy woman and her niece. I've added what little I've learned about them, but I'm sure you'll get to know more as time goes by. Any information my office receives will be passed on to you." He chortled. "And I can't imagine we'll get too much."

He stood up and reached his hand over the desk. "Good luck, Hauptmann Gruber. Enjoy Paris." They shook hands. "My sergeant will give you the transport details. You will be assigned a staff car in due course, but initially you will be taken to the property with an escort."

Gruber stood up, put his cap on and saluted with an outstretched arm. He then walked out of the office and stopped by the sergeant's desk.

"I believe you have the details for my move out to Montrouge?"

The sergeant nodded. "You will be picked up from your hotel after lunch, sir."

Gruber thanked him. "Oh, Major Heller wants any information that comes in for Madame Auroy and Charlotte de la Cour to be passed directly to me." He held up the file.

The sergeant acknowledge that. "Of course. Good luck."

Gruber walked out of the building feeling pleased with himself. Paris seemed to be exactly what he'd been told, and his assignment couldn't have been any easier.

***

Matilde had been listening to another broadcast from the BBC in London. She often imagined the sound of jackboots crashing through her front door as the Nazis came to arrest her for listening to broadcasts — a crime punishable by death. It was nonsense of course; no-one was going to get shot for listening to propaganda radio stations.

Her thoughts turned to Agata Stasiak. She hadn't seen Agata for several days and had no idea when she was likely to appear. Matilde had a way of letting Agata know if it was safe to come to the house. She had a plant pot outside the front door. The decoration on the plant pot was of flowers. Matilde would make sure the sunflower on the pot always faced outwards. And whenever she turned the pot, she would always make a show of brushing her porch, lifting the pot as she did, and leaving the sunflower showing if the house was clear.

And it was at that moment she heard the

unmistakable sound of a military vehicle. She immediately went to the window and looked out through the net curtain. She frowned as she saw a German *Kubelwagen* jeep pull up outside her front gate. In it were four soldiers. As it came to a halt, a German officer climbed out of the jeep, turned and said something to the driver, and then waited until the two men in the rear seats had climbed out. They were both carrying rifles.

Matilde clutched her hand to her chest in astonishment. Then she ran to the broom cupboard and took out a small brush. She hurried to the front door and immediately made a show of cleaning her porch, turning the flowerpot at the same time so the sunflower was no longer showing.

The soldiers pushed open the gate and stood aside as the officer came through. Matilde stood up in affected astonishment, which wasn't difficult at that moment, and stood there staring while holding the small brush in her hand. The officer came to a stop in front of her, stood smartly to attention, clicked his heels and gave the Nazi salute. He then turned to one of the armed soldiers who gave him an envelope. He turned back to Matilde.

"Madame Auroy, good afternoon," he said in French. "I have been assigned to your home as a live-in tenant. This is in accordance with the orders issued by the governing authority in Paris. The details are in there," he said, handing her the envelope.

Matilde took the envelope with a bewildered look on her face and opened it. She pulled the single sheet out and started reading. The order was printed in French and clearly stated that she would be responsible for housing Hauptmann Hans Grunberg until further notice. The rest of the detail became a blur as her mind fogged over and she started to feel sick.

She breathed in deeply to help overcome her reaction and thrust the letter back at Grunberg. "This is nonsense," she said. "I have had no notice of this. My house isn't ready and I'm not sure I can afford to accommodate you. It would mean an extra mouth to feed, and food is becoming scarcer every day. I cannot do it."

Grunberg bowed his head a little. "I can understand your frustration, Madame Auroy, but you have no choice. My tenancy will be paid for by the Wehrmacht Administration. Provisions will be provided."

Matilde almost found herself lost for words but knew that any argument or refusal to comply would more than likely end up in her arrest, and she wasn't prepared to let that happen — she had to bite her tongue.

"When would you expect to move in?" she asked.

He smiled. "Today, but I will come back if you like. It will give you time to prepare."

She thought that was a little unusual; the Nazi were renowned for not brooking any argument, she thought to herself, but here was a young man who was being considerate.

"No need. You can wait in the kitchen while I prepare a room for you," she told him and stood back in the hallway holding the door open.

He looked back at the jeep and nodded. Matilde saw the driver lift a suitcase from the jeep and carry it towards the house. Gruber stepped into the hallway as the driver arrived with the suitcase He dropped it there, gave Gruber a Nazi salute and went back to the jeep.

Matilde closed the door. "This way."

He followed her into the kitchen, looking around as he did so, and found himself admiring the antiquity of the place. She pointed to a chair. "Please don't wander around while I'm getting your room ready." She left him there and disappeared upstairs.

A strange, disquieting feeling came over Gruber as he sat there alone in the kitchen. It was as though he had tumbled down a rabbit hole, rather like Alice in Wonderland, and ended up in a place that was like nothing he'd encountered before. The kitchen could only be described as functional. There were a lot of pots and pans and other cooking utensils hanging from a row of hooks along one wall. A couple of herb bouquets were strung up at the end of the row. The table at which he was sitting was old and solid and had probably seen countless generations eat there.

He turned and looked over at the window above the sink, and despite Matilde's instruction not to move, he got up and went over to it. He put his hands on the edge of the stone sink and leaned forward so he was close to the net curtain that covered the window. He could see a yard and some sheds. A very small barn and what looked like a chicken coop. He wondered if Madame Auroy kept chickens.

He then turned away and walked slowly round the

room. He picked up a framed photograph and studied it. It was of a woman and a man. The woman was obviously Madame Auroy. He assumed the man with her was her husband who he knew from the file was currently a prisoner in Germany.

He sighed and put the photo back. Next to it was another framed photo. Two women, one a lot older than the other. He assumed the younger one was Charlotte de la Cour, and the woman with her was probably her mother who he knew was in England.

He went back to the table and tried to imagine what it must be like to have your lives turned upside down and, in a lot of cases, destroyed because of the awfulness of what had befallen them; for despite Gruber's birthright and the uniform he was wearing, he despised everything the Nazis stood for.

Chapter 21

Charlotte's thoughts as she cycled home from her shift at the Metropole were not about the German Officers she served or the value of the lip-reading she'd accumulated from them, but about the revelation of Jacques Garnier's link to London. She'd stopped stock still the moment she realised what he'd said, and the fact there was no way, other than through Jefson, that he was privy to the contents of her letters to her mother. All this had flashed through her mind in a few seconds before she spun round and looked at him with shock written all over her face. And at that precise moment, Camille came running down the corridor and pulled up next to Charlotte. She was quite breathless.

"Have you heard, Charlotte?" she said gasping. "The bastards are rationing food now."

Charlotte turned towards her, not sure that she wanted a conversation with Camille. Then she looked quickly at Jacques, her face still registering shock.

"I'll catch up with you later, Charlotte," he said, and walked past the two women, smiling at them as he walked by.

Charlotte had to force her mind back on to Camille. "No, I hadn't heard," she told her. When did you find this out?"

"My mother. There's a notice outside the townhall. Everything will be rationed — eggs, milk, butter, bread." She paused to take a breath. "Most things," she added shaking her head. "We have to apply to the townhall in person to collect our tickets."

Charlotte frowned. "When?"

"It supposed to start this Monday." She shook her head. "It will be bloody chaos, Charlotte, chaos."

The light was almost gone in the late September afternoon as Charlotte peddled furiously with these thoughts running through her mind. She could not imagine the staff at the Mairie, the townhall, being able to cope with the initial rush; it would be bedlam. Another thought that crossed her mind was that she was sure the Germans would not go without, which meant the Metropole was unlikely to suffer any rationing.

She reached her Aunt's smallholding and pushed her bicycle into the shed where she aways kept it, locked the door, and hurried across the yard to the front door. And that was when she noticed the flowerpot had been turned; there was no sunflower. She stopped and frowned. Had her Aunt forgotten?

She opened the front door and called out as she hung her topcoat up and removed her shoes, changing into a pair of casual slip-ons. She went through to the kitchen where she came to a sudden stop. Sitting at the kitchen table was her aunt and a German Officer.

Charlotte's heart rate immediately went up a notch. "What…"

Matilde got up from the table. Gruber stood too. He faced Charlotte, bowed his head, and clicked his heels.

Matilde introduced him. "Charlotte, this is Hauptmann Hans Gruber. He will be staying with us as a tenant."

"Good evening, Mademoiselle de la Cour."

Charlotte's mouth opened in surprise. She was almost speechless. Then she rallied and asked her aunt for how long. Matilde looked at Gruber for an answer.

Gruber walked over to Charlotte with his hand extended. "I know your aunt introduced me by my rank, but my name is Hans. And I will be staying until my commanding officer thinks otherwise."

"But you don't know for how long?"

He shook his head. "No."

Charlotte let her eyes wander over him briefly. She liked what she saw, but then she'd seen quite a few German Officers who she liked the look of. But Gruber was standing quite still as though he was giving her the opportunity to make up her mind about him. He was definitely attractive, and if circumstances had been different, she thought she might have encouraged a relationship with him. His height, his features and his general countenance somehow stripped away the Nazi uniform and revealed a young man who was at ease within himself and pleasing to the eye.

"Excuse me," she said, and turned towards her aunt. "Have you heard about the rationing, Matilde?" she asked.

Matilde said she had. "Simone told me about it this morning." She shook her head and sat down at the table. "We have to get our tickets from the Mairie."

"Mairie?" Gruber asked.

"The townhall."

He smiled. "Oh, that was one I must have missed during my French lessons."

"Your French is very good though," Charlotte told

him. "Where did you learn?"

"In France." He could tell by the look on their faces they were surprised. "I worked at the Fragonard perfume factory at Eze in the South before I went to university." He could tell they wanted to know more. He pointed at the table. "Do you mind if we sit down."

"Oh, yes, of course," Charlotte said, and sat down beside Matilde.

Once they were all seated, Gruber went on. "My family business is perfume. My father thought it would be beneficial for me and our business to learn from the masters. I studied there for a year."

Neither of the women knew what to say next. Matilde was bewildered to think she was listening to a Nazi officer in her own home who acted and spoke in such a friendly and personable manner. It made her feel uncomfortable as she recalled her encounter with Major Heller who gave her the information about her husband's imprisonment. She felt she was being sucked into a comfort zone that was like a Venus fly trap. It unsettled her, but at the same time it was a relief not to be tense and under stress in the close company of a German.

Charlotte on the other hand found herself warming to the man. He didn't look much older than her — mid-twenties maybe, she thought, her generation but on opposite sides of the fence. Then she thought of Nicolas and his rough edges. She wondered if Hans Gruber was hiding any rough edges beneath that charming manner he was showing.

Matilde thought about the lateness of the hour.

"Hauptmann Gruber," she said suddenly. "We usually eat around seven o'clock."

He stopped her. "Don't worry about me," he told her and looked at his watch. "I've instructed my driver to pick me up in about twenty minutes. I'll be going back into Paris and staying with a friend for the weekend," he explained. He stood up. "I'll go up to my room now, Madame Auroy. One or two things I need to do before I leave. Perhaps you'll show me?"

Matilde pushed her chair back and stood up. "Will you be back tomorrow?"

"Yes," he said. "Tomorrow evening. And I will bring provisions for dinner."

Matilde managed to thank him and then looked at Charlotte. She didn't say anything but turned away, beckoning Gruber to follow.

Charlotte watched them go. When they'd gone, she wondered if it had all really happened. It was surreal: a German officer, a Nazi at that, sitting at their table and chatting away like old friends. Warm, hospitable, pleasant. And then she thought of the risks to herself and her Aunt, and what a slip of the tongue could lead to. Then there was Agata to consider and how a chance encounter with Hans Gruber could lead to imprisonment, no matter how nice and pleasant he sounded. Her one thought then was to ask Jacques Garnier to somehow warn Agata of the real danger to them all because of the uncomfortable turn of events. And Charlotte wasn't even sure Jacques had any connection with Agata; it was all assumption on her part.

Her mind was still on the dangers and risks when Matilde walked back into the room. She looked flustered and flopped down on to the chair beside Charlotte. She grabbed Charlotte's hand.

"*Mon Dieu*," she said a little breathlessly, holding a hand against her breast. "I wasn't ready for that. He showed up without warning. We will have to warn Agata."

"How can we do that?" Charlotte couldn't say anything about Jacques Garnier and her previous thoughts. It seemed ridiculous but even her aunt had told her to trust no-one.

Matilde shook her head. "We can't unless she comes when Gruber's not here."

Charlotte lowered her voice to little more than a whisper. "But what will he be doing? Will he live here like a family member or be out all day?"

Matilde just fluttered her hands. "I don't know. Perhaps he'll tell us."

"Well he seemed pleasant enough."

"He's still a Nazi," Matilde said sharply. "My Pierre is locked up by the bastards, so whether he's pleasant or not, he is still a Nazi. Don't forget that, Charlotte."

Charlotte could see her aunt was clearly rattled by Gruber's presence. Her own attitude however was a little ambivalent, probably because of her association with so many of them at the hotel. She thought it would be wise to keep her opinion to herself.

"I will do my best, Matilde, and I'm sure we'll cope somehow."

Matilde looked forlorn. "My God, I hope so. My

poor Pierre would be horrified to think I'm sharing our home with one of them."

Charlotte noticed how her aunt had dispensed with the use of Gruber's name or rank, nor calling him a Nazi, but had consigned him to a place in her mind where only despicable and unmentionable vermin lived. It made her wonder just how long peace and calm would prevail, or would her aunt make life intolerable for all three of them.

Charlotte left her aunt and went through to her room to freshen up before their evening meal. Matilde was making bouillabaisse soup which Charlotte always enjoyed. They would have fresh baked rolls with it, but this time there was to be a hint of sadness, not simply because of Hans Gruber's arrival, but the fact that they would need ration cards the following week which would seriously limit their expectations in the kitchen.

Thirty minutes later they were sat at the table eating when Hans Gruber walked in. He stood at the table and lifted his head and sniffed.

"That smells wonderful, Madame Auroy," he said. "It makes me wish I was eating with you tonight rather than my colleague."

Matilde glanced up at him and made a grudging reply of thanks. Charlotte felt decidedly uncomfortable at her aunt's reaction.

"But on Monday, you will have provisions and maybe you can produce something just as lovely."

He moved away from the table and walked over to the door, but before he opened it, he turned.

"Auf Wiedersehen." He then put his hand up. "Oh,

Madame Auroy, I will bring your ration cards for you; there will be no need for you to queue up at the Mairie."

Both Matilde and Charlotte gawped as the door closed behind the young German. Matilde looked at Charlotte in horror.

"What can I do?" she asked imploringly. "They act so nice and helpful that we know it's all a subterfuge. They are playing with us."

Charlotte didn't know what to say, but she did realise that her own attitude towards the Germans was a little less disturbing than her aunt's.

"All we can do, Matilde, is accept their good nature until they reveal their true colours. What else is there?"

"There is resistance," she hissed. "And we must do that willingly or we will stand condemned."

Charlotte knew things would not improve for anyone in Paris until the Germans were defeated, and she knew that her aunt stood the risk of being accused of collaboration through no fault of her own. And she wondered what lay in store for them.

***

Saturday morning and Margot Aveline cycled to work at the catacombs beneath the Louvre where most of the stolen works of art and treasures were being stored for her and her colleague, Oliver Benoist, to verify and catalogue.

The catacombs, or Ossuaries as they used to be known, were built during the 18th century to cope with the overflowing cemeteries and dead corpses rotting out in the open. They were started at Montrouge, south of the city centre, but eventually spread over an area of several kilometres, reaching almost to the doors of the Louvre.

Access to the catacombs from there was now prohibited to the general public by the Germans, and a team of cleaners had been tasked with clearing those places where they intended to store the art treasures they were planning to ship to Berlin. Since the Vichy government had declared that all French Jews who had fled from the country were no longer citizens, it gave carte blanche to the Germans to remove all art from many of the Jewish galleries that proliferated around Paris. Almost all of the most prestigious galleries and homes had been raided and emptied of everything and anything that could be construed as valuable works of art.

It was a bitter disappointment to Margot as she had no choice but to identify those pieces that were of the highest value, all of which were being shipped out on the orders of Herman Goering. Goering had paid several visits to the Louvre and had shown Margot a remarkable knowledge and insight into the classic masterpieces under her care. She hated him and everything he stood for of course, and she knew she was facing imprisonment if she was caught falsely branding a painting or a sculpture as a worthless forgery or a poor copy.

Margot wheeled her bicycle through the doors of the Louvre and headed towards the steps that led to the catacombs beneath the city. The steps were guarded from the general public by a pair of solid doors, always closed, and the only people with rights of access were herself and Oliver Benoist, the Director of the Louvre, but now several German staff officers regarded the catacombs as their own personal fiefdom, and it wasn't unusual for Margot to find at least one of them already in one of the rooms fussing over a piece of art.

But now that had changed, much like the walls of the Louvre which were practically bare of many works of art, all waiting below for Margot's attention. She left her bicycle at the bottom of the stairs and walked along the poorly lit tunnel where much of the art work was haphazardly stored. Margot worried that they would suffer from the changed environment, but the only hope of salvation was to get them packed and shipped out.

When she reached her office she was a little surprised to see a German officer sitting at her small desk. He stood up as she walked in.

"Good morning, Mademoiselle Aveline," he said with a snappy click of his heels.

At least he was polite, Margot thought to herself. "Good morning, Major. What can I do for you?"

"A Renoir was brought in yesterday — Dance in the City?"

Margot nodded her head slowly and affected a thoughtful expression. "Yes, I remember, I had a look at it, but I will need to check it once more before I can validate the authenticity."

"Could we do that now?" he asked. "We have a train leaving Paris at noon, and I particularly wanted that Renoir to go with the current shipment."

Margot always tried to delay any movement of art to Berlin, no matter how small the delay, and she was keen to delay every single Masterpiece that passed through her hands.

She indicated to him that she wanted to get to her desk, so he moved out of the way. She sat down, produced a set of keys and opened one of the lower drawers in the desk. She pulled out a large folder and began turning the pages.

She looked up at him. "I need to check it once more before I can issue the validation. It's in the first room." She stood up. "We'll go there now."

Margot's heart rate quickened as she walked down the tunnel with the Major following closely. When they reached the storeroom where the painting had been placed, Margot went straight over to the piece which was covered in a cloth and propped up against the wall like something that had no worth.

She pulled back the cloth, pulled a small magnifying glass from her pocket and began studying the painting. It was of two people, a man and a woman, dancing. It was a simple piece, but it was a Renoir, and that made it special. What Margot was about to do, particularly if the Major was an art expert himself, could cost her dearly. Her heart rate increased yet again as she stood up and put the magnifying glass back in her pocket.

"I'm afraid I cannot validate this painting because I believe it's a copy."

The Major looked shocked. "A copy? How so?"

She pointed to the painting. "This has been painted by a right-handed painter. Renoir was left-handed."

He stepped forward and looked closely at the painting. "How can you be so sure? How can you tell?"

Margot knew then that the Major was no expert." I cannot confirm it as a copy until my colleague has checked it, just to make sure."

"Well, go and get him. I want this on that train."

"I can't. He is not working today, and for all I know he may not even be at home." She tried to make light of it. "But still, on Monday I'm sure Monsieur Benoist will confirm or reject my appraisal. It's only a couple of days away. I don't believe Berlin are holding their breath for something which, despite being a 'Renoir' — " She made air quotes with her fingers — "is really an inconsequential work of art in the Renoir collection."

The Major puffed his cheeks out and shook his head. "That is a pity. But it wouldn't look good for me, or for you," he added, "if the painting was declared a forgery and ended up in Berlin."

Margot shook his head. "I didn't say it was a forgery, merely a copy. There is a difference you know." She hoped he would accept there was such a difference. "So, if you will excuse me, Major, I have a lot of work to do."

He gave her a downbeat look and thanked her. Then he walked hurriedly from the office.

Margot sat down and breathed a sigh of relief. She'd just got away with a massive gamble by feeding the man with a lot of bullshit, just to gain a couple days and add another small delay that would frustrate them all in their plans to steal the Louvre's treasured works of art.

Margot waited several minutes before moving from behind her desk. She sat listening at first to the sound of the Major's receding footsteps until there was nothing but silence. When she was satisfied there was no-one else wandering about in the tunnels, she set about printing out a validation for the Renoir. There was nothing wrong with it of course; it was a perfectly genuine masterpiece. Then she printed a copy and went through to the room where the painting rested up against the wall and began the task of packing it carefully for transportation to Berlin. The whole process took Margot about an hour after which she retreated to her office and made herself a coffee before moving on to the next work of art.

As much as Margot had little to fear from anything or anyone while she was down in the catacombs on her own, the sense of not being alone was always present. It was as though the spirits of those dead people had been cursed and left to wander the tunnels for all eternity, and Margot knew that, as much as it was nonsense, it still made her feel uneasy.

She heard footsteps, faint at first but getting louder and nearer. She drained her cup and waited until her colleague, Oliver Benoist, walked through the open doorway. She sighed heavily and breathed a sigh of relief.

"Oh my God, Oliver, I'm so glad you decided not to come in early."

He frowned and looked quite worried. "Why, what's the matter, Margot?"

She laughed softly and explained the whole charade with the German Major and her dissertation about right and left-handed painters.

"I told him you was away and wouldn't be in until

Monday. I was so afraid you walk in while I was lying to him."

He laughed too and sat down opposite her. "You're either very brave or very foolish, Margot," he said, "but it something we all have to learn to do now."

She liked Oliver. He was what she would call a real academic, both in looks and demeanour. He was a lot older than her, in his sixties, and showed signs in his girth of a liking for cognac and patisseries. He was losing his hair as well.

"So, what news?" she asked.

His expression darkened. "As you know I was at the *Musée de L'Homme* earlier. The team are doing wonders but at such a risk."

The team Benoist was talking about were the museum curators and librarians, no more than about five people, who were risking everything by helping escaped prisoners of war and downed pilots by getting them across the border into the Vichy controlled Free Zone. They were the first group who were acting as resisters to the Germans and secretly publishing and distributing posters, newsletters and a journal called *Résistance*. Both he and Margot were members of that team, and it was from the very office in which they were sitting that Margot was printing single sheets of the team's newsletter.

"And there is something else, Margot,"

She shrugged. "What could be worse than living like this?"

"The police have been ordered to arrest all known Communists."

Margot looked shocked and immediately thought of Nicolas Escoffier. "Who ordered this?" she asked. "The Germans?"

He shook his head. "No, it was our own Vichy Government."

Margot's head dropped and a deep sadness invaded her soul. "Oh my God; they're reacting to the opposition they face. They've already started on the Jews, now the Communists. Who's next?"

"People like us, Margot — so-called middle-class intellectuals. Stalin did it, and the Nazis are simply following suit."

"Then we have to be prepared to fight or die," she said.

"Yes," he said. "Resistance should no longer be a headline on a piece of paper."

Chapter 22

Jacques Garnier pushed open the single door at the rear entrance to his sister's brothel and closed it behind him as he stepped into the corridor. He could hear familiar noises emanating from somewhere inside the front lounge area, and although they might have sounded familiar, they were the voices of the brothel's German customers who would be sitting around, no doubt drinking an aperitif, smoking and full of humour as they waited their turn for a visit to one of the upper rooms.

He smiled to himself and walked up to the door of his sister's office and knocked softly a couple of times. He heard shuffling from behind the door and a few seconds later it was opened by one of the girls.

"Morning, Suzzane, how are you today?"

Jacques did not know all the girls of course, only the few that had remained behind when the majority of them had fled Paris.

Suzanne stepped back and let him in. He went over to his sister who had turned in her chair and kissed her on both cheeks.

"Morning, Lilliane. How's business?"

Lilliane looked over at Suzzane. "Be a dear and bring Jacques a cognac," she said.

Jacques pulled a chair over and sat down. He waited for his sister's response.

"It's been manic. I've had to advertise for girls, believe it or not." She shook her head. "We've never had to do that before, Jacques, but the demand for the girls has rocketed. Almost all our customers are Germans. All ranks, by the way; not just officers."

"That busy?"

"Yesterday one of the girls…" She paused to think. "Mimi," she said eventually. "Pretty little thing. She did sixty tricks. That's over nine hours on her back, poor sod."

Jacques knew that the word 'Tricks' was the slang term for a session with a prostitute. He chuckled. "You're not sorry for her, Lilliane, surely?"

Lilliane shook her head, and a smile broke out on her face. "I gave her the day off, told her to have a lie-in." They both laughed at that. The poor girl had been 'lying in' all day. "She'll be in this afternoon though," Lilliane said. "Needs the money."

"Ah, yes, of course," Jacques said.

"But listen, Jacques, my girls could earn more, but I want to try and keep us above those places in the Place Pigalle. Suzanne has a friend who was on her back one hundred and fifty times working from nine in the morning until two o'clock the following morning. That seventeen hours servicing horny men. I can't have my girls reduced to that. I simply can't."

Jacques knew that the red-light district in the Place Pigalle was populated with dozens of brothels, and not all as clean and hygienic as his sister's rather grandiose *maison d'illusion* as the brothels were often called.

The door opened and Suzanne came in with a glass of cognac. She handed it to Jacques and left the room.

Jacques took a sip of the cognac. "Have you got anything for me?" he asked.

Lilliane shook her head. "It's too soon, Jacques. The girls have had no time to get comfortable with their regulars. Not that any of them have had much time with the same customer."

"Well, things are hotting up out there," he said, pointing back over his shoulder with his thumb. "They've banned the Communist Party, so it won't be too long before we see some arrests. There are more patrols now, I've noticed, despite the fact that the police are supposed to be running the show."

"Only for their German masters," Lilliane said. "We don't get any French police in here, so we're unlikely to get pillow-talk from that source. Once we've established a better understanding with our current crop of Germans, we may be able to ferret out some information, but we need to cultivate some of the Officers, and for that I need some fairly shrewd, dependable girls."

"So, you've nothing for me to pass on to London?"

She shook her head. "No, I'm sorry, Jacques, but it's going to take a long time."

He thanked his sister and left her with the kind of headache she wouldn't get from an illness, and hurried out to make sure his other responsibility was still eating from his nosebag.

He gave Charles a friendly pat on the neck and lifted the nosebag away. Then climbed up on to the carriage and turned towards the Hotel Metropole where he intended to intercept Charlotte and put some flesh on the bones of their secret and extremely dangerous partnership.

***

The news of the Communist Party ban had filtered through to the hotel bringing with it consternation and worry for Charlotte over Nicolas. She had tried to judge the mood of the Germans as they ate their meals and talked over all manner of things, oblivious to any risk of being overheard by the staff. From Charlotte's point of view it was as though none of the waitresses were visible, which went along with the way the Germans stupidly considered women as incapable of duplicity. Her lip-reading skills were not really helping, but she got a sudden lift in her spirits when she saw Nicolas's friend, Bobby, come into the hotel with his dad, Eugene Bayard.

Camille was standing up against the buffet when she saw Bobby. She glanced over at Charlotte who was serving at a table, and raised her eyes, giving an almost imperceptible nod in Bobby's direction. Charlotte responded and went over to the Bayard's table. It was inevitable that at least one senior Staff Officer would come over to Bobby's father. Charlotte had to stand a reasonable distance away while she waited for the Staff Officer to finish the small talk.

Bobby lifted a hand and acknowledged her, then got up from the table. He side-stepped his father and the officer and came up beside her.

"Hello, Charlotte. You looked worried," he said showing some concern. "Anything wrong?"

She glanced quickly from side to side and then spoke in a whisper. "I'm worried about Nicolas. The news today?"

Bobby grinned. "Oh that. Ignore it," he said. "Nicolas can look after himself." He touched her elbow. "Listen, Nicolas isn't even a paid member of the party; just a hothead who sees great things in his Communist ideology, so don't worry."

At that moment the Staff Officer clicked his heels and turned, almost tripping over Bobby and Charlotte. He looked at the two of them with a knowing smile on his face. "Excuse me," he said to Bobby and walked away.

Eugene Bayard told Bobby to order while he popped through to Armand's office. He acknowledged Charlotte as Bobby sat down at the table.

"Charlotte, make it look as though I can't make up my mind. Scribble something on your notepad."

Charlotte smiled sweetly and began scribbling. "I have to see Nicolas," she told him. "But I can't until after work. Is he at home?"

"He was there last night. Margot was with him and another guy who I've never seen before." He suddenly became very serious. "Charlotte, please be careful who you speak to and who you spend time with. You could get swept up in something that is nothing to do with you. It could be dangerous."

Charlotte smirked. "How about having a German Officer living with me and my aunt?" she said. "Do you think I'll be in any danger there?"

He looked shocked. "You have a …"

She grinned and nodded her head. "Yes. He arrived yesterday and will take up residence on Monday. My aunt is furious."

"And you?"

She shrugged. "I'm just a simple waitress who has no impact at all in this phoney war, so long as I keep myself to myself. And I'm likely to get sacked if I spend any more time chatting with you."

He laughed. "Don't worry; my dad has some influence here. You'll be okay."

"So, what would you like?"

"Two coffees and two patisseries. And a kiss when you are not too busy."

Charlotte felt her colour coming up. "I'll put that on the order. Maybe the chef will come out and give you one." Then she turned away with a grin on her face she was desperately trying to hide. But at least she felt a little happier.

But as she walked past a table on which four German officers were sitting, Charlotte heard one of them say: "We've set up the first listening station."

A table close by had been vacated, so she stopped and started clearing away the debris, while watching the four officers. There was no real need for Charlotte to use her lip-reading skills because they were quite animated in their discussion about this latest development. Charlotte couldn't believe how ingenuous they were; talking quite openly while she was working that close to them.

She came away from the tables and into the kitchen with a mixture of alarm and disgust — alarm because of the threat the listening station would pose to agents like Agata, and disgust that by implication, Charlotte's presence at the nearby table meant nothing to the four officers. When she went back into the dining room, the officers were no longer there, and their table was being cleared by Camille.

From what Charlotte had picked up by listening and lip-reading, the new listening station would be eavesdropping on transmissions and had the capacity to pinpoint the approximate location of the wireless from which the signals were being transmitted. She knew that she needed to get this information to Agata as soon as possible because Agata transmitted regularly to London from the smallholding. It was always done under the cover of darkness, although never at regular intervals, and only in brief spells, but the risk of detection was now more serious, which meant the two of them: Matilde and herself, would be arrested if Agata was caught.

The worry of what she imagined would be the consequences of discovery kept playing on Charlotte's mind throughout the remainder of her shift, and she was finding it difficult to concentrate. Added to that was her concern over Nicolas and the need to see him. But now this latest development had changed her priorities, and she decided to forget Nicolas and get home to her aunt as quickly as possible.

When her shift had finished, Charlotte hurried away from the hotel, unlocked her bicycle and began peddling furiously towards Montrouge, but she hadn't gone too far down the road when she saw Jacques Garnier. He had stopped his carriage facing the way she would come, which meant Charlotte could not possibly avoid him. And because of his revelation that he was to be her contact with Jefson in London, she knew then she had to stop and tell him what she'd heard.

She pulled up a little breathlessly and straddled her bicycle. "Hello, Jacques. What are you doing here?"

He jumped down from the seat, came up beside her and leaned up against the carriage in that nonchalant stance he seemed to embrace so naturally. "I knew you would come this way, and I needed to speak to you."

"About 'toodle-pip'. Yes, I know. You're my contact, aren't you?"

He smiled, changing his lined, aged complexion into a pleasant face with warm, sparkling blue eyes: eyes that missed nothing.

"Are you surprised?"

She gave him a puzzled look. "I was," she said, "until I think back to our chance meeting the day I arrived in Paris. You knew I'd be there. And getting a job with Armand at the Metropole: that was already set up, wasn't it?"

"And seeing Agata at your Aunt Matilde's house," he added, raising his eyebrows.

Charlotte sagged visibly. "Well, that means I am a member of a fledgling resistance group, I suppose. Which means I need to tell you something, and you have to warn Agata."

She then told him of what she'd learned about the German's listening post.

"It had to happen, Charlotte. It was inevitable. But you will have to tell Matilde; I cannot just turn up at her door unexpectedly."

"There won't be any door to turn up to if Agata gets

caught," she retorted angrily. "And me and Matilde will be arrested, you do understand that don't you?"

"That's why it's called war, Charlotte. We are all involved whether we want to be or not."

She shook her head. "You know, Jacques, what made me furious was not so much the risk we now face, but those bloody Germans couldn't have cared less that I was standing just a few feet away and could practically hear everything they said." She screwed her face up. "Are they really that stupid? To think I was invisible and couldn't hear them?"

Jacques chuckled. "Don't take it as a personal insult, Charlotte. That's how they regard women, particularly French women."

"I have to tell you something else too," she said. "We now have a German Officer billeted with us. He takes up residence on Monday."

He sighed heavily. "That's bad news. It will stop Agata, I think. But good news for you if it forces her to move somewhere else."

"Somewhere else? Where?"

He shrugged. "That, I'm afraid is Agata's problem. She's been trained for it."

Charlotte glanced up at the sky. The daylight was fading and with it the temperature. Although she had a coat on, she was beginning to feel the chill seeping into her bones.

"I need to go now, Jacques; I'm getting cold and I'm anxious about Matilde."

Jacques pushed himself away from the carriage and climbed up on to the seat.

"How am I supposed to contact you, Jacques, if I have something important to pass on?" she asked.

He gave it some thought. "We'll need a drop-off point — somewhere not too obvious. I'll think of something and get back to you."

"Well, don't leave it too long, Jacques. We may not have much time left."

He touched the brim of his ragged cap. "Au revoir." He flicked the reins and urged the horse forward. "Charles will see us through this," he called back as the carriage moved away.

"Which one, Jacques?" she called. "There are only two."

He laughed and shouted back. "The one with any sense."

Charlotte grinned, but the expression hid the concern she was feeling. At the start of her shift and after her moment with Bobby Bayard, she felt good. Now she felt as though intractable things were closing in around her, threatening to derail and devastate her reasonably comfortable existence.

Chapter 23

It was mid-afternoon on the Monday when Hauptmann Hans Gruber turned up at the smallholding. True to his word he had brought with him more than just an armful of provisions, but also Matilde's ration books. There were several books for different foods: bread, meat, cheese, fats (lard, oil, etc.), sugar, milk, chocolate, and milled products. When he handed the books to Matilde, he clicked his heels and bowed his head forward in the usual polite manner that Matilde found so annoying. She wanted to throw the books back in his face, but she was a realist too, knowing that without them, she would soon find life very difficult.

"Thank you, Hauptmann," she said trying to keep the grudging resonance out her voice.

"Please call me Hans," he said to her.

Matilde's eyes hooded over, and she shook her head. "I'm sorry; I can't."

He smiled. "I understand, but in time I hope you will."

Suddenly she heard the sound of several engines breaking the relative peace and quiet of the village. She looked at Gruber in shock and then brushed past him to run outside. She saw what she thought was a tank roaring by belching black exhaust fumes into the air. It was followed by several scout cars. Each one with four soldiers carrying rifles.

Gruber came up beside her. She looked up at him in shock.

"What's going on?" she asked.

He breathed heavily. "The Wehrmacht wish to show their presence in the suburbs and outlying villages," he told her. "So, they come bearing goodwill and gifts."

"That's some show of goodwill." She said angrily. "All they are doing is frightening the lives out of everybody."

"It is not a show of strength," he said. "I can assure you."

"Well it looks like it to me," she said testily, and left him standing there as she hurried back inside.

Gruber watched the small convoy of vehicles go by and then went back inside where he found Matilde unpacking the boxes of provisions he'd brought with him. He went to help but she stopped him.

"No need for that," she said sarcastically. "It wouldn't do for a German Officer to be seen doing a woman's work."

He touched her elbow and stopped her. "Matilde, wearing this uniform does not make me a monster. I am no less a man because of it, and all I want to do is help."

Matilde closed her eyes and leaned forward against the table, her arms outstretched for support. Her emotions were all over the place now. She felt humiliated because of her attitude towards him, and the fact that she was receiving kindness from someone who, despite his words, wore a uniform that represented the worst kind of enemy she could imagine.

She took a deep breath and turned to face him. "I'm sorry. Okay, you can help me put these things away and then I'll make us a coffee."

His face lit up. "Thank you, Matilde; that would be lovely."

***

Charlotte was on her way home, her mind filtering the events over the past few hours at work. She still hadn't seen Nicolas, and that concerned her. She just hoped he hadn't been arrested because of some ill-thought act against the Germans because of the Communist Party ban. There had been precious little she could learn from her shift at the Metropole, despite desperately trying to eavesdrop on the diners at the hotel.

But those thoughts were soon displaced by the curious sight of German military vehicles along her route home. It was obvious there was no intimidation going on and no soldiers swooping on unsuspecting homes. Instead she could see youngsters laughing and joking around with several of the Germans soldiers. She could see some of the young girls behaving in much the same way as they would with young French boys. She also wondered what it was the soldiers were handing out but guessed it must have been sweets or something simple. It was a puzzle for her, but a pleasant one. She wondered what her Aunt Matilde would think about it when she told her.

With these thoughts buzzing through her mind, she arrived at the smallholding where she saw a Kübelwagen parked close to the gate. She dismounted and wheeled her bike through and into the small shed, then hurried back to the house. For some reason she didn't knock as she usually did, probably because her mind was on the German Jeep, but opened the front door, pulled her headscarf off and hurried through to the kitchen.

Matilde and Gruber were sitting at the table, a cup of coffee each. They were laughing over something Gruber had said when they heard Charlotte walk into the room. They turned round.

Charlotte froze on the spot when she saw her aunt's face light up as she laughed. Gruber stood up immediately. His uniform jacket was unbuttoned. He clicked his heels together and bowed his head.

"Mademoiselle Charlotte."

Charlotte took a step forward, her face a puzzle.

Matilde could see the dilemma in her expression. "Charlotte," she cried. "Home already?" She looked up at Gruber. "Hauptmann Gruber and I —" She stopped when she saw Gruber look quickly at her. "Sorry — Hans and I were just enjoying a coffee. Would you like one?"

Charlotte didn't answer immediately but continued to stare at the two of them as she stepped closer in slow, careful steps. When she reached her aunt, she leaned forward and kissed her on both cheeks. She didn't take her eyes off Gruber; such was her stunned surprise at seeing him there.

"Did you want a coffee?" her aunt asked again.

.Charlotte dragged her eyes away from Gruber. "Oh, yes please, Matilde."

Gruber started buttoning his jacket. "I will leave you two alone. I have paperwork I need to catch up on." He picked up his cap. "I'll do that in my room." Probably by force of habit, he clicked his heels together and left them there.

Charlotte waited until the door closed behind him before turning to her aunt and sitting down. Matilde made a coffee and put in front of her.

"You're probably wondering what happened?" Matilde said to her. Charlotte simply nodded her head. Matilde carried on and told her of how the events had unfolded once Gruber arrived home. She got up from the table and went over to the cupboard that was up against the kitchen wall. She pulled the doors open.

Charlotte's gasped when she saw the shelves literally bulging with provisions. "What on earth…"

Matilde closed the doors and came back to the table. "He also gave me my ration cards." She shook her head mournfully. "I was furious with him. I wanted to throw it all back in his face. He asked me to call him Hans, but I wouldn't. It made me almost sick to my stomach that I was being offered so much by a Nazi. It made me feel violated." She took a breath. "But you know what he said to me? Wearing this uniform did not make him a monster. He said he was no less a man because of it, and all he wanted to do was help."

"So you called him Hans. For that?"

Matilde put her hand on Charlotte's. "He's only a boy. Well, a young man. I don't even think he belongs in that uniform." She shrugged. "But I didn't want to offend him for what he saw as generosity and kindness towards us. And he will be living with us for some time. I needed to remember that."

Charlotte lifted the cup to her lips and drank some of the coffee. She put the cup down. "Well, I hope you don't expect me to fall into his lap like a puppy —" She stopped when she saw the hurt on her aunt's face. "I'm sorry, Matilde," she said. "I didn't mean that. It was unforgiveable of me."

Matilde shook her head. "Give it time, Charlotte. I'm sure you will find a middle ground where you can meet him on your terms. And you are both about the same age; something might work for you that makes it just a little easier, don't you think?"

"I will do my best, Matilde. I promise."

***

Charlotte's opportunity to keep her promise came that evening after the rather sumptuous meal Matilde was able to serve because of Gruber's generosity. And even as the two women ate, they both wondered how their neighbours might react if they knew just what Gruber was doing for them.

Gruber said he would like to help with the dishes, but Matilde was having none of that. She literally ordered him and Charlotte to the front room where they could at least have a cognac and talk. Charlotte realised it was her duty to cultivate some kind of relationship with him because of her position as an SOE agent, albeit a relatively inactive one.

"Why did you join the Wehrmacht?" Charlotte asked when they were settled with their drinks.

He pursed his lips and thought for a while. "There's no easy answer to that, Charlotte. I didn't want to, but I had my family's honour to consider."

Charlotte looked puzzled. "Honour?"

"I have two brothers: Jurgen and Karl. Jurgen is the

oldest, I am in the middle and Karl is the youngest."

"No sisters?"

He smiled fondly. "Giselle. She is sixteen. Teases me mercilessly but I love her to bits."

"That's an English expression," Charlotte pointed out.

He nodded. "Probably something I learned from my colloquial English lessons at college." He puffed a breath out. "But, back to my brothers: Jurgen wanted to join the Wehrmacht immediately, but he wasn't allowed to do so."

"Why not?"

"My father's Company is a manufacturing outlet. We put liquid in bottles — perfume. But we have been ordered to turn our production over to glucose, so instead of putting perfume in bottles, we now put in liquid glucose. Bigger bottles of course," he added with a chuckle. "Jurgen practically runs the business, which was why he was not allowed to join the Army. My kid brother, Karl, was champing at the bit to join, but he failed on medical grounds. Which left me."

"You?"

He looked at Charlotte, a wry smile on his face. "Yes, me. I didn't want to join but as a member of an important family in Bavaria, I had to uphold the family honour and represent our name as a member of our glorious Wehrmacht." Charlotte thought she detected a note of cynicism in the way he said that. He looked at her, his face set in a grim expression. "But I'm not a Nazi." He lifted his cognac glass and downed the drink, putting the glass down rather firmly.

Charlotte could see what Matilde saw. He was merely a boy in a man's world. She suddenly felt this overwhelming compassion for him, and it unsettled her. There was no way she wanted or needed to feel sorry for the enemy, despite most of them being ordinary people as were those they were oppressing. It was a sobering moment for her. She finished her cognac and got up from the chair. Gruber stood up immediately.

"I'm going to bed, Hauptmann. I think we both have an early start in the morning. Thank you for the conversation. Goodnight."

As she turned, he spoke her name. "Charlotte. If there is one thing I want to achieve in this war before it kills me, it is that you will call me Hans." He bowed. "Goodnight."

Chapter 24

Gruber was up early the following morning. He had a spring in his step because of the improvement in the relationship with Matilde and Charlotte. He really liked Charlotte. In other circumstances he would have made it his main objective in life to develop something more than just knowing her. It was a forlorn hope though, as he well understood, so it was consigned to the back of his mind where he hoped it would wither and die.

He told Matilde he would skip breakfast and just make do with a coffee. Within thirty minutes of waking, he was outside the smallholding dismissing the sentry who had been stationed there. It was a development that was necessary; a security post had been set up in the local Prefecture building where the soldiers would be based. It allowed for sentries to be relieved during the course of their night shift, something which was essential to maintain their vigilance and provide security for Gruber who was to be their Commanding Officer for the area around Montrouge.

Gruber's own thoughts on the development were not important. He knew his SD boss, Major Heller, had received orders to establish security points at each *Arrondisement* in Paris, and it was for this reason that Gruber found himself in a position he never really wanted.

He climbed into the Jeep and started the engine, then glanced back at the smallholding as he pulled away and headed back to Paris. He knew he probably wouldn't have to do this journey too often once he'd established his office in the Prefecture.

As he motored into the city, he could see it was coming to life. No doubt, he thought, in much the same way as it would have done before the Occupation. It pleased him because it fitted in with how he really wanted his war to go: safe, comfortable and without too many difficulties.

He parked the Jeep and climbed the stairs to his office after showing his ID to a guard on the main entrance. He opened the door marked *Sicherheitsdienst* and pushed it open. Sergeant Witborg, the desk sergeant, leapt to his feet and threw up a stiff arm.

"Morning, Herr Hauptmann."

Gruber lifted his arm, a little loosely compared to the sergeant. "Good morning, Wilhelm." It was another ill-disciplined act of Gruber's that he should refer to his sergeant by his Christian name, but it was his way of trying to observe some normality in a totally screwed up world. "Anything for me?"

Witborg had some folders on the desk. He rifled through these until he came to one that was sealed. It had Charlotte's name on the cover. He handed it to Gruber together with another folder. Gruber flicked open this folder and scribbled his name in the column as the person accepting responsibility and handed it back to Witborg. He then broke the seal on Charlotte's folder and flipped it open. And as the words unfolded in his mind and the implication of what he was reading began to sink in, he closed the folder.

"When did this come in?" he asked.

"Last night, sir."

"So, why didn't you pass it on to Major Heller?"

Witborg lifted his shoulders in a small shrug. "The Major said to pass it on to you seeing as you are billeted with the girl and her aunt. And it is within your remit, Herr Hauptmann. I don't think he felt there was anything of great importance in it."

Gruber accepted the sergeant's appraisal and tucked the file under his arm. "And nothing else for me?"

Witborg pointed to a wall on which was an open cabinet with large pigeon hole in which various files had been placed for the attention of others within the SD building.

"Nothing in your slot, sir, except general orders for your deployment at Montrouge."

Gruber thanked him and went over to the cabinet and withdrew his folder. "Is Major Heller in?" he asked.

Witborg shook his head. "He won't be in until later this morning. Something to do with an appointment with one of the senior staff officers."

Gruber thanked him. "I'll sit at his desk and read these.Then I'll probably head back to Montrouge."

Witborg dipped his head as Gruber disappeared into Major Heller's office. And he wondered what it was Gruber had seen in that folder because he'd never seen the kind of reaction Gruber had to its contents. None of his business though, he thought, and got on with the work already piling up on his desk.

***

Charlotte arrived at the hotel about an hour after Gruber had sat reading her file. Naturally, she was unaware of that; had she been, she would have fled Paris and make an attempt to get back to England. But in blissful ignorance, she locked her bicycle and went through to the changing rooms where she found Camille smoking a cigarette before her shift started. Charlotte could tell by the way Camille was smoking that she was agitated.

"Are you okay, Camille?" she asked as she unlocked her slim cupboard.

"It's my brother," she answered, breathing out a stream of smoke. "He's a Freemason."

Charlotte glanced at her as she pulled an apron over her head. "I thought they were banned."

Camille nodded. "Yes, but it doesn't stop you being one. He's been raging against that anti-Masonic exhibition the Nazis have opened in the Petit Palais. He wants to demonstrate against it."

Charlotte had heard of the measures taken by the Germans to eradicate Freemasonry, which the Vichy government had banned, by stealing many works of art and treasures from the Masons and demonising them by an exhibition of the stolen treasures.

"They came to his house yesterday. Four of them: all wearing the uniforms of the SS." She spat the words out. "They threatened to arrest him and send him to prison."

Charlotte was truly shocked. "What on earth for? It's not as if the Masons are trying to overthrow the government."

"What government?" Camille asked.

"Why didn't they arrest him?" Charlotte asked, ignoring Camille's cynical question.

"He proved to them that he wasn't an important member of the Masonic lodge he attends. Or used to attend," she added. "And he had Jeanne and the baby at home, so maybe they felt sorry for him."

Charlotte laughed. "The Nazis feeling sorry for someone? Never. Sounds like he was lucky though."

Camille drew heavily on the cigarette and crushed it into the ashtray. "But for how long? They've started making the Jews wear that bloody yellow star on their clothes now. Where is it going to end?"

She stood up and brushed some ash off her apron. "Will you help me burn the Petit Palais down, Charlotte? We could do it secretly one night."

Charlotte laughed. "Arson — that would be fun."

Camille hooked her arm into Charlotte's. "Come on, let's go and pretend we really like the robbing bastards."

The day rolled on in much the same way as ever. The restaurant was busy of course, and Charlotte was listening and lip-reading as best she could but with little success. Her mind was on Nicolas Escoffier and her need to speak to him, particularly after Camille's revelation about her brother, and this tended to deflect from the real job she was supposed to be doing — spying for the British.

But even that was becoming something of a malaise for her. There was no meat on the bones and precious little she could learn that might have an impact on the war. And the less she learned, and the longer it went on, Charlotte realised she was sinking into a normalised way of life, if that was possible in Paris now, and felt less energised about the job. Added to that was the fact that she had to go to the Mairie for her ration cards: another boring but essential diversion for her to negotiate.

Finally her shift ended and within minutes she was peddling furiously over to Nicolas's apartment in the Latin Quarter. The late October sun was fast disappearing behind the Paris skyline letting the chill of the autumn air drift into the streets, which seemed to dull their usual vibrance. But she knew that would change come evening.

As she peddled on her way, she saw more and more of the young women that had been imported into Paris by the Germans. They wore grey uniforms with forage type hats and had been dubbed 'Grey mice' by the Parisiennes. They were employed in all manner of jobs to compensate for the absence of the people who had fled and failed to return. But they were managing to bring some sense of normality to life on the streets in the way in which they conducted themselves and how they would often be seen arm in arm with young German soldiers.

She reached Nicolas's apartment building and pressed the assigned button. She waited, fingers tapping on the handlebars, hoping against hope that he would be in. Suddenly a voice came over the speaker.

"Oui?"

Charlotte didn't realise she'd been holding her breath, but as soon as she heard him, she breathed out sharply.

"Nicolas, it's Charlotte."

The door lock buzzed, and Charlotte pushed the door open, then wheeled her bicycle into the small hallway where she left it locked and propped up against the wall. Nicolas was waiting for her at the open door of his apartment.

Charlotte was puffing a little after her hurried climb up the stairs. "I'm so glad you're in, Nicolas," she said as he kissed her on both cheeks.

"Why? Is something wrong?"

He stood back and let her through into the small corridor, closing the door behind them.

Charlotte turned briefly. "No, not really. I was concerned about you since they announced the ban of the Communist Party."

He chuckled. "But I'm not a paid member, Charlotte, which I could claim calls into question any allegiance I have to them."

"Yes," she said. "I know; Bobby told me."

"So, let me get you a coffee and you can tell me why you're worried."

Charlotte sat down at the small dining table while she waited for her coffee, mulling over the reason for her concern. But the truth was, she had more than just a liking for Nicolas. Although he was a friend, they had become closer over the last few weeks, and she harboured warm, sentimental thoughts about him. She believed it was his reckless nature that stirred the emotion within her. He was like a wild child, and it somehow appealed to her. But his recklessness was dangerous in the current existence under the Nazi Occupation, and that was her main worry.

He brought the coffee over and sat down at the table. "Now, Charlotte, why not tell me why you are so concerned about me."

She sipped her coffee, looking over the top of the cup at him. She put the cup down. "I don't want you to do something stupid and get hurt. Or get arrested."

"And how would I do that?"

"By going to secret meetings. Somone told me there are a lot of German spies in Paris."

He nodded. "It would be naïve not to believe that, Charlotte. But I believe we all have a duty to make life as difficult as we can for them, spies or no spies."

"Are you in the Resistance?" she asked him.

He raised his eyebrows. "If I was, I certainly wouldn't tell you," he said. "Unless you was an active member of the group yourself."

Charlotte realised then it was all about trust. As much as she trusted those people she had come to know and regard as friends, she could never be sure if any of them had been coerced into working for the Nazis.

"Will you promise me you will be careful? Otherwise I will worry about you."

His eyes lit up; for him it was a declaration of more than just friendship. He took hold of her hands across the table. "I will do my best, Charlotte, but I cannot promise."

Charlotte knew that was all she was going to get from him, and she could understand it. She stood up and came round to him. He looked a little uncertain, then knew why. He stood up too and put his arms around her. She smiled and kissed him. It was more than just a friendly kiss; there was passion in it. She pulled away.

"I'm going now, Nicolas," she said, her voice faltering. "Before I change my mind."

He knew what she meant; the way she kissed him told him more than a verbal declaration of love. He let her go.

"Goodbye, Charlotte. Please don't leave it too long before you come and see me. I promise you I will do my best to be careful because you have now given me a reason."

Charlotte managed to get out of the apartment before changing her mind, hoping against hope that the two of them could see this damn war out and survive together.

***

It was mid-day when Gruber received a call from Sergeant Witborg at SD Headquarters. Gruber had been using his time to organise and make sense of the new arrangements at the Montrouge Préfecture when the call came ordering him back to HQ where he would be accompanying Major Heller to a meeting with SS Hauptsturmführer Theo Dietrich. He was annoyed at being called away simply to attend a meeting. Whenever he'd been to anything like that, he'd struggled to hide his indifference to what was generally little more than an elevated council meeting.

He arrived at HQ where Major Heller was waiting for him. Naturally he asked the Major what the meeting was about and why it was necessary for his involvement. Heller looked at his watch and asked Gruber to sit down.

"Hauptsturmführer Dietrich has arrived in Paris to

oversee the Jewish question. He reports back to Adolf Eichmann in Berlin and consequently to Heydrich and Himmler."

Gruber had heard of Dietrich. He was SS and only twenty-seven years of age, and to have such an important role at such a young age meant he carried a fair bit of influence back in the corridors of power in Berlin.

"Berlin has authorised further movement on the Jewish question, and because we are responsible for Security, it falls on us to be involved at the planning stage. I tried to find a good reason to leave us out, but Dietrich calls the shots here, so we must go."

The two men then left for Avenue Foch where Dietrich had appropriated offices for himself. He had also set up another office in Rue de Sussaies. When they arrived, Gruber was surprised to see just four men seated at a large conference table beneath high windows that allowed the dull sunlight to brighten the room.

Both he and the Major gave snappy Heil Hitler salutes, and then Major Heller introduced himself and Gruber to Dietrich. After that brief formality it was handshakes all round and getting down to business.

"Gentlemen," Dietrich began. "I now have complete authority to deal with the Jewish question, some of which has already been implicated, as I'm sure you will all know. However, we cannot manage the entire question without the help of the French. To that end I have sequestered the help of Commissaire de Police, Monsieur Francois. He has at his disposal a staff of sixty, but also the entire police force and *gendarmerie* as well. He has started the census on the Jews domiciled in Paris and the Occupied Zone. The Vichy government have already begun sequestering Jewish businesses." He pointed around the table. "You will see that each of you has a folder there. You will find everything you need — heads of departments, both in Paris and the French zone, and what their responsibilities are. I have been given various figures for the number of Jews in France, from 200,000 to 800,000, but I'm sure with the help and dedication of everyone on that list we will eradicate the entire Jewish population from France."

The meeting rolled on for a couple of hours. Gruber was bored stiff with it all. It was mostly about Dietrich revealing how obsessed he was with the task and practically grandstanding on his ability to wipe out so many undeserving people.

Gruber asked if was true that the majority of Jews left in France were mainly working class, and to remove them would be to create a vacuum that could have a detrimental effect on the entire workforce and French economy. Dietrich was having none of it, so blinkered was he about his role.

And it was practically the last statement he made before the meeting closed that he would wipe out every single Jew and anyone who had a Jewish ancestry that gave Gruber the most concern. Not the statement itself, but the knowledge of Charlotte's heritage in the folder that Sergeant Witborg had handed to him.

Chapter 25

It was quite dark when Charlotte arrived home. As she wheeled her bicycle over to the small shed where she always kept it, she was surprised to see Matilde walking towards her from the direction of the barn. Normally her aunt would be in the house at this time of night. In the summer it would have been different.

Charlotte frowned at her in the poor light. "Not working, are you, Matilde?"

"The chickens sounded restless," Matilde told her. She lifted her head a little and looked somewhere beyond the fence. "I wondered if any of those soldiers had been nosing about."

"Have you seen many of them?"

Matilde nodded briefly. "They've been flying around most of the day. Goodness knows what they're up to."

"Is Hans here?"

"Gruber?" She shook her head. "Haven't seen him since he left this morning."

They reached the small shed. Charlotte unlocked and it and stowed her bicycle. Once it was in and the shed door was locked, the two women hurried into the house. Matilde turned the flowerpot round and stepped through the front door.

"He'll be in soon, I shouldn't wonder. We have to be careful for Agata's sake."

As she closed and locked the door, Charlotte caught her arm, thinking about why her aunt was coming back from the chicken coop when she got home.

"Agata? We can't have her here anymore, Matilde. Not with Hans around."

"I know. She will have to go somewhere else."

Charlotte took her coat off and hung it on one of the coat hooks, then followed her aunt into the kitchen.

"Did you get to the Mairie for your ration cards?" Matilde asked as she was filling a jug with water.

Charlotte sat down, shaking her head. "No. I tried but it was late, and the queue was far too long."

Matilde put the jug on the stove. "Why was you late? Armand keep you there?"

"No. I went to see Nicolas. I wanted to make sure he understood how dangerous it would be to attend any Communist Party meetings."

"Did you think he wasn't aware of that, Charlotte? Or is it simply because you think a lot of the boy and worry like any woman would."

Charlotte felt the heat rising in her neck. She put her hand there and rubbed it gently. "I'm fond of him, Matilde, I must admit. But he can be reckless at times."

Matilde put some coffee beans into a hand grinder and rotated the handle. "That's something we may all have to do," she said, rotating the handle furiously. "Bloody Germans."

Charlotte could see the tension in her aunt as she worked it out on the coffee grinder. "Has something happened today, Matilde?" she asked. "You seem tense."

Matilde stopped grinding and turned round. "You asked if I'd seen many Germans today." She brushed her hand across her forehead. "I popped into the village earlier to see Brigitte Goldsmith. She's been told she must put a Star of David on her shop window."

Charlotte looked horrified. "Why?"

"Because she and Benjamin are Jews for goodness sake." She flapped her hand in the air. "All Jewish businesses have to do it now."

She turned back to the coffee grinder and put a spoonful of the ground coffee into the cups. Then she took the jug off the stove and poured the boiling water over the coffee beans.

Charlotte watched as her aunt went through the process in silence, but she could see her shoulders shaking as she cried. Charlotte got up and went over to her. She put her arms around her and kept them there until her aunt sniffed loudly and pushed her gently away.

"Sorry about that," she said, and took the cups over to the table. She sat down, and poured a little cream into her cup. "Brigitte and Benjamin have owned that shop for almost forty years. Why must they be treated like that?"

Suddenly there was a loud knocking at the front door. It startled both women. Matilde looked at Charlotte and got up.

"That will be Gruber," she said.

Charlotte noticed she had used his surname. "Well, perhaps he will be able to tell you why the Goldsmiths are being singled out like that."

Matilde grunted. "Hmmph! Fat chance," she said as she swept past Charlotte and out of the kitchen.

Charlotte listened to the sound her aunt's footsteps and then Gruber's voice as he stepped into the hallway. He followed Matilde into the kitchen and said good evening to Charlotte. He bowed his head a little and clicked his heels together but without the harsh sound of leather on leather.

"Good evening, Charlotte." He removed his cap and spoke to Matilde. "I will go to my room, freshen up and join you for dinner."

Matilde brushed past him. "Dinner will be at seven o'clock."

He smiled. Charlotte thought he had a lovely smile. "Perhaps you wouldn't mind if I join you before that? Just for a chat."

Matilde nodded. "Please yourself."

He glanced at Charlotte. "I'll see you in a little while."

Charlotte waited until he had gone. She stared at her aunt for a while. "Matilde, I know it's difficult for you, but it isn't his fault that the Goldsmiths have to put a Star of David on their window. I deal with lots of them at the hotel and believe me, they are not all bad. I hate having to be nice to them, but some of them can be really pleasant. So, why don't you give Hans a chance and try not to blame him?"

Matilde glared at her and then visibly softened. "For the sake of harmony, Charlotte, but only that."

Charlotte went to her aunt and gave her a hug. "I'm off to my room. I'll see you later."

Matilde grabbed her hand. "Make sure you don't leave me on my own with him. It will help if you are there."

Charlotte smiled. "I will." And then she was gone.

***

Their evening meal was a little tense. Charlotte could sense her aunt's hostility towards Gruber. Any responses she made to his questions were short and, in most cases, non-committal. When the meal was finished, Matilde made the excuse that she had a headache and would retire early. Charlotte knew her aunt expected her to remain with Gruber, for a while at least.

When Matilde had gone, Charlotte got up from the table and started picking up the dirty dishes. Gruber immediately started helping her.

"There's no need for that, Hans. I can manage."

"But I want to help," he told her. "It helps instil a little normality into my life."

Charlotte chuckled. "If that's all it takes," she said as she piled the dishes into the sink, "perhaps a little domesticity will help bring this wretched war to an end." She filled a jug with cold water and took it across to the stove which was throwing a fair of amount of heat into the room. She put the jug on top of it and went back to the table.

"You long for normality, do you, Hans?"

"No-one, particularly the French, could deny it," he said. "One year ago I was working for my father. I had a girlfriend who I would see every day. We would go dancing, watch football together and enjoy our kind of normality. And what about you, Charlotte? What was you doing a year ago? What was your normality."

She lifted her head a little as she recalled her days at Oxford. "I was at university and loving every minute of it."

Gruber knew Charlotte's history because of the file he had on her. "And now the world has gone mad," he said with a sigh. "I would like to have met you when you was at Oxford."

"Have you ever been?"

He shook his head. "No. I've never been to England. I was told it was too drab."

Charlotte laughed. "The English can be very correct in their manner. Unlike us French who love the *Joie de vivre*. But drab?" She shook her head. "Never; it's a lovely country and the people are lovely too. Unlike…" She looked at him with a speculative expression on her face.

"The Germans?"

She laughed. "Sorry, Hans. I'm sure you are very much like all of us."

"Except for the Lederhosen and Steins of beer," he said with a chuckle.

Charlotte got up from the table and retrieved the jug of hot water from the stove. She poured it over the dishes in the sink and began washing them after putting rubber gloves on. When she'd finished, she wiped her hands and sniffed at them.

"They never smell clean," she said, fluttering her hands in the air. "Back at Oxford I never had to do any washing up, so I always managed to keep my hands smelling pleasant."

"With what?" he asked.

"Cream. And a little dab of perfume on the neck. It did wonders for my self-esteem."

"And now?"

She looked at him scornfully. "Oh come on, Hans. You Germans have emptied our shops and taken everything home. Or are trying to at least. And for us to do any shopping now is virtually impossible because of the rationing."

He stood up. "In that case, I have something for you," he said. "Wait there."

She watched him leave the room. She had a frown on her face, wondering what he was up to. When he came back, he had something in his hand. He offered it to her.

"I want you to have this." It was a small bottle of perfume.

Charlotte took it from him, pulled the small stopper from the bottle and held it to her nose. She'd never smelt anything like it before; it was gorgeous. She put her finger tip on the opening, turned the bottle and allowed a couple of drops out. Then she touched the side of her neck. She put the stopper back and handed the perfume to him.

"Thank you, Hans. That's lovely."

He shook his head and thrust the bottle back in her hand. "No, no. I want you to have it. Someone as beautiful as you deserves something that's a little different."

Charlotte felt her colour coming up. "Hans, I can't possibly accept this from you. I …" She started stuttering, unable to get the words out.

"Couldn't possibly accept something like a gift of perfume from a German?" he said.

She was stymied; he said exactly what she had been thinking. "What on earth will my friends say — what would Matilde say?"

He smiled. "You can lie. Tell your friends you bought the perfume when you was at Oxford. You can buy it in England, by the way. You don't have to tell them the truth."

Charlotte, like most young women, thought the idea of wearing perfume was the most natural thing in the world. And even the German propaganda machine had started telling the French women that they should never give up on the French woman's ability to remain poised, elegant and very feminine. And she knew she could lie; it was something she'd been doing quite successfully since she had returned to France. She closed her hand around the bottle.

"You won't say anything to Matilde, will you, Hans?"

He shook his head. "It will be our secret." He took hold of her hand. "And Charlotte, I promise you I will not be seeking any favours in exchange for the gift. You have my word on that." He released her hand. "I'm going to bed. Goodnight."

And in that brief moment, she wanted to reach up and kiss him, but resisted the thought and bid him goodnight, her voice barely audible above the thumping heart beneath her breast.

***

Matilde opened her eyes and rolled over on to her back.

It was quite dark in her bedroom, although a hint of moonlight peeked through the edges of the curtains. Moonlight was the last thing she wanted, but there was nothing she could do about it. She pulled the covers aside and swung her legs out of bed, sliding her feet into a pair of slippers. She stood up and reached for the dressing gown which was looped over the bed rail. She put it on and wrapped it tightly round her making sure the cord was secure.

She walked carefully over to the bedroom door and opened it, then glanced into the passage as a precaution. She stood there listening for any sounds that might be coming from Gruber's room, but there was nothing but silence. She then went through to the kitchen and over to the stove where she'd left the cooking pot in which she'd cooked their evening meal. There was still some warmth coming from the old ironwork, which pleased her.

Although it was the middle of the night, a faint light from the open curtains by the sink picked out the room with faint shadows. Matilde went to a cupboard and removed a small pot. It had a screw-on lid. She took this over to the stove and spooned a generous amount of the stew into the pot. Then she attached the lid tightly and went to the food cupboard for bread, which she stuffed into her dressing gown pocket.

Once Matilde was satisfied she had everything, she made her way through a door at the rear of the kitchen that led into a scullery. There were no windows in there, which meant she had to feel her way in complete darkness until she came to the back door. She put the pot on the floor and unlocked the door, opening it very carefully until she could chance putting her head outside and listening for any sounds that might tell her someone was in the yard. She knew there was a sentry posted out the front of the smallholding, but she had to take the chance the soldier was not feeling inclined to wander about.

She picked up the pot and walked across the yard to the barn and unlocked the padlock, which she left hanging, then she went over to the chicken coop. It was there that she stood most chance of being discovered if she disturbed the chickens. But she pushed on and walked round to the rear of the coop and stopped beside a mesh door.

She called out softly. "Agata?"

She heard a rustling sound as Agata appeared behind the mesh. The small space she stood in was the rear entrance to the coop; it acted as a walk-in before gaining access to the coop itself. Matilde pulled the door open.

"Are you okay?" she asked.

"I've been better," Agata said. "Is Gruber here?"

"Yes. You need to leave us. I'm afraid the risk is too great."

Agata stepped through the opening. "Can we go to the barn?"

Matilde nodded. "The guard won't see us; he's probably asleep in Gruber's jeep."

The two women hurried across the yard and into the barn. Matilde handed Agata the pot and the bread.

Agata sat on a small crate and opened the pot. She

tore the bread into pieces and began eating the stew. "God, I'm hungry," she said. "This is lovely, Matilde. I'll come back after the war and live with you."

"Fine," Matilde said, "but I do need to know when you can leave." Agata didn't answer so she waited for her to finish the stew.

Agata put the pot to her mouth and drained it, then put the pot on the ground by the crate — the crate that they had brought back from the Lysander with the transmitter and hand guns in it.

"I have to make one more transmission, Matilde," she said. "But I have to meet someone before I can send anything. I'm sorry, but I don't have another aerial, so I can't take my transmitter with me. It means I'll have to use the barn again. But once I've done that, I'll find somewhere else, I promise."

"When do you plan to transmit?" She asked.

"It can be any time," Agata told her. "But I need to be back here before daylight."

Matilde nodded in the darkness. "Gruber will probably be away before eight o'clock this morning. Make sure you are back before that. Leave the padlock on the floor so I'll know you're back. Then I can come over and lock it."

"Thank you, Matilde. You'd better go now."

"If we can manage it, Agata, you can come into the house for fifteen minutes, get cleaned up. But only if it's safe."

She walked away and hurried back to the rear door of the scullery, into the kitchen and then back to her room. And as she sat on the bed waiting for her heart rate to drop, she cursed everything about the war, the Nazis and Gruber, and thought about poor Agata and what she was having to put up with, risking her life and probably her sanity in the cause of freedom.

She slipped her dressing gown off, threw it over the bottom of the bed and climbed under the covers. She laid on her back and started thinking about her husband, Pierre, and wondering how long it would be before they were all free again. Her eyes drooped and she fell asleep, dreaming of chicken coops, wire netting and someone unrecognisable as a woman drinking stew from an old, blackened pot.

Chapter 26

Gruber left before eight o'clock, and because the whole of France was on Berlin time, it meant that the darkness lasted long enough for Matilde to get Agata into her house so the poor girl could clean herself up. Once that was done, Matilde was able to get her into the barn unseen, and as she was locking the barn door, Agata wished her *au revoir*. It was a sad moment for Matilde because she realised that it was unlikely she would ever see her again once she'd transmitted and made her way somewhere into France to find another safe place where she could transmit her vital information back to London.

Agata at least felt a little more comfortable than she had done for the previous twenty-four hours. But now the discomfort was to begin again as she manoeuvred herself into the small space from where she would make her transmission. Much of the space was taken up by the transmitter, which was concealed in a suitcase almost two feet long. It weighed thirty pounds. Once opened up it was attached to an aerial seventy feet long. Agata had managed to put the aerial up several days earlier when the German presence in Montrouge was negligible. She knew of agents who had climbed trees to put an aerial up so they could transmit. Her transmissions had been short. She used the poem written on silk by Jefson's team as the code on which the information she transmitted was based. Once she was ready, she tried to make herself as comfortable as possible in the confined space. There was no preset time for transmissions; she knew London would be listening, as would the Germans. And it was while she was sending her coded message, she knew she would be at her most vulnerable and open to detection.

Hans Gruber arrived at SD headquarters a little after eight o'clock. He was in a reasonable frame of mind, particularly after his pleasant encounter with Charlotte the evening before, but he knew that was likely to change once he'd spent time in Major Heller's company. What irritated Gruber more was the fact that Heller insisted he came into the office every morning. It tended to make a mockery of the fact that he been billeted out at Montrouge to establish a secure detachment of soldiers to help maintain order and security there. He believed he could achieve more by being there than touching base with the Major, but he managed to spin it out and was relieved when Heller told him he could leave.

Once Gruber had gone, Heller left the SD Headquarters and made his way to the listening station that the Wehrmacht had installed at the top of the building. Despite his rank and seniority, none of the five operators acknowledged him when he entered the room. Their job was to listen for transmissions and not waste vital moments leaping to their feet and slinging up a stiff-arm salute every time an officer walked in.

Heller acknowledged Feldwebel Schloss, the senior sergeant there and began strolling up the line watching the operators turning the dials on their instruments, searching for anything that might reveal an illegal transmission from whatever source. He'd been there about ten minutes when suddenly, one of the radio operators lifted his arm.

"Hier."

Schloss immediately went over to the operator and stood behind him. Suddenly the operator removed his headset and spun in his chair. "Montrouge."

Heller's ears pricked up. "Montrouge? That's Gruber's area." He looked at Schloss. "Do they have a detector van at Montrouge?"

Schloss nodded. "Yes sir."

"Get on to them now." He pointed back at the radio set on which the signal had been picked up. "Can you pinpoint the transmission?"

Schloss shook his head. "We have to triangulate. Get an intersection from us and Montrouge." He had the field telephone to his ear as he spoke and shouted hurried instructions before he put the phone down. "They're on it, sir. We should make a pinpoint reference providing the transmission doesn't stop."

Agata had to give the transmitter a few minutes to come to life before she could transmit. While she was waiting she removed the piece of silk on which her poem had been embroidered. Silk was used instead of paper so it could be hidden in the lining of a coat, for example, and not be detected when searched by hand, whereas any paper concealed in a coat lining would make a rustling noise when touched.

She checked the message she had prepared, written on a one-time notepad, and reached down to the transmitter dial. Then she moved her hand to the morse key and began to transmit. It was to be a long message, and she prayed it would get through before being picked up by the German listening stations.

Gruber heard the shout as his senior Feldwebel came hurrying to his office at the police station in Montrouge.

"Sir, we have a transmission. SD have confirmed it is here in Montrouge."

He got up from his desk and hurried out of his office, following the sergeant to the detector van. Behind the van were four jeeps with armed soldiers in them. Gruber leapt into the detector van and urged the driver to go.

Almost immediately the radio operator clutched at his headphones. "Sergeant, we're triangulating on a source one kilometre from here."

The sergeant put a hand on the operator's shoulder. "Can you get us close?"

The operator moved the dial slowly, millimetre by millimetre. "Seven hundred metres."

Gruber looked at the sergeant. "What will we be looking for?"

The sergeant shrugged. "Could be a house, a garden shed, a barn or maybe out in the fields somewhere, particularly if there are trees."

"Sergeant," the operator called. "I think it's close to the Auroy smallholding."

Gruber felt his whole body slump. He knew what his duty was as the officer leading the hunt for the agent or whoever it was that was sending something.

"Take us there," he said.

Agata finished her transmission and breathed a sigh

of relief, but it lasted just a few seconds as she felt rumbling coming through the thin walls of the small space in which she was confined. She screwed her face up and listened, straining her ears. It sounded like a lot of traffic, which may have meant nothing, but so heightened were her senses that she feared the worst, particularly as she'd been transmitting. She disconnected the aerial and closed the suitcase lid slowly and as quietly as she could. She began to feel small beads of sweat forming beneath her armpits and on her forehead. Her breathing sounded ragged, and she tried taking deep, slow breaths to control it. But all she could do was wait.

Matilde was working in the kitchen when she heard the sound of military vehicles pulling up outside her smallholding. She also heard the distinctive guttural sounds of the German soldiers. She put the knife down she had been using, wiped her hands on her apron and went to the front door. What she saw made her stop and almost freeze in horror as she watched the German soldiers clambering out of their jeeps and taking up various positions along the fence. Then she saw Gruber.

"Madame Auroy, we believe there is an agent transmitting close by," he said as he reached her. "You could save us a lot of time by telling us if you have an agent concealed here."

Matilde kept her hand on her chest beneath which her heart was pounding mercilessly. She thought she was going to faint but kept her hand on the door lintel to stop herself from toppling.

"No, no." It was all she could manage.

Gruber turned and beckoned the soldiers, pointing to the small buildings around yard. "Search them all," he shouted.

The senior sergeant came running over. "We must search the house, sir."

Gruber knew he could not prevent it, as much as he believed he would be violating Matilde's home, her sanctuary and, after this, her sanity. He stepped aside and let the sergeant through with another soldier. Then he turned to Matilde.

"I'm sorry."

Agata knew. It was almost as if she was standing out in the yard as a spectator watching the events unfold. She felt sick. If they found her, she knew they would arrest her and put her in prison. Then would come the pain of torture and death. She wished she had a gun, not that she could fight her way out against armed soldiers, but she had a knife, which she was determined to use if anyone touched her. Her mind went back to her home in Poland and the violation visited upon her country by the hated Nazis. If she could take just one soldier to his death, she believed she would be vanquished and forgiven in the afterlife. But one other thing she had was a cyanide pill. All SOE agents were giving one for obvious reasons. Agatha shuddered at the thought of making that final choice, but it was either that or fight and die. She took the knife from her coat, unsheathed it and waited

"The barn has a padlock on it, Major!"

Gruber looked at Matilde. "We can smash our way in, Madame Auroy, or you could open the door for us."

Matilde pushed herself away from the door and walked over to the barn. She unlocked the padlock and stood aside as Gruber went in with four armed soldiers.

Agata heard them coming in. She visualised the layout of the barn and could literally see where the soldiers were searching.

Matilde stood inside the doorway. She'd already wet herself in fear because she knew that if they found Agata, they would be arrested, and that would be the end. Charlotte would be arrested as well. She felt tears come to her eyes and she brushed angrily at them, cursing the men searching for Agata.

As she brushed her eyes, she looked down and saw the stew pot on the floor beside a crate. She gasped and put her hand to her forehead in a dramatic show and slumped down on to the crate. Gruber looked at her, a frown on his face. Matilde hoped that he hadn't see the pot. He called one of the soldiers over and spoke to him. Then he turned back to Matilde.

"Could you get up please?"

Matilde had no choice and stood up. The soldier immediately eased her to one side and lifted the lid off the crate. It was empty, which Matilde expected anyway. But then the soldier shoved the crate. It knocked the pot over which rolled a short distance away. Then the soldier scraped his foot over the floor that had been covered by the crate and shook his head.

"Nein, Hauptsturmführer."

Matilde realised Gruber suspected the crate may have been covering a hatchway.

Suddenly one of the soldiers shouted and pointed to

the floor where he was standing at the far corner of the barn. He brushed away some straw with his foot to reveal a trapdoor. In the small space where she was hiding, Agata could almost feel his feet scraping away the rubbish.

Gruber walked over to where the soldier was scraping his feet. He could see the trapdoor clearly. He stopped, turned the small inset lever and lifted the trapdoor. He pushed it up against the wall where it rested at an angle. Then he pointed to the dark, black opening and nodded to the sergeant.

The soldier stepped forward, pointed his rifle into the opening and fired several shots into the void.

Agata almost screamed but kept her hand clamped firmly over her mouth as she felt the impact of the bullets thudding into the bottom of the void in which the soldier had fired his gun. She was now trembling with fear and had also wet herself. It was a small mercy that she had emptied her bowels that morning. Her body shook until her bones felt like rocks beneath her flesh. And then she fainted.

The soldier looked at Gruber who nodded his head. The signal was obvious, and the soldier climbed down into the cellar. One minute later his head popped up. "Nein, Herr Hauptmann. Empty."

Gruber almost breathed a sigh of relief. He spun on his heels and hurried out of the barn, taking his troops with him.

"No-one here," he called out. "We'll carry on searching the area."

Matilde watched them all leave and carefully

relocked the barn door. Then she went back into the house and collapsed on to a chair, her whole body practically shredded of any dignity after what she had just witnessed.

***

An hour passed in which time, Matilde had cleaned herself up, finished off preparing the meal for that evening and occasionally peered out of the window at the front of the house to see if there was any activity. Once she was satisfied the soldiers had definitely left the area, she walked over to the barn and let herself in. She pulled the door shut and slid the bolt into position. Then she went over to the trap door and lowered it back into place. She could still smell the cordite from the gunfire. Then she tapped on the panel that had been covered by the trap door leaning up against it.

"Agata?"

She waited before tapping the panel again. Then she heard movement, and it opened inwards. Agata slid the panel away and crawled out of the small space on her hands and knees. She stood up, put her hands behind her and arched her back, stretching her limbs to get the discomfort from them.

Matilde waited until Agata relaxed and then swept her into a big bear hug.

"*Mon Dieu*, How are you?"

They held each other for a while before Agata pulled away. "I was terrified," she said. "Why did they not find me? I was shaking so badly I thought they would be able to hear my bones rattling." She looked down at her trousers. "I wet myself I was so frightened."

"You weren't alone in that," Matilde said. "But I've been able to clean myself up." She stooped down behind Agata and pulled the panel back into place. "You know you won't be able to stay now, Agata, don't you."

"Yes, I know."

"Where will you go?"

"You know I can't tell you that, Matilde," she said. "But don't worry, you won't see me again."

They walked to the barn door. Matilde stooped and picked up the pot from where it had stopped rolling when the soldier had shoved the crate to one side. She looked carefully from the open door and checked first to make sure the coast was clear, before hurrying across the yard to the house. Once they were inside, Agata disappeared to get herself cleaned up. Matilde provided her with a change of clothes and fed her. All the while she was doing this, Matilde had the fear in the back of her mind that Gruber would suddenly return, and she found herself wishing that he would not come back at all — ever. But she knew he would, and she had to act as if nothing had happened other than he had made an unfortunate mistake and frightened her to within an inch of her life.

Chapter 27

Charlotte arrived home from work that afternoon. She greeted her aunt with a kiss and went through to her room for a few minutes before returning to the kitchen where Matilde had made a cup of coffee for her.

"How was work?" Matilde asked.

Charlotte sighed heavily. "I'm bored," she said.

Matilde's eyebrows lifted in surprise. "Bored?"

Charlotte puffed air out of her mouth. "Everything is so repetitious," she said. "I go to work, serve the Germans with their meals. Listen to their chatter, their jokes and, sometimes, the invitations for you know what. There's no excitement anymore. The war has sucked the life out of us. Well, me," she added. "Once upon a time we could go dancing, go to the cinema. Enjoy walking in the park. I went to see Nicolas a couple of days ago as you know. I like his company and would love to spend more time with him, but I think his mind is set on rebellion and not on more prosaic things. Don't you feel the same, Matilde?"

Matilde wanted to tell Charlotte how her world had almost collapsed around her, and how the fear she'd experienced had aged her to a degree she thought impossible. But she saw no reason to shatter her niece's complacent view of life under the Nazis; not while she was unaware of how close they had both come to being taken away and put in prison because of Agata.

"Did you get your ration cards?" she asked instead.

Charlotte chuckled. "Oh yes; another exciting

moment in my life. Queued for ages. Now it seems I have to get one of them changed."

"Why?"

"They spelt my name wrong on one of the cards," she said. "Bloody idiots. "I went back into the Mairie, but they said I could come back another day or get it changed at the Prefecture because they were too busy to do it." She shook her head irritably. "A bloody ration card! Why couldn't they have done it for me while I was there?"

"Had you left the queue?"

Charlotte nodded irritably. "Yeah."

"So what will you do then?"

Charlotte lifted her cup and drained it. "I'll pop into the village and get it done. Do you want to come with me?"

Matilde thought it would make a change to have a walk into the village with Charlotte, rather than stay in the house. She wasn't worried about Gruber; if he showed up while they were out, she thought it wouldn't hurt for him to sit outside and wait. She actually liked that idea too.

"Yes, okay. I'll be with you in a couple of minutes."

Charlotte waited until her aunt came back and together they linked arms and set off for the centre of the small town, which everyone insisted on calling the village, and headed towards the Prefecture so Charlotte could get her ration card amended.

"There's a lot of soldiers about," Charlotte said, looking up and down the street as they walked.

"No more than usual," Matilde answered, not

wanting to offer up an explanation. "You don't come into the village that often, it's about normal." It was a lie of course but Matilde was still trying to protect Charlotte from the reason she believed there were more soldiers patrolling the streets.

They reached the Prefecture. Matilde told Charlotte she would pop into the Goldsmith's shop for a chat while Charlotte was getting her card sorted. Charlotte gave her a quick kiss on the cheek and stepped into the police station.

The moment Charlotte stepped into the building; she sensed a change in the atmosphere. It was as though an unseen tension was rippling through the walls. She frowned and wondered if it was because she rarely came into the place and hadn't been in there of over two years. But something was different; she could tell.

She walked over to the reception desk where a uniformed officer was talking to a colleague. Alongside them were two German soldiers. Charlotte wasn't familiar with the rank badges, but she believed they were non-commissioned officers. She wondered if Gruber would be there, which made her think about asking him to help. Then she dismissed that idea as quickly as it had entered her head and explained to one of the police officers why she was there.

Then suddenly she heard raised voices coming from somewhere beyond the area in which she was standing. They were men's voices that she could hear. Angry voices too. Then a scream that lasted no more than a moment: brief but chilling.

"Yes, mademoiselle?"

Charlotte snapped out of the moment and looked at the police officer.

"What is it you want?"

She glanced over his shoulder to where the sounds had come from. "Sorry," she said. "I was distracted by that scream.

The young man looked back over his shoulder and then at Charlotte. "A prisoner. The Germans picked her up an hour ago." He shrugged. "Now, what can I do for you?"

Ten minutes after walking into the Prefecture, Charlotte walked into the Goldsmith's shop. Her aunt had her back to her talking to Brigitte Goldsmith. The elderly shop owner glanced up and then said something to Matilde who turned round.

Charlotte couldn't believe the stunned look on her aunt's face. She took a step forward to see if her aunt was okay but had to stop when Matilde grabbed her.

"We have to go home, Charlotte," she said hurriedly. "Come on." She literally dragged Charlotte out of the shop and into the street, who had no option but to follow.

"What's going on, Matilde?" he asked, her voice stuttering as her aunt pulled her. She stopped and stood there firmly.

Matilde turned round. "Quickly, Charlotte. We have to get home. I'll explain everything then."

Charlotte could see her aunt was in some kind of distress and knew she had to go with her.

They reached the smallholding within five minutes, but instead of going up to the front door, Matilde went straight over to the barn. She yanked open the door and ran inside.

Charlotte watched, a puzzled look on her face as her aunt went to the far end of the barn and immediately got on to her knees and started scrabbling her hands over part of the lower wall. Charlotte got to her as Matilde pulled back the panel behind which Agata had been hiding. She leaned inside, was still for a moment, and then settled back on her heels.

"Oh, the silly girl; she's taken it with her."

Charlotte put her hands on her shoulders. "What are you talking about?"

Matilde's body sagged. "Agata had her transmitter in here. It was there this morning when she transmitted. Now it's gone, and I think the Germans have caught her. Brigitte Goldsmith said the news of someone being captured had gone round the village like a whirlwind." Her head dropped and she started crying. "Poor Agata."

Charlotte straightened, her mind in shock when she realised that the scream she'd heard in the Prefecture could only have been that of Jefson's SOE agent, Agata Stasiak.

***

Charlotte pedalled away from the house with her aunt's words ringing in her ears. *"If Agata is tortured and reveals everything, you and I will be arrested."*

Her legs were pumping like mad as she pushed herself to get into Paris as quickly as she could. There was still plenty of life in the streets, but she had no time to take any of that in because her one thought was to get to Jacques Garnier and to let him know what had happened. It was more in hope than certainty that she thought he would have some answers, but if it was to be a pointless journey, she knew her and Matilde would have to leave Paris and find their way to sanctuary somewhere.

She reached Jacques' home and was relieved to see the carriage in his yard. There was no sign of the horse. She pushed the gate open and wheeled her bicycle in, dropped it on the ground and rapped her knuckles on the front door. What seemed like an eternity passed before she heard footsteps, and the door was pulled open.

"Oh, Jacques," she said breathlessly. "I need help."

He stood back and let her literally fall through the doorway. He could see she was in a dreadful state. Her breathing was harsh and, even in the half light from the single bulb above them, he could see she was quite flushed and had beads of sweat on her forehead.

He closed the door and took her by the elbow, helping her into his kitchen. The heat thrown out from the stove in there made the room lovely and warm. He helped her into a chair at the long wooden table. The remains of a meal was evident. He sat down and put both his hands up, holding them palms outwards.

"Now, Charlotte, calm down and tell me what the problem is."

Charlotte didn't really know how or where to start, so she began with the news that Agata had been arrested and was locked up in the Prefecture at Montrouge.

"My aunt says we will be arrested if Agata tells the Germans about us." She put her hand on her chest. "I didn't even know Agata was transmitting from Matilde's barn, Jacques, but I would still be arrested as an accomplice."

He stopped her there. "So, what is it you are asking?"

Her breathing was beginning to settle down, but her heart rate wasn't. "Matilde says the Germans must not be allowed to question her because she is afraid that Agata will crack under torture. She is terrified, Jacques. And so am I."

He blew his cheeks out. "Let me get you a cognac. Then you can go home and tell your aunt I will be doing my best to deal with this."

He got up from the table and went across to a cabinet from which he took a bottle of cognac and two glasses. He brought them over, filled the glasses and put one in front of Charlotte.

"Drink that and go home."

She looked up at him and frowned. "Can I help?"

He shook his head. "Yes, by drinking that and going home. You're no good to me in the state you're in, and we need you back at the Metropole in the morning, which is what Jefson sent you out here for. Now drink up."

He watched as Charlotte lifted her glass. Then he raised his and swallowed the cognac in one go. Charlotte did the same. The she got up, thanked him and left him there.

He went to the front door and opened it to see Charlotte leaving on her bicycle. Then he went back into the house, picked his long coat, pulled on a pair of boots and set off for the only person he knew who might be able to help.

***

Margot Aveline heard the knock at her door and wondered who that could be; she wasn't expecting anyone, and at that time of night, although still early evening, there was never a good reason for anyone to call unless invited. She closed the book she was reading and set it down on the small table beside her armchair, got up and went through to the front door.

"Good evening, Margot."

Margot's expression changed to one of surprise, and then darkened when she saw Jacques Garnier standing at the open door. She stood back and let him in, closing the door behind him. She followed him through to the lounge where he was now standing with his cap in his hands.

"Jacques, what a surprise. Can I get you anything?"

He shook his head. "No thank you, Margot. I need something else."

She sat down in her armchair. "What is it?"

"How quickly can you get a team together?"

This brought a gasp from Margot. Getting a team together was risky, difficult and almost impossible now the German presence was increasing daily. She knew Jacques would not waste her time; he would come straight to the point.

"Go on," she said.

"The Germans have captured an SOE agent in Montrouge. If she is taken to Gestapo headquarters, she will be tortured and will almost certainly expose a safehouse plus an important agent that London have embedded right in the heart of the German hierarchy. We need to stop that."

"Where is she at this moment?"

"She is in the Prefecture at Montrouge."

"And do you know when they will be transferring her?"

He shook his head. "No, but I think it's unlikely they will keep her at Montrouge for long."

She sighed heavily. "If it's tonight, it won't be until after the curfew; the streets are emptier then."

He nodded. "Of course."

"And you want this woman rescued?"

Jacques gave Margot a forlorn look. "She must never reach Gestapo HQ alive. If she can't be rescued, she must be killed."

Margot said nothing, just simply ran the options through her mind, her head moving up and down slowly as she began debating the chances of success or failure. Then she stood up.

"Leave this with me, Jacques. If I can put a team together, I will, but I make no promises. What is the agent's name?"

"Agata Stasiak."

"Dead or alive," she said, her eyebrows raised in question.

"Either."

She reached her arm out and put her hand on his shoulder. "You'd better go now, Jacques. I'll do my best."

He thanked her and left the house more in hope than

expectation, but he'd done what he could, knowing that if Margot could not get a team together, it would be the end for Matilde and Charlotte.

***

Agata lay asleep, virtually unconscious, on a hard, unforgiving stone floor. She was vaguely aware of pain all over her body and discomfort from where she could feel the pressure from the weight of her body on the stone. Her memory of being captured was limited because of the beating she'd received at the hands of the German guards. She recalled scrabbling through her clothing looking for the cyanide pill, but the soldiers had practically stripped her and found the pill. It was her last hope: one that she did not want, but death was to be the result of her capture whether it was from the cyanide poison of the torture she knew would happen, and there was no way she could survive that.

She heard footsteps and then the sound of her cell door being opened. Someone shoved a cloth bag over her head and pulled her to her feet. She cried out in pain as she was dragged from her cell. She had no shoes on her feet, and because she was very weak, her feet dragged on the floor. She heard an exchange of German voices and then the sudden chill of the night air as they bundled her outside and into a waiting jeep.

What Agata couldn't see were the two armed, German soldiers sitting in the front of the jeep. She was literally thrown into the back seats and felt two bodies squeeze in either side of her. Her hands were handcuffed behind her, which meant she couldn't sit back without a great deal of pain. Then the unmistakeable order to the driver, and the jeep lurched forward, heading into the empty streets and towards Gestapo Headquarters.

Agata knew there was now no hope. She prayed that they would kill her before she gave up the names of Matilde and Charlotte. She didn't care about revealing anything connected to her role as an SOE agent; she was a disposable asset as far as London was concerned, but that was the price she had to be willing to pay.

The noise of the jeep was almost like a comfort to her, knowing that once it stopped, so would her life. She still had the hood over her head, and as a result of her pain, her beating and her hunger, she allowed herself to sink in the hope she could shut her eyes and conjure up dreams of her homeland, her childhood and her family.

It was as Agata was going through this almost catatonic state that she heard the sound of gunfire and shouting. The jeep stalled as a bullet tore through the radiator and into the engine. She was thrown to one side as the jeep veered into the kerb and slammed to a halt. The two soldiers who were pressed up against her on either side moved away quickly, but suddenly another shot rang out and something fell against her in a deadweight. She knew instinctively it was the body of one of the German soldiers.

There was a lot more shouting and gunfire, and then silence followed by the sound of running feet. Agata felt someone's hands pushing underneath her armpits as she was lifted bodily out of the car. Then she was in someone's arms and could feel the thud of his footsteps slamming into her bruised and battered body.

Then she was gently lowered on to something soft as someone shouted in French. *"Vite alors!"*. Her body rolled back as the car moved forward with the sounds of triumphant French voices and a great deal of laughter.

Then Agata's hood was removed, and she felt someone trying to giver water, It dribbled round her mouth and on to her neck, but she drank greedily and thankfully until she was sated. Then she stopped, the bottle was taken away and a calming, female voice spoke to her.

"You are safe now, Agata."

Chapter 28

Margot Aveline hurried out of her apartment, holding the collar of her coat up against her neck to help ward off the chill of the stiff evening breeze that funnelled along the dark waters of the River Seine. She was wearing a divided skirt, which was becoming fashionable in Paris because a bicycle was the only practical means of transport. The luxury of pulling your car into a petrol station for fuel had disappeared with the advent of the German Occupation. And because the Paris women were being encouraged to not let their standards drop, it had become *de rigeur* to wear what was basically a Culotte, but strategically designed to allow the wearer the comfort of riding a bicycle and remaining chic as most ladies in Paris managed with some elegance.

But for Margot, fashion was not on her mind as she pedalled towards the store rooms where she worked during the day on sorting out the priceless art treasures that had been moved from the Louvre and stored safely in catacombs beneath the city streets. She had an appointment that she had to keep, one that exposed her to the risk of imprisonment and eventual dispatch to the Concentration camps in Germany if she was discovered.

She turned into a narrow street along which was the unobtrusive door that led into the depths of the catacombs. She unlocked the door trying to ignore the few people who were walking by. Thankfully there were no German soldiers around; darkness and narrow streets were places of risk for them.

She pushed open the door, wheeled her bicycle into the dark passageway and locked the door behind her, sliding the top and bottom bolts into place. She removed a small torch from her pocket and turned it on. Using the small beam she walked along the tunnel until she was a safe distance from the door and turned the lights on.

Once her eyes adjusted to the gloom, she turned the torch off and made her way down some steps until she came to a room on which there was no door. She stepped inside, turned the light on and looked at a scene that was very familiar to her because this was her place of work when she was cataloguing and labelling the artwork that was stored further along the catacombs in larger rooms. The official entrance, and the accepted way in, was from the Louvre. Use of the small street door through which Margot had entered was not encouraged, and there was usually no reason to use it because the staff only worked there during daylight hours. It wasn't a secret door; simply one that no-one ever used — except Margot and her colleague from the Louvre, Oliver Benoist.

Margot's first thought was to remove the dust cover from the printing machine that was used to print labels of Provenance and Art verification. She turn the power on and waited for the machine to hum and then whirr into action. Then she went to a safe that was standing up against a wall. She opened it, pulled out a folder, smiled and took it across to the machine. She fed a piece of old, slightly stained card into the machine, then inserted small cast iron alphabet letters and waited for the result to be printed. Once that was done, she opened her purse, took out a small photograph and, using a very sharp blade, trimmed the photo and attached it to the card. Once she had done this, she closed everything up and put the dust cover back on the machine.

Whenever Margot printed out a false identity document, she felt an overwhelming sense of satisfaction coupled with an inordinate sense of fear. And there was a good reason for that.

She checked her watch, nodded thoughtfully to herself and walked out of the room and deeper into the catacombs to a room that she hoped was that far away from prying eyes that it would be too scary for anyone to even venture down there, particularly at night.

***

Agata lay awake, her eyes closed but aware of a faint candlelight that threw flickering shadows against the dull, dry wall of the room. She was wrapped in something, she knew not what, but she was warm and comfortable. She still ached abominably from the beating she'd taken at Montrouge, but that was to be borne in exchange for the luxury of relative freedom.

Her mind went back to the moments the jeep had been attacked, the gunfire and the shouting voices. Then the sudden crash and a pair of hands lifting her. And finally a woman's voice telling her she was safe.

She heard footsteps in the tunnel and lifted her head. A woman walked into the room. She was carrying something in her hand.

"Hello, Agata. I have a coffee for you. Are you okay?"

Agata sat up and let her cover fall away as she took the cup from the woman's hand. She took a mouthful, then lowered the cup.

"I'm okay," she said. "Who are you?"

"Who I am does not matter. Just drink that and then we'll be leaving."

Margot glanced around the room which was quite empty. Agata had been in that room for twenty-four hours with nothing to eat other than a croissant Margot had given her the night before and had slept on a hard bench with a blanket thrown over her. There was a small pot which she'd used to relieve herself. Margot had told her she would remove it later. Then she took Agata's hand and walked her out of the room and back along the tunnel to the small front door where she had left her bicycle.

"This is your identity card. Put it somewhere safe," she said to Agata handing her the card. "Do it now so I can see it is done." She watched as the card disappeared into the folds of Agata's trousers. "When we step out into the street, we will walk arm in arm like friends. There will be no Germans out there, and the French police will not bother us, you can be sure of that. We only have a short way to go. Come on."

They stepped out into the street. Agata grabbed Margot's hand. Margot could feel the tension in her grip. They started walking with Margot wheeling her bike until they came to a small café. She stopped and asked Agata to hold the door for her as she wheeled her bike through. She immediately acknowledged the man standing behind the bar and sat down at a table. She made sure she was facing the interior of the café.

"*Deux cafés*, Padron," she called, holding two fingers up.

She looked back at Agata and smiled. She could see her eyes flicking back and forth, bewildered and in fear. Margot could understand it; Agata needed help to escape across the border into the so-called free Vichy France territory and from there to Spain.

Suddenly, Margot stiffened slightly as she saw an elderly woman walk through a beaded curtain alongside the bar. She touched Agata's hand.

"Don't turn round, but in a moment you will see an elderly lady walking out of the café. You must follow her into the street. She will be waiting there. On no account must you linger here over farewells and thanks; just get up, kiss me on the cheek and leave. You will never see me again. Now go."

Agata got up, kissed Margot on the cheek. "I will come back to Paris one day whoever you are and find you. *Au revoir*."

Margot watched her go and breathed a sigh of relief. Now it was up to the elderly lady.

***

Agata fell into step beside the elderly woman who was wearing a knee length coat. She had a headscarf covering her hair. The scarf was tied beneath her chin.

"Hold on to my arm like any young woman would do with an elderly relative," she said to Agata.

"What is your name?" Agata asked.

"My name isn't important, but you can call me Simone."

"Where are we going?"

"To a safe place outside Paris where I will hand you over to someone else." She turned her face towards Agata and smiled. "But don't worry, you will be safely across the border into the Free Zone. In two days you should be in Spain."

There was little conversation after that. Agata understood the need for secrecy; the need not to know anyone's real name in case you were picked up by the police or the Germans. Names could easily be revealed under torture, which was why the elderly woman was called Simone — it was simply a name.

Within ten minutes of leaving the café, Simone steered Agata towards a narrow street along which was a short row of garages. She went to one and unlocked the doors, swung them open and climbed into an old Citroen CV. She made Agata wait until she had driven the car out and locked the garage doors behind her. Then she beckoned Agata to the car and pulled out into the Paris night.

Agata had no idea where they were going of course, but as the streets became less populated, so she managed to relax a little. Simone said nothing other than a mild oath when something unexpected happened, like a drunken cyclists wobbling about in the road as he or she negotiated an unsteady ride home. But after about thirty minutes of driving, Simone pulled over and stopped. She turned the ignition off and sat there for a moment, waiting.

Agata could see a parked car on the opposite side of the road. A tall man wearing a coat and a trilby hat stepped out of the car and walked over. Simone put the window down.

"This is Agata: your responsibility from here."

He nodded and came round to the passenger side of the car. Simone watched him and then spoke to Agata.

"Go with God's speed and good luck." Agata went to say something, but Simone stopped her. "Say nothing. Good bye."

She watched as the man took Agata across to his car and drove away. Then she started the car and headed back to Paris. As she drove, Simone reflected on the work she'd been doing since before the Germans actually arrived. For a while it had been fairly straightforward with very little risk, but now the stakes were higher and the danger increasingly close. But it was the least she could do for anyone who wanted to flee the Nazi terror.

She arrived back at the garage, put the car away and cycled back to the Hotel Metropole, where she locked the bicycle up against the racks, and walked into the hotel through the staff entrance.

She was still wearing her coat and headscarf as Armand came out of his office. He took the coat and scarf from her.

"Thank you, Armand. I told you I would be back before the curfew," she said. "Goodnight."

He smiled. "Goodnight, Countess Lipovsky. Sleep well."

Chapter 29

It was less than forty eight hours since Charlotte had cycled into Paris and told Jacques Garnier of the prisoner at Montrouge. The full implication of what could have happened to her and her aunt hadn't really sunk in, despite the increased police activity in the area, and she was still holding on to the fantasy that everything was relatively normal, which meant her life was still boring.

Charlotte was on a late start that day; the resident waitresses at the hotel served breakfast, leaving the outlying staff, like herself and Camille to work a luncheon shift that ended with high tea. The lunch period had been extremely busy. Charlotte had waited on Major Heller's table, and it was obvious to her from Heller's group and their heated conversation that not all was right in the surreal world of Nazi Paris. She'd managed to pick out some stuff, but the officers were keeping their voices down, which meant she had to rely on lip-reading, and that was limited. What she did manage to pick out was the need for increased German presence and the need, therefore, for more troops to be sent into Paris.

Soon, it was time for a short break for her. She breezed into the changing room to freshen up and have a coffee. Camille came in just as Charlotte was putting a dab of perfume on her neck.

Camille came straight over. "Wow, that's smells gorgeous," she exclaimed. "What is it? Where did you get it?"

Charlotte turned to her, a smug look on her face. "I could tell you," she said, "but then I would have to kill you."

They both laughed. Camille took the bottle from Charlotte's hand and tried it on herself. Where did you get this? Not in Paris I'll bet."

Charlotte retrieved the bottle and put it back in her locker. "I bought it in England," she lied, thinking about Hans Gruber and his suggestion.

Camille gave her a look that said she knew Charlotte was lying. "Come on; I won't tell."

Charlotte pulled on her apron and fastened it behind her back. She closed her locker door. "I've got to go to work, Camille."

Camille nudged her on the shoulder. "I will find out, you know. You can't keep any secrets from me," she said. "You know you can't."

Charlotte smiled. If only Camille knew, she thought to herself.

***

Major Heller had been back at his desk for a couple of hours after his lunch. His main problem was the recent attack on the escorts bringing Agata Stasiak to Gestapo Headquarters. He'd had an angry exchange of words with Hans Gruber about the attack, and the impact of his own words still resonated with him.

"What do you mean, the soldiers were disarmed?" he'd shouted down the phone to Gruber.

"They were relieved of their weapons, Major," Gruber replied simply.

"All of them?"

"Yes, Major. Although one of the soldiers was injured and is in hospital. He wasn't seriously wounded."

"I want those men charged, Hauptmann, do you understand?"

"Yes, Major."

The conversation had them morphed into the reasons why it happened, how and were there any leaks to the security team at Montrouge for which Gruber was responsible; none of which Gruber could answer. Heller had ended the phone call with the thought on his mind that Gruber should be replaced with a more diligent officer.

His phone rang. He picked it up. "Heller."

It was Hauptmann Gruber. "Major, we believe we have located the safehouse here in Montrouge from where Agata Stasiak had been operating."

Heller's spirits lifted a little with the news. "When will you raid it?"

"We will wait until it is dark. In about an hour. Do you want to be with us for this?"

Heller shook his head. "No, but don't blow this, Gruber; it may give you and your men a chance to redeem themselves. Search the house thoroughly and report back to me immediately." He put the phone down.

At that precise moment, Charlotte was called into Armand's office. When she got there, he was bent over his desk writing something. He looked up as Charlotte came in.

"Ah, Charlotte, I want you to do something for me. You know Roland Metier, don't you?"

Charlotte nodded. Metier was one of the Commie chefs at the Metropole. He was a lot older than Charlotte and always fun to talk to.

"Yes," she said.

Armand folded up the note that he'd been writing and rolled it into a small tube. He then wrapped an elastic band around it and handed it to her.

"Roland lives near you at Montrouge. He's at 12, Rue Antibes. Do you know it?"

She nodded. "Yes, I know the street," she said as she took the rolled up note from him.

"Will you drop this off to him on your way home, please?" he asked.

She nodded and put the note into the pocket of her apron. She was about to walk away when Armand stopped her.

"Take it now, please, Charlotte. Don't worry about finishing your shift."

She arched her eyebrows. "Okay. Thank you, Armand."

She went back to the staff room and changed out of her uniform and hurried out of the hotel as the afternoon light was almost gone and darkness was settling in.

Charlotte found the address on Rue Antibes without too much difficulty. Unknown to Charlotte was the fact that Roland Metier was the leader of a fledgling Resistance Group, many of which were springing up all over France. These brave people risked their lives daily, which meant Charlotte, unknowingly, was risking a lot simply by association. But being unaware of Metier's secret; she simply believed she was taking an uncompromising message to him probably about rescheduling his work times.

The architecture in Rue Antibes proclaimed its heritage: tall apartment blocks of four stories, dull brown in colour with ageing sash windows lined up on either side of the street. Steps led up to the front doors from the street; steps that would have been used by the tenants to congregate in small groups if the weather was good and talk about life in general. But now these were empty; no-one ventured outside unless it was absolutely necessary for fear of being picked on by groups of German soldiers wandering the streets looking for anyone they could question and abuse.

Charlotte padlocked her bicycle to the railings and rattled her knuckles on the front door. Within a few minutes the door was opened a crack and a man's face appeared.

"Oui?"

"Roland?"

He looked beyond Charlotte, searching for anyone else who might be waiting there. He pulled the door open. "Bring your cycle in," he told her.

Charlotte wheeled it in and propped it up against a damp, mouldering wall as Metier closed the door. He pointed upstairs. She followed him up two flights of stairs and in through a door that led into his apartment. The room was quite large. A round table covered in a dark red patterned cloth stood in the centre of the room. The carpet was worn and had little of its original design showing. There was an empty fruit bowl on the table, a testimony to the lack of fruit in Paris. On one side of the room was a book case with a few books laying on the almost empty shelves. Beneath the shelves were two cupboard doors.

Charlotte watched Metier go over to the one window and peered cautiously into the street below. He turned and looked at her.

"No-one followed you?"

Charlotte frowned. "Why would anyone want to follow me?"

"Why would they not?" was his strange reply. "It is true that women are allowed to move a little more freely around Paris rather than the men, but not all the Nazis believe our women are harmless." He pointed at Charlotte's small shoulder bag that hung by her waist. "You have a message for me?"

She opened the small bag and took out the note. She handed it to him. He scanned the message quickly, then he tore the note into small pieces and stuffed them into his mouth. Charlotte looked on in amazement as Metier chewed and swallowed the message.

"Thank you," he said. "Now you had better go."

Charlotte needed to go to the toilet. Her bladder had protested as she'd cycled through the streets to get there, and she wasn't sure she would make it home without wetting herself.

"Do you mind if I go to the toilet? I'm desperate."

He pointed to a door. "Through there."

Charlotte thanked him and went through the open door into a small hallway. There were three doors and a small corridor, no more than few feet in length, which was where she found the toilet. She hurried in, closing the door behind her and slipped the flimsy bolt into place. Then she pulled her trousers and panties down and settled in relief on to the brown wooden seat.

And as she felt herself and her mind relaxing, she suddenly heard men's voices and the sound of rushing feet pounding up the stairs. Then there was a crash and shouts in German ordering Metier to get down. Charlotte stiffened in absolute terror knowing that within seconds the toilet door would be smashed open, and she would be dragged out without ceremony.

There was nothing she could do despite a brief thought that she should run, although she didn't know where she could run to. By the time she'd got her panties up and unlocked the door, they would be on her. She could feel her hands shaking violently as her heart thumped in her chest. Her breathing became laboured, and she thought she was going to pass out.

She could hear the thud of footsteps and in her mind could see them moving around the apartment and into the small hallway. The voices quietened but she could hear them searching and literally destroying the apartment as they obviously looked for something. She knew she would soon be found.

Then the voices faded, and she heard one say he would check. Then there was silence, but she sensed, rather than heard, a presence beyond the door. Her eyes widened as she fixed them on the door knob. It turned slowly. She started shaking violently as the door knob rotated to a stop. Then the door moved; just a little until it was held by the flimsy bolt. Charlotte wanted to scream but all her senses were slamming themselves against her muscles and she had no voice, just a sense of terror.

The bolt did not yield and whoever was trying to open the door gave up. The door knob rotated back as the searcher let it go. Then Charlotte heard a muffled voice. "Alles in ordnung?"

"Ja!"

She heard footsteps again, but they were receding, moving away from the hallway. She sat there, her mouth open wide, her breathing harsh in her chest and listened until there was complete silence. She waited like that for fifteen minutes, not daring to move or to find out if they had gone. But eventually she stood up, pulled up her panties and trousers. She was now ready to step out and wondered if she would walk straight into the arms of the waiting Germans. But one of them must have known there was someone in the toilet, so why did they stop?

She didn't linger on the unanswerable question but opened the door carefully and tip-toed into the main room. The damage there was horrendous. Everything had been knocked over, torn open and the contents scattered all over the floor. There was no sign of Metier and no sign of any waiting German soldiers.

She hurried down the steps to the front door, which was open, and looked out into the street. The Germans had gone. She let out a deep sigh of relief and unlocked her bicycle. Then she was off and peddling down the street, trying not to hurry but with all the imaginary demons chasing after her.

**

Charlotte arrived home in quite a state. She was still shaking from the fright she'd had at almost being plucked out of the toilet and arrested. She was also angry with Armand for putting her in such a dangerous situation. But she had survived and that was the important thing. She now needed to put it behind her and be more guarded in her daily life.

Her aunt welcomed her in the usual fashion and asked the usual questions. Charlotte did not want Matilde to see how shaken she was, so she made and excuse and took herself off to her bedroom. She emerged fifteen minutes later having composed herself and fought off all the madness that was going through her mind.

She sat at the table as Matilde put the meal she'd prepared in front of her. It was a potato broth seasoned with whatever herbs and vegetables she dared add to it. Charlotte cut off a chunk of bread and began using that to scoop the broth into her mouth.

"How was your day, Charlotte?" Matilde asked.

Charlotte realised there was no way her aunt would have heard of the raid on Metier's apartment because news does not travel that fast. She had no doubt that it would be all round the village by morning though.

"Same as ever, Matilde: usual stuff. Boring of course."

Matilde managed a smile. "Thank goodness we're not in a war zone. At least we are reasonably safe here from any bombing. Unlike your poor mother in

England."

"I think we need not worry too much. Mother lives in a rural area. It's of no interest to Hitler and his bombs."

The conversation drifted then. Because of the way in which their lives were no longer their own, there was precious little to fill the day except for news of how the war was going.

Suddenly, there was a knock at the door. Charlotte's heart leapt and she almost dropped her bread into the broth.

Matilde got up. "That will be Gruber," she said.

Charlotte closed her eyes and breathed in and out slowly, hoping her aunt did not notice. It wasn't the fact that Gruber was coming in, but the sound of the loud knock. She opened her eyes as he walked into the kitchen and affected a welcoming smile for him, which was a lot more than Matilde could do.

"Evening, Herr Gruber. Are you ready for your meal?"

"Thank you, Matilde; yes, I'm starving." He pointed towards the door. "I'll just go through to my room, freshen up."

Matilde watched him go and gave Charlotte a withering look. "I wish he would freshen up away from here permanently," she snapped.

Charlotte grinned. "He will when the war is over, Matilde."

Matilde grunted something and brought over a plate and the broth. She put a chunk of bread and some fruit there and sat down.

"When I've served his food, Charlotte," she said softly. "I'm going to leave him with you. I have things I must do."

Charlotte knew it was because her aunt could never forget that her husband was being held captive by men who wore the same uniform as Hauptmann Gruber.

He came back in and sat down at the table. Matilde made her excuses and left the two of them.

"How was your day, Charlotte?" he asked in that pleasant, comforting voice of his.

"Same as ever," she said. "Nothing out of the ordinary. Usual stuff."

He looked at her as he scooped some broth up with the bread. "We had a very unusual day," he told her. "I won't be giving any secrets away either because the whole village will be talking about it by morning."

Charlotte affected a look of innocence. "Oh, what was it? I haven't heard anything."

He finished his mouthful and pushed his plate to one side.

"Our security people discovered a safehouse that we believe had been used by the British agent we captured a couple of days ago." He said nothing of the attack on Agata's journey to Gestapo HQ and that she had been snatched away by an armed gang. "We raided it earlier this evening."

Charlotte didn't say anything; not that she could, and she certainly wasn't going to congratulate him for his success.

"It's quite amazing what you discover on these raids." He shook his head. "Quite amazing," he repeated. Then he stood up. "I have to go back to the Prefecture, Charlotte. I will stay there this evening, so you can lock up when I've gone."

He buttoned his tunic and picked up his hat. Then he paused and looked at her with an expression on his face that Charlotte found hard to decipher. Until he spoke.

"I'm pleased you're wearing that perfume I gave you. It gives off a most beautiful fragrance. Goodnight, Charlotte."

And then he was gone, and Charlotte knew.

Chapter 30

Gruber arrived at SD Headquarters the following morning and hurried up the stairs to Major Heller's office. He acknowledged Sergeant Witborg and asked if there was anything for him, but the sergeant shook his head. He shrugged that off and knocked on Major Heller's door.

Heller looked up as Gruber walked in. He was writing but put his pen down as Gruber gave him the usual 'Heil Hitler' and the stiff arm salute, although in Gruber's case there was precious little stiffness in his arm.

"Sit down, Hans."

Gruber sat as instructed and waited for Heller to say something. The Major pulled a folder towards him and flipped it open. "I've decided to pull you out of Montrouge. I think you're wasted there; the senior Feldwebel can manage."

"Is there any particular reason, Major?" He wondered if the Agata Stasiak incident was the reason for the decision.

Heller sniffed and flipped open the folder. "Your record shows that you have a higher than average ability when it comes to leading a troop in the field, so to speak. I shall need that kind of leadership on November 11th."

"November 11th, sir?"

Heller breathed in and out heavily. "It's Armistice Day. The French always have a remembrance service at the tomb of the unknown soldier." He lifted his head a little and glanced over at the window. "At the Arc de Triomphe. We are expecting trouble because, as you know, all assemblies are banned, but we don't expect the Parisiennes to take any notice of that, particularly the students. We know they are planning something, so we'll be increasing the number of soldiers to police the situation. I want you to liaise with Feldwebel Schumacher and provide Officer cover for that day."

"And Montrouge, Major?"

Heller shook his head. "No, I have decided to recommend you for a transfer to somewhere more useful than ministering and wet nursing a bunch of villagers in Montrouge." He looked at the calendar on his desk. "The eleventh is in one week. I want you finished down there and back here by, let's say, the ninth."

Gruber tried not to show his disappointment. He was happy at Montrouge, particularly being billeted in the same house as Charlotte. He'd nursed the hope that they could develop a relationship that would rise above the conflict; one they could continue once the war was over. It was a forlorn hope really judging by the Major's decision to move him on.

"Is there anything else, Major?"

Heller shook his head. "No."

The interview was over, signalled by the fact that Heller lowered his head and got back to studying the paperwork on his desk. Gruber threw up a salute, clicked his heels and went away a disgruntled and disappointed man.

***

When Charlotte left for work the following morning she wasn't in a very happy frame of mind. The implications of what could have happened the previous day still stung her as the horror of it all kept popping into her head. And it was the fact that Armand had sent her into the lions' den that made her so angry that she decided to give him a piece of her mind when she got into work. But as she got nearer to the end of her relatively short ride to the hotel, she began to see things differently, and she realised she couldn't tell anyone. If she flew at Armand about almost getting caught, it would have been an admission that she was in Metier's house when the Germans raided it, and she could hardly claim that it was her perfume that saved her. Armand would have refused to believe that the Germans were so slack that they would not have bothered to search every single room and cupboard in the house including the toilet. The implication then would be that Charlotte was involved in some way with the enemy.

As Charlotte approached the hotel, she had digested her own misgivings and decided to say as little as possible and come up with a simple explanation that she arrived at the house while the raid was in progress.

Armand was in his office when she got in. He stopped writing as Charlotte knocked and opened the door. He put his pen down and leaned back in his chair.

"Morning, Charlotte. I heard about the raid."

News travels fast, Charlotte thought to herself. "I saw it happen," she said. "Practically watched it from across the road."

"Did you see Roland?"

She frowned. "No; I didn't go in the apartment."

"And the message I gave you?"

"I threw it away."

He seemed to settle visibly and sagged in the chair shaking his head. "Poor Roland. I doubt we'll see him again."

"Why?"

He simply looked at her and shrugged. "Go to work, Charlotte; I'll see if I can find out whether he will be released and be allowed back to work."

She turned to go, but as she reached the door, he called her.

"Charlotte."

She turned, her hand on the door handle. "Yes?"

He sighed heavily. "I'm so glad you were not there when they raided the house."

She knew what he meant. "Thank you, Armand," she said and left him pondering over the fact that he had nearly lost two employees, which would have been his fault for not acting with caution.

Arman waited until his door was shut before picking up the phone and ringing Eugene Bayard's number. He was the only person he could think of who would be able to ask Major Heller if there was any news of Roland Metier without risking any suspicion about his motives for asking. As the owner of the hotel and a neutral to boot, he would be perfect.

He got through to the Chateau within a short time and was eventually connected with Bayard. He explained the dilemma and needed to know if he would have to replace a very valuable member of the hotel staff, or would the Germans be releasing Metier. Bayard agreed to do this for him and promised he would make enquiries.

Armand put the phone down and again cursed his own fallibility. And he could only hope that Metier would say nothing about there being a connection between himself, Armand and the growing resistance in Paris.

Chapter 31

The days following Metier's arrest were a little tense for Armand, but Bayard had proved successful in getting him released. And once he was back on the kitchen staff at the Metropole, Armand could begin to relax.

For Charlotte though, it wasn't a case of relaxing. She was being lulled into a false sense of security because very little was happening in her life other than the boring routines she was obliged to follow. As the war raged between Germany and Britain, life in Paris was tolerably calm for those Parisiennes who were happy to embrace what of their former lives was available to them despite having to endure many restrictions like rationing, standing in lengthy queues and witnessing the Nazi orchestrated harassment of the Jews and the strict control of other nationals.

It was November 11th — Armistice Day, and Charlotte's day off just happened to fall on that day. She told her aunt she was going cycle into Paris and meet up with Nicolas and, despite the cold, try to find some comfort in each other's company.

Charlotte found herself becoming quite close to Nicolas: something she didn't mind at all, but she did wonder at times if those feelings were reciprocated by him. When they agreed to spend the day with each other, Nicolas had suggested they started their day outside the front of the hotel. She didn't mind, but did wonder why he hadn't agreed to her coming to his apartment. Not that she thought about it too much; it was just nice for her to think of being with him.

As she cycled into Paris, she became aware of an increasing amount of military traffic. Several jeeps and lorries with armed soldiers had passed her, and it wasn't until she arrived at the hotel that she could see the reason why. They were stationing lines of soldiers around the Place de la Concorde and all the way along the Champs Elysee. She took it all in before wheeling her bicycle round to the back of the hotel and locking it away. When she returned to the front, Nicolas was waiting for her.

She kissed him warmly on the cheek and gave him a hug. "What's going on?" she asked, nodding her head in the direction of the soldiers.

Nicolas grinned. "Armistice Day. They've banned all gatherings and ceremonies, and warned anyone who attempts to mount a parade or a march will be arrested and thrown in prison."

"So why all the soldiers?"

"It's the students. All the Lycée students will be marching up the Champs Elysee in defiance of the ban." His grin was getting wider. "We've been organising it for some time," he told her.

"We? You mean you are involved?" She saw him nod his head. "But you're not even a student, Nicolas, so why are you doing this?"

"Because the Germans must be shown that we will not be curbed. The Armistice Day is a day of remembrance for everyone. Even the bloody Germans must know this. After all, they lost thousands of men during the Great War." He took her hand. "Come on."

She allowed herself to be dragged along, not really sure she wanted to be involved in all this, but then she thought how she had described her own life as being tedious and boring, and thought this might liven it up for her.

It wasn't long before she heard the sound of strident voices calling out for freedom from Nazi tyranny. As they got closer, Nicolas increased the pace until they reached a large group of young students, many with homemade placards declaring against the Nazis and chanting slogans and epithets. There was a lot of pushing and shoving, nothing too violent because the soldiers were trying to control the protestors with the minimum show of strength.

Slowly the columns of students coming from different directions merged into an amorphous collection of young men and women singing, chanting, waving and pushing aside any soldiers who dared to step into the advancing column.

Charlotte started getting caught up in the groundswell of passion and anger that was growing within the mass, and she found her excitement level growing. The noise from the students was now drowning out the angry commands of the Germans. Even the loud hailers had no effect, not that it would have mattered; the students were determined to get to the place where the tomb of the unknown soldier lay and celebrate the tradition of remembrance.

And then someone fired a shot. The sound flew over their heads and echoed around the buildings. There were screams and many students fell to the ground instinctively, although no-one had been hit. But the effect was not what the Germans had expected because the students all seemed to surge forward in unison and began pushing and shoving the soldiers aside. People started struggling with the soldiers and fighting with them. Another shot rang out, but this just seemed to inflame the body of youngsters.

A jeep came roaring into the Place de la Concorde with more soldiers, but as it reached the body of students, it had to come to a halt. As soon as it did that, several students turned on the jeep and began rocking it from side to side. The soldiers jumped out and began clubbing those nearest with the butts of their rifles. A young officer with them, pulled his sidearm from it holster and started firing into the air.

Then a scout car came roaring up and more soldiers poured out, but this time they started dragging people away and bundling them into the vehicle. It wasn't too long before more armoured vehicles and troops were on the scene, and many battered and bloodied students were being dragged away.

Charlotte and Nicolas had the presence of mind though to hang back and keep away from the hardcore elements of the youngsters who were bent on fighting and giving the soldiers a good hiding. But against the guns and the overwhelming number of soldiers arriving, they never stood a chance. Eventually, Nicolas pulled Charlotte away.

"Come on," he said reluctantly. "We'd be better off away from here."

Charlotte didn't want to disagree although she was a little disappointed because she had started to enjoy herself. She started running with him. They were both laughing as they made their way to their favourite café along the banks of the River Seine.

They flopped down at an empty table and just looked at each other, wide grins on their faces.

"Well," Charlotte said breathlessly, "We won't forget this day in a hurry."

Nicolas laughed. "That's why it's called remembrance day."

Charlotte reached over and took his hand. "I'm glad we were together, Nicolas," she told him.

"Me too," he said.

And they both knew that by that admission, there was more to their relationship than just friendship.

They spent the day doing little else but wandering around hand in hand, talking, laughing, and making wishful plans. After they had lunch, Nicolas asked if she would stay the night with him. Charlotte wanted to, but she knew she had to refuse.

"If I don't get home before dark, my aunt will worry, especially if she has heard about the students' protests and arrests."

He looked into her face, his expression changing slowly to one of fatalistic acceptance. "But you want to, don't you, Charlotte."

She nodded. "One day," she said. "And soon."

He reached forward and pulled her close. "Then I will hang on to that promise and will not let you forget."

"I won't," she said. "And now I must go."

Nicolas watched her cycle away, a warm feeling in his heart and wondered if they would survive the war and find the happiness they both wanted; one that seemed so out of reach and far away.

***

They came for Margot Aveline the following day. There was no warning, just a hammering on her front door and an accusation read out to her of sedition and riotous assembly. Margot was too shocked to take any of the accusations in because they were so preposterous. She was given five minutes to get dressed and was then hauled off to a waiting scout car. They bundled her in and drove off.

Margot was stunned. Fifteen minutes earlier she had been eating her breakfast and listening to the radio with precious little on her mind other than the task she needed to complete at the Louvre; one which she had tried to delay for as long as she possibly could but was now just about ready to be signed off.

It didn't take long for the car to pull up outside the Prefecture in the heart of Paris. Margot was bewildered with the speed with which it had all happened. And the galling surprise was that it was the French police who had dragged her away from her comfortable apartment.

She was hustled into the police station and booked in at the front desk. She thought how odd it was at the formality. The desk sergeant took her ID from her, copied the details and handed the ID to one of the police officers who had brought her in. Then she was bundled into a police cell and left there. Nothing was said to her.

At that moment, Margot's colleague at the Louvre

and erstwhile boss, Oliver Benoist, received a phone call. He picked up the receiver.

"Oui?"

"Monsieur Benoist?" a woman's voice asked.

"Oui."

"Oh, good. This is Madame Brioche. I'm a neighbour of Margot Aveline. She may have spoken about me?"

He thought for a few moments. Then, "Ah, yes, Margot has spoken of you."

"Monsieur Benoist, I have to tell you that Margot was arrested this morning and taken away by the French police."

He frowned heavily. "Mon Dieu, arrested you say?"

"Yes. I heard the knock at her apartment door. I didn't take any notice at first, but within about ten minutes there such a lot of noise going on, I had to open my door and see what all the commotion was about."

"And that was when you saw her being taken away."

"Yes."

"So, why did you call me and no-one else?"

"Margot gave me your number in case anything happened to her. She has no family, you see."

He did see, which meant he had to do something, anything, to get Margot out of the clutches of the French police and, no doubt the Germans. He thanked Margot's neighbour and hung up. Then he sat down and began giving a lot of thought to how he would play this.

Margot looked up as her cell door was opened and a French police officer walked in. He had a pair of handcuffs with him, which he locked on to Margot's wrists. Then he led her away to an interview room which looked as cold as the sparse furniture there. She was told to sit at the table.

Another police officer came in, but this time he was accompanied by a German Feldwebel. The two men sat down, and the French officer started reading out the charges. He got to the sedition and riotous assembly bit when Margot's patience cracked.

"Stop there," she snapped. "This is damned ridiculous. What are you talking about? What have I got to do with riotous assembly for goodness sake?"

The German sergeant put his hand on the French officer's arm and leaned towards Margot.

"Yesterday in the city a large number of Lycée students demonstrated and rioted in an illegal assembly. The marches were organised by the student's colleges with the support of the instructors there."

Margot huffed loudly. "Bloody nonsense!" she said, finding it difficult not to laugh.

The Feldwebel was about to say something when a knock came at the door. Another German soldier walked in and whispered something in his ear. He looked at Margot and then spoke to the French officer. He left the room.

Waiting for him at the front desk was Oliver Benoist. The sergeant greeted him politely and asked his business.

Benoist began. "I believe you have Margot Aveline here under arrest for some reason." He waited until the sergeant nodded in affirmation before continuing. "Well, I need to inform you that Madame Aveline is a leading curator at the Louvre. I am her colleague and her boss. We are currently working on a shipment of art for Berlin. The Provenance of each piece has to be confirmed and signed off by Madame Aveline ready for transportation two days from now. Without Madame Aveline's signature, the shipment will not be allowed to go."

"So, get someone else to sign the Provenance," the sergeant said testily. "Shouldn't be that difficult, surely?"

"Well, as you know, Reichsmarschall des Grossdeutschen Reiches, Herman Goering, has a special interest in moving the most important works of art to Berlin. He is due in Paris this afternoon to ensure the certification has been completed. But he will not allow anyone other than myself and Madame Aveline to complete the certification on this particular shipment. He would be most upset if this precious cargo was delayed because, Feldwebel, you are holding Madame Aveline prisoner on a charge that she will contest and deny most vehemently. Unless you want to explain to Reichsmarschall Goering himself? I could have you at the Louvre this afternoon so you can speak to him. Would that help?"

He left it there and watched as the doubt crept up on the Feldwebel's face. Just the mention of falling foul of the second most powerful man in Nazi Germany was enough to send small tremors of uncertainty through the poor German's veins. He took a deep breath.

"Please wait here."

Benoist watched the man disappear. He heard raised

voices from the interview room before the man reappeared with Margot. He then formally discharged her to Benoist's company and handed back her ID.

The two of them walked out of the police station and climbed into Benoist's old Citroen.

Margot couldn't believe what had just happened. "How did you manage that?" she asked.

He started the motor and chuckled. "By coming up with the biggest load of bullshit I've ever had to come up with in my life." He told her what had gone on and then put the car into gear and drove away.

"Margot," he said eventually. "Don't ever put me through that again."

Chapter 32

Christmas was just two days away. Charlotte and Nicolas were now fully committed to their relationship, which meant Charlotte staying overnight at his apartment from time to time, and that particular day, they were going to a wedding. It was an invitation from Bobby. One of his American friends was getting married at his father's chateau, and he was to be the best man.

Charlotte had managed to buy herself something nice. It was a relief to find some pleasantness in her static life at the hotel. She had rarely been able to give Jacques Garnier any information that could be of any use to Jefson in London, and she had more or less come to the conclusion that Jefson expected nothing from her. Not now.

So, this innocent conclusion of Charlotte's only helped her to see life through the proverbial rose coloured glasses, and preparing for the wedding by shopping for something new was like therapy for her.

The Metro was now running in Paris, which helped to add a sense of normality to everyday for those willing to ignore the reality. But it was a bonus to be able to ride the Metro instead of finding one of the homemade trike taxis that had sprung up in the latter part of the year. Fortunately for Charlotte and Nicolas, Bobby was able to meet them at the station using his father's car. And it was because of his father's situation that petrol was not difficult to come by if and when he needed it.

The wedding ceremony had Charlotte thinking how nice it would be if she and Nicolas could get married at the Chateau. It wouldn't be as grand as Bobby's friends were having, but just the fairy tale notion of marrying Nicolas was enough to make her wish it could happen.

The meal was beyond expectation, and made Charlotte recall how horrified her aunt was when Hans Gruber provided her with 'Provisions'. After the toasts and the speeches came the party, and time to let go, let your hair down and forget there was a war on, people were getting killed, the Battle of Britain was raging, and convoys were being sunk in the Atlantic by the Wolf Packs as they brough vital provisions to the beleaguered United Kingdom. Yes, weddings were good for that, and as the drink flowed, the guests could let their hair down and party like there was no tomorrow.

And then it was time to go home. Back to reality. But Charlotte and Nicolas had both drunk a great deal and were having trouble walking in a straight line without the pair of them getting a fit of the giggles. They said their farewells and climbed into the car full of merriment and fun as Bobby drove them back to the Metro.

On the short journey home, Charlotte felt a contentment she hadn't felt for a long time. And she was happy. Nicolas, being a little worse for wear, showed the opposite. He was a man who could not really hold his drink, but it didn't bother Charlotte because they were heading straight home when they arrived in Paris.

And as they stepped out of the Gare du Nord, they walked into what looked like a riot going on between civilians, almost certainly French, and armed, German soldiers. Nicolas immediately ran towards the mob and started throwing punches at the soldiers. Charlotte, horrified by seeing him getting involved, ran after him with the intention of getting him away and taking him home. Until she saw a soldier use his rifle butt on Nicolas and club him to the ground. Charlotte's temper burst to the surface, and she threw herself at the soldier who immediately turned and clubbed her as well.

Nicolas scrambled to his feet and punched the soldier who toppled back. Nicolas threw himself on top of the man and started laying in to him. Charlotte tried then to grab Nicolas, but as she got to him, more soldiers piled in until Charlotte found herself swinging punches and kicking madly and furiously.

Then suddenly she was yanked away and dragged to a Scout Car. They threw her in without ceremony and handcuffed her. She toppled over and landed on the feet of other unfortunate people who, like her, were handcuffed and looking battered.

The journey to wherever they were being taken was short and unremitting. The hard suspension of the Scout car sent shockwaves up through Charlotte's body and into those painful areas where she'd been hit by boots and rifle butts. She managed to get to her feet and sat down on a hard bench where there was little room. She squeezed up beside someone, a young woman, who was sobbing. Charlotte could feel the young woman's terror and wondered what lay in store for them.

The Scout car came to a stop and with the usual, now familiar guttural shouts from the armed soldiers, they were screamed at and kicked towards a building that Charlotte had no hope of recognising in the dark and in the condition she was in. It soon became clear that it was a prison of sorts, which was confirmed when they were bundled into a prison cell and the cell door clanged shut.

There were other young people in there, most of them looking similarly beaten up as were those with whom Charlotte had arrived. It was obvious that the Germans had literally lost control, no longer able to handle protesters without inflicting violence upon them. They were getting tough, which meant they were getting dangerous.

Someone asked what was going to happen to them.

"They're going to shoot us, aren't they?" someone said.

"They haven't shot anyone yet," another voice chimed in.

"Bastards," said another voice. It was a weak rejoinder but said a great deal.

They'd been in there about thirty minutes when an armed guard opened the cell door. He didn't walk in but stood in the doorway and called out Charlotte's name.

"Charlotte de la Cour!"

Charlotte looked up sharply and held her hand up.

"Come with me," he beckoned, so Charlotte stood up and stepped carefully over some of the sprawled arms and legs to get to the door. The guard locked the door, grabbed her by the elbow and walked her down the lengthy corridor. He stopped at a door, knocked and opened it. Then he held his hand out ordering Charlotte to go in.

She stepped into a room in which there was a desk and a couple of chairs. She realised it was an interview room, and her body sagged under the expectation of an uncomfortable time of questioning. She lowered herself into one of the metal chairs at the table and waited. Two minutes later a door opened, and Hans Gruber walked in,

Charlotte stared open mouthed at him. "Hans?"

He sat down opposite her. "Yes, it's Hans." He reached over the table and took her hand. "Why did you get involved, Charlotte? Why?"

She looked down at the table, her eyes filling with tears. "I was drunk."

He smiled. "Drunk and disorderly, then. It's a lesser charge, but not one you're likely to get away with."

She lifted her head and looked at him, "Am I going to go to prison?"

He shook his head. "No, Charlotte; I'm going to take you home."

That was a complete, total shock to her. She was convinced she would be punished someway for getting involved in fighting with the German soldiers.

"Take me home?"

"Charlotte, what you did, and what many of the others in there did —" He pointed beyond Charlotte, "is being considered by my superiors as …" He let the words drift away. Then he straightened up. "Come on, before I change my mind."

"What about Nicolas? Can he come too?"

He shook his head. "Charlotte, you have to forget about Nicolas, I'm afraid."

"What…"

"I can do nothing for your friend."

"But…"

He put his hand up. "No more, Charlotte. Let's get you home."

Charlotte got to her feet. She felt weak and unsteady, but understood that Gruber was acting, if not strangely, then benevolently. And in that way, he was showing her that he could do nothing for Nicolas, only her.

She allowed herself to be taken out to his Jeep. He put his greatcoat over her shoulders because the night air was cold and there was a touch of frost on the ground. He helped her into the passenger seat and climbed in behind the steering wheel. Then he started the motor and pulled out into the road.

Nothing was said on the journey back to Montrouge. It was almost midnight when he pulled up outside the gate.

"You have your key with you, Charlotte?" he asked.

She nodded. "Yes. Thank you, Hans."

"Before you go, I want you to have this." He reached behind for his briefcase, which he always had with him, and flipped it open. He pulled a slim folder from the briefcase and handed it to her. "I want you to read this and then you must promise me that you will destroy it. It will explain everything. Goodbye."

She took the slim file from him, her face etched in

curiosity but said nothing other than muttering a word of thanks. She got out of the jeep and walked to the front door. As she reached into her pocket for her key, the door was pulled open and Matilde stood there, her arm outstretched and holding the door back.

"Charlotte? Oh my God, Charlotte, what happened?"

Charlotte could say nothing but fell into her aunt's embrace and started sobbing her heart out.

***

The following morning was Christmas Eve, and Charlotte had promised herself that she would cycle over to Nicolas's apartment to see if he had been released and was at home. But when she opened her eyes and looked at the clock, it was eight-thirty, which meant she had slept far too long.

She swung her legs out of bed and went through to the bathroom. Once she had relieved herself, she hurried downstairs to the kitchen where Matilde was eating her breakfast.

"Morning, Matilde. Why didn't you wake me?" she asked as she reached for the coffee pot.

Matilde chuckled. "The state you was in last night, it's a wonder you're up this early."

Charlotte brought her cup over to the table and sat down.

"It was quite a day, Matilde. It had everything in it: fun; laughter; dancing; drinking; fighting." She shook her head and had a rueful smile on her face. "In a way, I quite enjoyed it, but I wouldn't want to go through it again. Well, not the last part," she added.

"And there was the file that Gruber gave you," Matilde reminded her. "Quite a revelation."

The file had been the one handed to Gruber by Sergeant Witborg at SD Headquarters. It was the information provided by the traitor, Pierre Baudet, at the French Embassy in London detailing Charlotte's heritage from the Jewish line and the fact that she had been embedded in Paris by Jefson as an SOE agent. The file had come as a complete shock to them both, but on questioning the reason Gruber had risked his own life by handing it to Charlotte, it revealed something else.

"He was in love with me, wasn't he, Matilde? He knew what my fate would be if my Jewishness was revealed. He didn't want to see me put through that. He risked his life for me. If they found out what he'd done, they would have shot him."

She sighed heavily.

"Poor man. He must loathe having to wear that uniform just for the honour of his family."

She then told Matilde about the perfume and being in Metier's apartment during the raid. "He literally told me that he knew I was in the toilet because of the scent."

Matilde let the truth of Gruber's feelings for Charlotte sink in, bewildered that such a kind, tender man could wear the uniform of a Nazi.

"Have you burned the file?" she asked.

Charlotte nodded her head and looked over at the stove. "In there."

"So, what now, Charlotte."

Charlotte drew in a deep breath and sighed. "I need

to find Nicolas; see if he's okay."

"I'm sure he will be, Charlotte. They probably arrested a lot of hot heads like you two yesterday. I'm sure you will find him back at his apartment."

Charlotte smiled. "I hope so. It will be a lovely, early Christmas present."

Suddenly there was a loud knock at the door. The two women exchanged glances. Matilde wasn't expecting anybody. For a brief moment, Charlotte hoped it might be Nicolas.

Matilde got up and went to the door. Charlotte heard mumbled voices. Then Matilde came back in with Hans Gruber.

Charlotte frowned. "Morning, Hans," she said slowly, looking at the expression on his face and not liking what she saw. She went to get up, but he stopped her.

"Please, Charlotte, stay where you are."

He looked weary. His eyes had no life in them, and he hadn't even managed a smile; something he always did whenever he walked into the room. He didn't say anything for a while. In his mind he was struggling.

She wondered if he had come to arrest her and take her back to face punishment.

He stepped a little closer.

"Charlotte, I'm afraid have some sad news."

His eyes hooded over for a moment as he struggled to speak. "I'm sorry to have to tell you this, but your friend, Nicolas Escoffier, was shot this morning. He was executed by a firing squad at six o'clock."

Charlotte's body seemed to freeze in an instant as

the awful statement sank in. Her mouth fell open, and she started shaking her head.

"No, Hans. Please, no. It isn't true. Please say it isn't true." Her face reflected the horror of what he had just revealed.

He shrugged. "I am truly sorry, Charlotte, but the decision was made by someone senior to me."

She stood up. "But why, Hans? Why?"

His face said everything but revealed nothing. "I truly don't know, but I believe it was to set an example and show how dangerous it is to rebel against the German authority in Paris."

"But you only execute spies," Charlotte shouted at him as tears fell down her cheeks. She wiped her hand over her face in an angry gesture. "Nicolas wasn't a spy, Hans; you know he wasn't." Her voice reached a fever pitch. "You know he wasn't."

He frowned and shook his head wearily. "I never knew the man."

Charlotte was crushed. Her whole body shook as she sobbed. She didn't want this to be true. The life she believed they faced together had vanished. It made her feel empty. She looked up.

"I'm a spy," she said suddenly, "so why not arrest me and shoot me?"

Matilde leapt to her feet in shock, knowing that such a revelation would implicate her too.

"Charlotte!"

Charlotte didn't react to her aunt; her mind and eyes were focused on Gruber.

He gave her a curious look. "Really, Charlotte? Can

you prove it?"

"I've just told you," she said angrily.

"Do you have any proof?"

"What proof?" she snapped at him.

"Well, you could tell me the names of your contacts here in Paris, then I could arrest you all. That would earn me some kudos in the whole grand scheme of things, wouldn't it?"

Charlotte knew that naming names was never a reality. She was being stupid really, but her reasoning had gone, and she didn't even know why she'd said that to him. Her mind was so distraught she'd lost what little control she had. She said nothing else, just slumped back onto the chair and cried her eyes out.

"Charlotte."

She looked up.

"I'm going now. You will not see me again. So, let me ask you to think carefully how you will fight this war. Last night was the closest you'd come to being shot like your unfortunate friend. Don't be like him, a blunt instrument; show more subtlety."

He looked over at Matilde who was weeping and bowed his head,

"Matilde." Then he looked at Charlotte who was still sobbing her heart out. "Goodbye, Charlotte."

He turned round, the usual stiffness and formality gone, walked away and closed the door softly behind him.

THE END

Author Note

Despite the wishes of those in Berlin to turn Paris into a cosmopolitan city and enjoy a cosy, happy relationship with the Parisiennes, it was never going to happen. The reality of the Occupation of Paris by Nazi Germany was brought into the open by the execution of a young civil engineer, Jacques Bonsergent on December 23rd for striking a German soldier during a street scuffle for which he was arrested. The announcement was made on Christmas Eve by the Military Commander of France. It was the first execution publicly announced in 1940. I can imagine the shock to the people of Paris when the true nature of the Nazi beast was revealed so close to Christmas.

I realised as I researched this story that it would be impossible to finish with a 'happy ending' and conclude a war that took the lives of six million Jews and about ten times that number of non-Jewish people world-wide. Happy endings are Fairy Stories and have their rightful place in literature, but for a war story, a happy ending would be pure fiction. What I have tried to achieve with my book is to see the Occupation of Paris through the eyes and lives of the ordinary citizens and slowly reveal the tightrope on which the Parisiennes were forced to walk. I hope I have managed to convey some of that in the story and show that the true heroes and heroines were ordinary, honest working folk who were forced to draw on all their resourcefulness and fight an evil they never dreamed they would ever have to endure.

Michael Parker

Michael Parker's other books

North Slope
Shadow of the Wolf
Hell's Gate
Roselli's Gold
The Eagle's Covenant
A Covert War
The Devil's Trinity
The Boy From Berlin
A Song in The Night
Past Imperfect
Where The Wicked Dwell
No Time To Die
A Dangerous Game
Hunted

Writing as Emma Carney
Happy Lies The Heart
The Girl With No Name
Chapel Acre
Dare To Dream

Non-fiction
My Pat (A love Story)
What Happened After
A Word in Your Ear (How God changed my retirement plans)

You can read all about me and my books on my website at
www.michaelparkerbooks.com

Printed in Dunstable, United Kingdom